Exit Prohibited

A Memoir

Ellen Estilai

AN INLANDIA INSTITUTE PUBLICATION

RIVERSIDE, CALIFORNIA

Printed and bound in the United States
Distributed by Ingram

Author's Note: Some names have been changed or abbreviated to protect privacy.

Cover image: *The Lovers* by Riza-yi 'Abbasi (Iranian, ca. 1565–d. 1635), opaque watercolor, ink, and gold on paper, from the collection of the Metropolitan Museum of Art, New York

Book layout & design: Mark Givens
Publications Coordinator & editor: Maria Fernanda Vidaurrazaga

Library of Congress Cataloging-in-Publication Data

Names: Estilai, Ellen, author.
Title: Exit prohibited : a memoir / Ellen Estilai.
Identifiers: LCCN 2023036858 (print) | LCCN 2023036859 (ebook) | ISBN 9781955969178 (paperback) | ISBN 9781955969208 (ebook)
Subjects: LCSH: Estilai, Ellen. | Authors, American--21st century--Biography. | Americans--Iran--Biography. | Iran--Description and travel. | LCGFT: Autobiographies.
Classification: LCC PS3605.S7537 Z46 2024 (print) | LCC PS3605.S7537 (ebook) | DDC 955.05/42092 [B]--dc23/eng/20231003
LC record available at https://lccn.loc.gov/2023036858
LC ebook record available at https://lccn.loc.gov/2023036859

Published by Inlandia Institute
Riverside, California
www.InlandiaInstitute.org
First Edition

Exit Prohibited

Ellen Estilai

Table of Contents

PART IV: Revolution

PART V: Dislocation

PART VI: When Was the Last Time You Were in Iran?

For Ali, Samira, and Sarah

PART I: The End of the Beginning

1

.....

MEHRABAD

Tehran: July 29, 1980

"Look who's leaving and look who's staying," Ahmad says.

It's four a.m., and my husband Ali's younger brother is hunched over the steering wheel of our old Peykan, driving us through deserted Tehran streets to Mehrabad Airport. Ali sits stiffly in the shotgun seat. I'm in the back, with a sleepy girl on either side of me, both with dark brown braids. Our daughter Sarah, five years old, rests her head on my lap. Her older sister Samira is staring straight ahead into the darkness. Today is her seventh birthday. In the trunk are four suitcases, one per person—all that we are allowed to take.

Our leaving is just temporary, we tell ourselves.

Who else has left? The Shah of Iran, for one. Mohammad Reza Pahlavi left 559 days ago, ending his 37-year reign on the Peacock Throne. Although few Iranians had held out any hope that his absence would be temporary, it is definitely permanent now. He died two days ago in Cairo. Many of our friends have been gone for months. There were no good-bye parties, just a gradual drifting away. Colleagues have left the country as casually as they would leave for a conference or a vacation, but we know they're not coming back.

And who's staying? Ayatollah Ruhollah Khomeini, who arrived

from exile in Paris just 17 days after his followers helped to oust his archenemy, the shah. And the American embassy personnel who were taken hostage by militant Islamic students 271 days ago—they're staying, too.

We are on the Parkway, the modern highway the shah had built for the 1969 Asian Trade Fair. I first traveled this road when I arrived in Iran in September 1971. Ali's good friends Mahmoud and Mahine Fadaei picked us up at Mehrabad airport. The shah's lavish celebration of 2500 years of Iranian monarchy was in full swing, and the Parkway was ablaze with colored lights. Not really understanding how Mahmoud and his fellow drivers kept from crashing into each other, I held Ali's hand in a death grip, kept my eyes on the lights and avoided looking at the traffic.

"Look, Ellen," Mahmoud said gesturing at the dazzling display. "This is all for you."

* * *

"Look who's leaving and look who's staying," Ahmad mutters under his breath, to no one in particular. "This isn't right."

It wasn't right. We had resisted leaving. After almost nine years in Tehran, we were entrenched—engulfed by Ali's large family and enmeshed in our university jobs, our apartment with a mortgage, and the lives of good friends we planned to grow old with.

But the Islamic Republic had made us feel like strangers in our own home. The university had become highly politicized. We watched as old friends and colleagues segregated themselves into factions—Islamic fundamentalists, monarchists, leftists, and secular humanist democrats. The taking of the American embassy had solidified the mullahs' position and many people were only too eager to distance themselves from Americans and *gharbzadeh*,

West-toxified, Iranian intellectuals.

Of course, many hadn't distanced themselves—like Salman, the corner grocer. His shop was tiny—maybe 300 square feet at the most—with barely enough room for him and his assistant, let alone the two or three customers who could squeeze in between the counter and the bins of lentils, yellow split peas and rice. The arrangement of his wares defied logic. The walls were lined to the ceiling with a haphazard assortment of pineapple compote, tomato paste, hand soap and mayonnaise. The window display was a dusty collection of plastic colanders, flyswatters, and flashlights.

I was Salman's only foreign customer. I think he liked me because I had bothered to learn Persian. He also seemed to appreciate my childishly scrawled Persian shopping lists. So even when there were shortages—and there were many—he managed to set something aside for me—a few eggs or a small box of laundry detergent. If other people were in the store, he would scratch his stubbly beard and say, "*Nah, Khanum* (madam). We're out of detergent today." But he would fix his gaze at me just a second longer than necessary and raise one eyebrow almost imperceptibly. I would know then that I should come back when the other customers had gone, and he would have ready a small box of Tide neatly wrapped in brown paper.

But as anti-American sentiment increased, others had become less accepting. The usually friendly woman across the street suddenly stopped returning my *salaam*. And one day, when I called the Butane Gas Company to order another canister for the stove, the agent taking my order interrupted me to ask, "*Khanum*, are you a foreigner?"

"Why do you want to know?" I demanded, in Persian. He explained that he was asking only because so many of his foreign customers had been leaving, and he wanted to see which of his accounts were going to be closed. That was a plausible answer, but still…he knew where we lived.

We arrive at Mehrabad airport a little after four a.m. We'll meet Essie and Julie there, then travel on separate planes to Zurich, Switzerland. We'll need to pick up our Iranian passports at the airport police station. Travelers leaving the country are required to submit their passports to the airlines 48 hours ahead of departure. The airlines turn them over to the airport police, who then check to see if any holds have been placed on the documents. We have our Swiss Air tickets to Zurich, but our American Airlines tickets to Washington, D.C., will be waiting for us on the plane. The Swiss Embassy has finessed that.

But first our bags must be inspected.

After nine years in a country, what do you take with you when you are allowed only one bag? Well, if the country is the Islamic Republic of Iran, you certainly don't take money, gold or valuable antiques. We had seen too many nightly news broadcasts featuring people caught spiriting valuables—their own possessions—out of the country. The culprits stared sheepishly into the television lights as the camera panned over the loot: elaborate gold jewelry, candelabras, stacks of foreign currency. These "enemies of the state" were then led away to jail to await trial.

Officially, no one was executed for trying to abscond with his own valuables, but the regime was busy cleaning house. Our German friend Christa, who lived in the village of Evin, in the foothills just north of Tehran, told us of lying in bed at night hearing the executioner's rifle shots ringing out from nearby Evin Prison.

In news photographs, taken just minutes before their executions, the hapless men all had the same wry, ironic look of resignation. Rumpled and unshaven, they sat alone in their stark cells and stared half smiling at the camera lens, as if remembering long-ago family gatherings when they had joked with the photographer. *"Wait, Mr. Photo, let me put on some cologne first.... Please, just one more, Mr. Photo!"*

So we were careful. Not that we had much in the way of elaborate gold jewelry or other questionable booty. But we took the line of least resistance and packed family photographs and too many soon-to-be-outgrown children's clothes, my wedding dress, and audiotapes of Iranian classical and '70s American pop music.

Ali packed his chromosomes—well, pictures of them, at least. Tucked in among the reprints of scientific articles he had published over the previous ten years were the tangible evidence of his work—stacks of 8 x 10 inch black and white glossies of safflower, sunflower, saffron and cumin chromosomes, in various stages of cell division—coming together and separating like courtly dancers in some cellular gavotte.

However, as cautious as our packing strategy was, even we tempted fate, just a little. We were allowed to take only $500 per adult—a sum that would diminish quickly in Zurich, one of the most expensive cities in Europe. Before we left the apartment that morning, Ali carefully folded two one hundred-dollar bills and put them in the toe of my right shoe.

It is six-thirty in the morning now, and we find the line for the baggage checkpoint. As we watch the security personnel rifle through the bags of the sleepy travelers in front of us, we grow increasingly apprehensive. Apart from two sweaty one hundred dollar bills, we have no contraband, but somehow that doesn't matter. We feel guilty nonetheless.

"How much longer, Mommy?" asks Samira, who is gripping my hand tightly. Sarah, her arm around my leg, is whimpering softly, only just now realizing that she has neglected to retrieve one of her favorite dolls before we locked up the storeroom.

It's finally our turn at the baggage checkpoint. We heave our suitcases onto the inspection table. Without so much as a *salaam*, the bearded official, his collarless shirt buttoned up to his chin, opens each one. I cringe as his calloused hands skim over the linings, dart into side pockets, explore every shoe, and turn over every piece of underwear. *You touch those sanitary napkins, buddy*, I think to myself, *and they're yours*. I make a mental note to do laundry at the hotel.

Then he finds Ali's chromosomes.

Squinting, he turns one of the cell division photographs this way and that, first holding it at arm's length, then, his glasses raised to his forehead, slowly bringing it within an inch of his face. He looks at Ali as he takes another page from the sheaf of glossies, then another and another.

Clearly, he is trying to get some sense of perspective, of scale. *Are these Quonset huts in the middle of the desert? They could be aerial shots of...yes...perhaps a military installation.*

Then he starts pulling negatives out of their translucent paper sleeves, holding them up to the light, peering at rows of root tip cells looking for all the world like stacks of missiles.

"They're chromosomes," Ali explains.

"Huh?"

"Chromosomes…. DNA."

The baggage checker's eyes narrow. He stuffs the photos and negatives back in their folders, slams shut the last of the suitcases, scrawls a large X on each one with an indelible felt pen, and throws them onto the baggage cart.

"You can go," he says. His eyes follow us, yet another *gharbzadeh* (West-stricken) intellectual university professor and his American wife preparing to leave the Islamic Republic of Iran. *Good riddance.*

Free of our bags and relieved to have passed that hurdle, we make our way to the airport police station where we find Essie and Julie and their two girls in the waiting area. Mona, age 9, is bouncing around on the seat, brushing her yellow ringlets out of her eyes as she relates the plot of a book she has been reading. Ayda, age 4, a red-haired, pink-cheeked cream puff, begins flirting with Ali, with great success. It is Julie's birthday as well, and she and Samira exchange good wishes. "We'll celebrate tonight in Zurich," Julie tells her.

We compare notes. Essie has fared less well with the baggage checker. He tells us that when the agent searched his luggage, he got suspicious about some boxes of histological slides and confiscated several prized samples of rat and hedgehog brain tissue.

We all regroup in preparation for the next stage of our departure, the retrieval of our Iranian passports. The children are on my passport. Even in the shah's era, a woman needed her husband's consent each time she wanted to leave the country. However, as soon as we arrived in Tehran in 1971, Ali wrote a letter to the authorities giving me permanent permission to leave the country any time I wanted. He also made sure to deposit half of his paycheck in my bank account, so that I would always have access to funds if he were away. Of course, that permission letter was just insurance. I never wanted to leave the country without him.

Julie and I tend to the children as Ali and Essie give all our names to the officer behind the counter. He hands Essie his wife and children's passport and gives the girls' and mine to Ali. Then he disappears into an adjoining room to look for Ali and Essie's passports. He comes back empty-handed, except for two official-looking envelopes that he hands to them. Ali is very quiet. I move over to the counter and stand next to him as the officer leafs through a huge ledger with neatly handwritten entries.

"You're on the list, sir," he says to Ali.

"OK, that's great," I say.

Ali is very pale. He doesn't look at me as he says, "That's the *mamnou'ol khorudj* list."

Mamnou'ol khorudj. Exit prohibited.

"There must be some mistake," Ali says. "We have letters from the university allowing us to leave."

"No sir," the officer replies. "There's no mistake."

I cannot move. I cannot hear. The clamor of the airport is just white noise. All around me people are busily gathering their children, their bags, their last-minute gifts. They head toward the departure lounge, calling out to children to hurry up, negotiating the cumbersome sacks of pistachios and sweets that well-meaning relatives have pressed into their hands at the last minute. I hear nothing, see nothing except Ali, who in one fluid motion, spins away from the counter, opens his briefcase, and begins taking out documents.

"OK, here are your passports and the Swiss Air tickets," he says, pressing them into my hand.

"What do you mean?" I ask him. "You can't be serious. We can't go without you."

"You can't stay," he says. "You and the girls have to get out of here."

"But when will we see you again?" I ask.

"I'll join you as soon as I can," he answers impatiently.

"What's in that envelope?" I ask him. "Why is this happening?"

"It's a letter from the Prime Minister's office," he explains. "Essie and I have to go there now to find out why we're *mamnou'ol khorudj.*"

I'm suddenly aware of Samira and Sarah standing next to us, their eyes filling with tears. Just over Ali's shoulder, I see Essie talking to Julie, her arms folded tightly across her chest, her eyes trained on the floor, listening. Essie comes over to us. "Ali *jaan,*" he says, using a term of endearment for family and close friends. "Let's go try to retrieve our luggage and get everyone home. We can sort this out later."

Ali puts his hand on Essie's shoulder. "Listen, Essie *jaan,*" he says, in measured tones. "You and I need to focus on getting our exit visas. It's better for our wives and children to be safely out of here. Give Julie the tickets and put your family on that plane."

So we regroup. Julie and her children are taking an earlier flight. We make plans to meet in the Zurich airport. I leave the children with Ali and head across the main concourse to the women's restroom. As I push the door open I see a large room with a row of sinks and about ten cubicles along the wall, the usual drab, poorly lit Mehrabad Airport restroom. But there are men standing among the women waiting to use the stalls—lots of men, perhaps more men than women. The men glance at me sheepishly as I stand in the doorway. I go out again and check the door sign, sure that, in my distress, I have made a mistake. But no, it is indeed the women's restroom. Another sign, handwritten and taped to the wall beside the door, announces that, "due to construction, the men's restroom is unavailable. Please use the women's restroom."

So here in the Islamic Republic of Iran, where very soon, every woman's modesty will be protected by *hijab* because the sight of her hair or her ankles may arouse men, where male and female university students will be separated, where doctors may not examine patients of the opposite sex, it is acceptable for both sexes to use the same restroom.

I decide to wait for Swiss Air.

Ali walks us to the checkpoint near the departure lounge. Samira and Sarah are sobbing now, loud choking sobs. We say goodbye to him and watch as he turns and disappears down the concourse and out into the morning sunlight.

I used to enjoy Mehrabad Airport. Mehrabad means "place of kindness." Before the children were born, Ali and I would go there sometimes in the evening to drink Nescafe and watch people. Being there made me feel so cosmopolitan, so grown up. I especially loved watching families, with their shared features and mannerisms. I would try to figure out their relationships and ethnicities and guess at their professions and destinations. I would sit across from Ali in the busy airport café, grateful for his kindness and for this gift he had given me—the opportunity to know a different culture and a different side of myself, to inhabit two worlds at once.

Place of kindness. This morning, Mehrabad has nothing to do with kindness

2

....

SATANIC SAFFRON AND ZIONIST MICE

Tehran: July 29, 1980

After Ali and Essie leave the airport, the girls and I make our way to the final checkpoint where a woman in a large gray headscarf and black manteau searches our hand luggage. She pats me down perfunctorily, and, smiling, wishes us a safe trip and waves us through the electronic security gate. My hundred-dollar bills, still tucked in my shoe, mock me. Only a few hours ago, they were my major concern. Now they are just a sweaty, vaguely discomforting reminder of my naiveté.

Silently, I settle the children into seats in the sunlit departure lounge where we wait for our Swiss Air flight to Zurich. Hungry and tired, the girls are still whimpering, tear-stained and very, very scared. Other parents smile and nod sympathetically. Are those just the complicit glances of the fraternity of weary parents or do these people know what has just happened to us? I feel exposed, as if everyone in that lounge has been a witness to our family drama.

I gather the girls to me and try to reassure them, burying my face in their shiny hair and whispering soothing encouragements. *Don't worry. We'll see Daddy soon. Everything will be all right.* But my hollow ministrations only serve to launch another crying spell. I resolve to sound more convincing, even if I don't completely believe what I am telling them.

I look up to see someone standing in front of us. *What now?* But it is one of the other mothers with a package of biscuits in her outstretched hand.

"These are for the girls," she says in Persian, smiling. Right behind her is another Iranian passenger, this time one of the fathers, bearing coloring books and crayons for the children.

"These will keep them busy," he says cheerfully.

The biscuits seem to revive the girls enough for them to get started, albeit halfheartedly, on the coloring books. After a few minutes, Samira gets up from her seat and comes over to me, whispering in a serious, big girl voice, "Mommy *jaan*, I'm sorry I cried."

Finally it's time to board the plane. We find our seats and settle in for our five-hour flight to Zurich. I ask the flight attendant if she has our American Airlines tickets to Washington, D.C., and she goes to find them. When she returns with all four tickets, including Ali's, in their bright red Swiss Air envelopes, the Iranian woman behind me leans over the back of my seat and asks me how we got those tickets onto the plane. I just close my eyes and, with a slight shake of my head, give her a weary smile. She backs off. *Great,* I think, *after nine years in Iran, I've finally learned how to be indirect and ambiguous. Too bad it's on the day I am leaving.*

Things are quiet in the cabin as the passengers make themselves comfortable. The flight attendants begin their ceremony, their hands tracing arcs in the air as they gesture toward the exit doors, their faces intent as they lift the oxygen masks like chalices to their faces. The familiarity of this ritual is soothing. For once, the image of the children and me clinging to our seat cushions in the middle of the ocean doesn't capture my imagination; instead, my maudlin flights of fancy take me back to Tehran and the Prime Minister's

Office and some faceless person who wishes us ill.

About an hour into our flight, a cabin attendant announces in French, English and Persian that since we are now out of Iranian airspace, beverage service—including cocktails—will begin shortly. At this news, the mostly Iranian passengers burst into applause. There is a definite change in the atmosphere—a perceptible energy that wasn't there a minute ago. Soon the beverage cart appears between the aisles. I order juice for the girls and tea for myself.

Slowly the cabin fills with the smell of alcohol. I look across the aisle and see the coloring book man, the beginning of a smile on his face, studying his plastic tumbler of whiskey. Seeing me, he nods and raises his glass in a salute. I nod back, thinking, *"Nush-e jaan,"* nectar for your soul. It may be only nine in the morning in Tehran, but here, just outside of Iranian airspace, it is cocktail hour.

I lean back in my seat and think about what awaits us in Zurich. Driving to the airport only hours before, we were so sure that our biggest hurdle was not going to be getting Ali out of Iran but rather getting him into the United States. Even after 10 years of marriage to an American, Ali did not have a green card, or permanent residency status. This deficit was not the result of procrastination. Ali's not having a green card was a point of honor for us, a political statement.

It was also hubris.

Although he had spent 1965–1971 in California, first learning English, then getting his Master's and Ph.D. at UC Davis, he had never planned to settle in the States. Of course, he was obligated to return to Iran; because he was the recipient of a first student scholarship, the government had paid for his tuition and all his expenses. In exchange, Ali's father was required to put the family home up for collateral to insure his son's return.

But it wasn't just saving the family property that drove him back to Iran. After all, Iranian academics in similar situations often simply paid off their debt to the government with their foreign salaries. Rather, it was his deep and abiding desire to serve his country—specifically as a professor of Plant Genetics at Tehran University.

For most of the seventies, it was so easy for Iranians to get visas to the United States that Ali and I never thought he would need a green card for our biennial visits. Ali was easily able to get a tourist visa, or, for his sabbatical, a J-1 exchange visitor visa. We never really discussed getting permanent resident status for him because we were so unequivocally permanent residents in Iran.

Cynical folks might assume that Iranian men marry American women largely for that perk. One such cynic was a student in my English Conversation class at Tehran University.

There is definitely something about a conversation class that makes instructors vulnerable to students' relentless curiosity about their personal lives. Maybe it's the easygoing camaraderie we affect in an attempt to approximate conversation between friends. Or maybe it's the directive to draw on experiences from real life, things we're interested in. Whatever it is, suddenly everyone wants to tackle the interrogative mood, and what better, more entertaining way than to ask potentially embarrassing personal questions of the instructor?

"What is your salary, Khanum?"

"How long have you been married, Khanum?"—followed closely by *"How old were you when you got married, Khanum?"*

"Khanum, do you like your mother-in-law?"

But of course, in the uncertain days after the revolution, this playful banter could easily escalate to reveal repressed resentment. I shouldn't have been surprised when one of my students decided to unleash the interrogative mood and score more than just the usual points for that day's conversation grade.

She was a young woman, probably 18 or 19, with a face like the Madonna of Michelangelo's *Pieta*. That face was encircled by a black *maghna'eh*, or wimple, worn under a black *chador*, a redundancy of modesty that amplified her religious and revolutionary dedication.

"Khanum, you are American?" she asked.

Yes.

"And your husband, he is Iranian?"

Right again.

"Well, is it not true that Iranian men marry with American women just for to get the green card?"

"Actually," I said, with studied indifference, "I've been married 10 years, and my husband has yet to bother to get a green card. But it's better to say, '*marry American women just to get a green card.*'"

She stared at me in shocked silence as I turned to write the correct construction on the board.

Two hours into the flight, the children have calmed down. We are exhausted, still stunned by what just happened at the airport police station.

"Where's Daddy now?" Samira asks, her face rigid with worry.

"He's with Uncle Essie," I explain, trying to sound positive. "I'm sure that right now they're on their way to the Prime Minister's

Office to straighten things out."

Satisfied for the moment, Samira returns to the coloring book. She and Sarah are occupied for the time being, working in resigned harmony.

But my mind is racing. I desperately sift through the events of the past few months, trying to figure out how we got to this point. I close my eyes and see a motley parade of suspects. Every slight, every misunderstanding, every sidelong glance now assumes a new importance. Was it one person or a combination of people?

Who would want to prevent Ali from leaving Iran? Which officious bureaucrat, which backbiting colleague, which sly neighbor could have written the letter or made the phone call? And just what is Ali being accused of? Having an American wife? Not being Islamic enough? Working on saffron?

Ali had worked on plenty of other, more utilitarian crops over the last nine years: safflower, sunflower, flax, cumin—cumin, the earthiest and most plebeian of all herbs, wild and abundant in Kerman. It is so plentiful there that the Persian equivalent of "carrying coals to Newcastle" is "carrying cumin to Kerman."

But saffron...ah, that's another story.

No other spice packs the emotional punch of saffron. The ancient Welsh believed it could cure melancholy. Iranians believe that saffron is a mood elevator, so much so that excessive amounts could cause a person to die laughing. To dispel unhappiness or grief, some devout Iranians write prayers in saffron ink, soak the prayer sheets, and then drink the saffron-tinged water left behind.[1] And, after much personal research, I became convinced that saffron is an

---

1. Grami, Bahram, *Gol va giah dar hezar sal sh'er e farsi (Flowers and Plants in a Thousand Years of Persian Poetry)*, Tehran: Sokhan Publishing Co., 2nd ed., 2009, p. 146.

aphrodisiac, at least when it figures in paella or cioppino.

But beyond its emotional baggage, saffron has a sociological status. While it is used liberally in the kitchens of the middle and upper classes, it is a non-essential frill largely out of the reach of the downtrodden masses—except for the traditional *shol e zard*, the saffron rice pudding that the wealthy give to the poor on certain Muslim holy days, especially days of mourning. In the months after the revolution, for those looking to unmask the *taaghooti* tendencies in society, saffron was an easy target.

In the early days of the Islamic Republic, we heard the attribute *taaghooti* constantly. It was used by proponents of the regime to describe anything they thought ran counter to egalitarian Islamic principles—from expensive restaurants and fancy apartments to neckties and high heels. Among our close friends, we even began to jokingly refer to ourselves and our lifestyles as *taaghooti*, as in, "You're not going to wear that *taaghooti* suit, are you?" or "While you're out, pick up a kilo of that *taaghooti* pastry."

In the haphazard, contextual manner in which I learned most of my Persian, I just assumed *taaghooti* meant "elitist," or "overly Westernized"—something akin to *gharbzadeh*, West-toxified. As it was being used in post-revolution Iran, *taaghooti* definitely had those connotations, but the word was far more damning than that.

Taaghoot, the noun, is the name of a pre-Islamic idol in Mecca, and, in Persian, is synonymous with an idol. A *taaghoot* is a false deity that could be anything from the sun and the moon, to stone idols, to Satan himself. It also includes prophets, rulers and other leaders who are falsely worshipped.[2] Therefore, anything related to the shah, his politics or his lifestyle was *taaghooti*.

Taaghoot comes from the Arabic verb *taghaa*, to transgress, in the sense of going beyond the limits of law and regulation. What had been merely Westernized and elitist before the revolution was now idolatrous. People who lived in modern, expensive houses in the north of Tehran and went to nightclubs were idolatrous. Uncovered women in high heels and Western dress were idolatrous. Men in neckties were idolatrous. That the hardliners chose an Arabic word from the Qur'an rather than a Persian one to differentiate these supposed transgressors from the faithful is significant. They might have used a Persian word like *gonaahkar* (transgressor) to describe their enemies. Instead, their choice of *taaghoot* not only underscored their preference for the culture of Islam over that of the conquered civilization of the Zoroastrian Persians and their more secular descendants, but also elevated the conflict to a discussion of the most basic article of faith.

In the Qur'an, the first obligation of a Muslim, indeed of mankind, is to reject the *taaghoot* (false deity) and worship only Allah. *La Ilaha Illallah*—there is no God but God—is the first pillar of faith. God said, "And we have indeed sent every nation a messenger (saying): 'Worship God alone and avoid the *Taaghoot*.'"[3] The first obligation of the hardliners in the Institute of Biochemistry and Biophysics (IBB) was to demonize the professors whom they deemed to be insufficiently Islamic by classifying their research as *taaghooti*.

2. Al-Hilali, Mohammad Taqi-ud-Din and Mohammad Muhsin Khan, Translation of the meanings of the Noble Qur'an in the English Language, King Fahd Complex for the Printing of the Holy Qur'an, Madinah, K. S. A. Appendix, p. 885.

3. Qu'ran, Surah Al-Nahl: 36.

Some of Ali's colleagues had recently come under fire for their research choices. Ali had told me about a meeting a few months before of the newly created post-revolutionary IBB Coordinating Committee. Ali was one of three professors serving on the committee, along with three students and three staff members. The militant student representatives had mocked another professor's genetic research using mealy bugs, a scourge of the citrus industry. To these detractors, mealy bugs lacked sufficient gravitas, but they were unaware of their unique genetic make-up that made them particularly well suited for molecular genetic research.

The militants had also castigated Essie for importing Zionist mice. Apparently, Essie had paid for a shipment of mice from the Weizmann Institute in Rehovot, near Tel Aviv, with a personal check. He had been given authority to use IBB funds to purchase laboratory supplies. To expedite these purchases, he was told to open an account under his name in an American bank.

Some of Essie's colleagues needed a special breed of mice that were hairless and athymic, i.e. lacking a thymus gland. These mice, available only from the Weizmann Institute, were to be used for immunological research conducted by other professors, not for his own research. To speed up the ordering process, Essie issued a personal check drawn on that American account. After the revolution, the militant students found out about the mice and began circulating rumors that Essie was an agent of Israel.

Behind Ali's back, the militant students must have been criticizing his research on saffron as well. However, perhaps because Ali was present, one of the students on the committee set about, as Iranians would say, putting watermelons under Ali's arms—that is, puffing him up by patronizing him with compliments.

"It's true that Dr. Estilai works on saffron, a *taaghooti* crop," the student said, "but he justifies his existence by working on oil seed crops as well."

Ali would have none of that. He responded to this backhanded compliment with a story about Plato.

"One day a young man came to a gathering at Plato's house," Ali began, fixing the hapless student with a steady gaze. "The young man told the philosopher that he had just come from a party at which one of the guests, a famously fatuous and uneducated person, had been lavishly praising him, saying that he was the greatest philosopher and that there had never been anyone like him.

"Plato began to cry. When the man asked him what he had said to make him so unhappy, Plato replied, 'I don't know what I've done that this ignorant person is praising me, but I vow never to do it again.'

"And understand this," Ali told the student, breaking the shocked silence, "Dr. Tehrani and Dr. Meisami are engaged in important basic research—far more complex than my own."

For the past seven years, Ali had been working on *Crocus sativas L.*, the flowers of which produce saffron, the world's most expensive spice. A chance conversation with one of his graduate students spurred him to investigate the crop. For generations, the student's very traditional and religious family had been farming that *taaghooti* crop in Gonabad, a town in Khorasan Province, a major center of Iranian saffron production. Saffron farming in Iran was primarily a family-run operation. During the short harvest period in October, children helped gather the flowers in the early morning and returned from school in the afternoon to begin the laborious process of liberating the saffron-bearing stigmas, the part of the flower that produces the aromatic red strands, from the mounds of purple perianths spread on cloths in the middle of their living room floor. The average saffron picker could process 600 flowers an hour—yielding only three to four grams of the precious filaments. In 1971, when I first arrived in Iran, this labor-intensive crop commanded 350 rial per *mesghal*, or a dollar per gram in the marketplace.

While an undergraduate, this student had asked Ali if he would supervise his master's thesis research on saffron. Ali told him that he knew nothing about saffron, but he was eager to learn. He asked the student to bring some saffron bulbs so he could grow them in his office for observation. He also promised to review the literature on saffron and think of a research project.

The student went back to his family's farm in Gonabad and returned with a few bulbs, which Ali kept in pots in his office while his greenhouse was being built. As he watched the slender leaves slowly push out of the potting soil and the pale purple flowers unfurl, he began to fall in love with the plant.

Fortunately, Ali was going to the States that summer to present a paper and had the opportunity to do a thorough library search on saffron. He returned with several possible projects that would eventually keep four graduate students busy on their master's theses over the next seven years.

Ali asked his student if he had ever seen any plants with more than three stigmas. At first, he said no. However, the next day he rushed into Ali's office to tell him that he did indeed remember as a child finding flowers with four and five stigmas among the piles of blooms on the living room floor.

"Each time I found an extra stigma, my father would give me one rial and say, 'This is a good omen. The prophet Khezr must have passed through our saffron field.'"

That was all Ali needed to hear. It was possible the prophet

Khezr had made more frequent visits. Ali immediately set about making plans to research the crop to see if he could find these rare types and replicate the genetic mutation to increase the yield.

After a field trip to collect bulbs from Gonabad, Ali established a three-hectare saffron plot on land owned by the Faculty of Science near the college of Agriculture in Karaj. This field produced enough saffron not only for his experiments but also for the enjoyment of members of the Institute. Saffron left over from his students' research projects was divided into packets of two to five grams and given to all the Institute's graduate students, faculty, and staff.

My thoughts drift back to an October afternoon in our rented apartment in Kooy e Gisha—the architect-designed one with the stained-glass sliding doors opening onto the sunny, expansive living room. That morning, Ali had spread a sheet on our living room carpet onto which he emptied a basketful of light purple saffron flowers, filling the room with a heavy, heady, throat-catching perfume, at once salty and honey-like. During the day, Samira and Sarah, barefoot and diapered, occasionally wandered onto the flowery display, only to be gently pulled back and sent away, victoriously grasping a stray flower in their pudgy, sticky hands.

That afternoon, after tea, Ali taught me how to pluck the filaments, consisting of a style and three stigmas, from the flowers. He had become somewhat adept, but I was hopeless—far less competent than a six-year-old Gonabadi saffron picker. After more than an hour's work, the two of us had amassed just a minuscule amount of saffron—barely enough to enhance a small rice pilaf. As we proudly set our harvest to dry on a tiny saucer in the pantry, I had a newfound respect for saffron and the farmers who worked so hard to get it to my table.

But it's not just the saffron, I realize suddenly. *It's what he does with the saffron that might be the problem.*

Although his work had practical applications, Ali's research was not just about a plant's productivity but also about its evolution. In fact, he taught all the courses in evolution at the Faculty of Science and IBB. While there were certainly many among the faithful—some theologians included—who believed that the teaching of evolution was not only consistent with Islam but was described in the Qur'an, there were still many students in the university who considered the teaching of evolution to be blasphemy.

Ali told me about one such student who challenged him to "look at the complex structure of the human eye. How could that be the result of accident, of natural selection?" With the rest of the class looking on intently, Ali asked the young man to imagine a 747 aircraft.

"If you had never seen any other airplane before," he explained, "you would assume that the creation of this plane was the result of a superhuman intelligence. But if you were to travel to the Air and Space Museum in Washington, D.C., you would see that the 747 evolved over time through trial and error from many, extremely primitive structures.

"It's the same with the human eye," he continued. "While it's not even the most complex organ in the human body, it's certainly highly developed. But if you look at primeval organisms, like planarians, that have the ability to sense light, you will see how the eye could have developed from such primitive forms."

Central to evolution is the slow process of weeding out organisms that cannot adapt to environmental changes. Was Ali like one of those maladaptive organisms? Were the Islamic revolutionaries in his classes targeting him for extinction?

I suddenly remember another encounter between Ali and some fundamentalist students—one that I didn't think much of at the time. The previous spring, Ali had caught two students in his probability and statistics class cheating during an open book final exam. He had told the class that they could use any source material, but they could not consult each other. While he was grading papers, he noticed that two of the students had given several identical wrong answers. Applying the same laws of probability that he had imparted to his class, Ali decided that the likelihood of two students independently arriving at so many of the same wrong answers was nearly zero. He asked several of his trusted students if these two had been cheating, and they confirmed his suspicions.

Ali could have failed the culprits, but instead he gave those students incompletes and told them they would have to take the course over again the following year. They immediately contacted the university administration and complained that Ali was anti-Islamic. When the matter was referred to a committee, a mathematics professor investigating the incident called Ali to say that, while he agreed with Ali's analysis, the political climate was such that he didn't want to take a stand. However, Ali stood by his decision.

Something Ali said during the last few weeks of the spring semester takes on new importance, something about slanderous screeds against professors posted on the IBB corridor walls. The signs, hand-written by students, accused some faculty members of being pro-Shah or colluding with the CIA.

"What did they say about you," I asked him.

"Nothing specific," he answered. "But they posted that photo of me receiving the research award from empress."

I had seen that photo. It was nothing incriminating, just Ali in a book-lined room shaking the hand of Empress Farah as ten or so colleagues, themselves honorees, looked on. We both shrugged off the incident, but perhaps we should have paid more attention. Did these disgruntled students have a hand in holding up Ali's passport? Who knew we were planning to leave? We hadn't broadcast our intentions. Besides family and a few friends, we had not discussed our travel plans with anyone. Certainly, our second-floor neighbors, Ashkan and Ladan, knew we were leaving. But would they have contacted the authorities?

Now disjointed images flood my consciousness—images of events that I had pushed to the back of my mind. I see the sullen face of the *chadori* student to whom I had given a failing grade the previous fall. I see the neighbor woman down the block look the other way when I wave hello. I remember waking up one night to see the neighbor across the street glaring at me from his balcony. I had fallen asleep in the La-Z-Boy recliner with the curtains open while the rest of the neighborhood poured out of their apartments to stand on rooftops and balconies and shout anti-American slogans in support of the Islamic Republic. Or maybe he was glaring at me simply because—asleep or awake—I am American.

A chill passes over me as I realize how careless I had been. Now I see myself as my neighbors must have seen me, framed in my kitchen window or asleep on the La-Z-Boy, blithely going about my business, my foreigner's business, oblivious to thinly veiled resentments and old prejudices.

I remember a strange, late night phone call I received from an acquaintance just a few weeks before we left. Oliver, a visiting professor at the university, had called to chat. I was surprised to hear his voice. We didn't know him well and hadn't heard from him for months—in fact we weren't even certain he was still in Tehran.

Oliver was the son of an Iranian father and British mother. Raised and educated in England, he spoke no Persian and had had very little contact with Iranian culture. In fact, with his silver hair, his ascots, and his plummy Oxbridge accent, he radiated an effete British elegance. His American wife was at least 15 years his junior. Tall and thin, with a porcelain blondness, she seemed to be playing at being a grownup. Her expensive, tastefully preppy clothes hung on her gangly, delicate frame as if they were a size too large, and her shoes seemed to gap at the heels, all giving the general impression that she had raided her mother's closet to play dress-up. It looked as if she were trying the marriage on for size as well. Husband and wife appeared congenial with one another but not really close.

Oliver said he was calling to say goodbye. When he told me that his wife had already left months before, I wasn't entirely surprised.

"It was a personal decision," he volunteered tersely, apparently meaning that it was not the result of the political situation.

When he quickly asked, "What's new with you?" I assumed he was merely deflecting the attention away from his marital woes. I told him that we were also thinking of leaving and that several of our mutual friends had already left.

"Who else is planning to leave? Tell me their names," he quickly demanded, his tone suddenly becoming brusque and businesslike.

I stared at the receiver in stunned silence.

"Oh, sorry, I know that sounded strange," he said, backpedalling furiously. "It's not as if I'm going to use this information. I was just wondering who would be left here."

If Oliver is some kind of a spy, I thought, he's a pretty inept one. At any rate, I pleaded ignorance about anyone else's travel plans and cut the conversation short.

It is chilling now to remember these encounters. Had we been wrong about everyone? Was there anyone left we could trust? I think of Ali and Essie, alone in Tehran, trying to figure all this out. Who would give them the answers they needed?

3

....

ZURICH

Zurich: July 29, 1980

As our plane speeds toward Zurich, I try to imagine what I will say to the US consular official who, the Swiss Embassy has told us, will meet our plane.

Meet our plane. Just like in a movie.

I close my eyes and see Julie and me, and the four girls, standing waiflike, in the middle of the crowded airport, bags in hand. Suddenly, across the concourse, a tall, thin man in a trench coat appears—looking maybe just a little like Gregory Peck—rushing toward us, his briefcase parting the crowd like a blade. Out of breath, he apologizes profusely for being late.

"Your government is here to help you ladies," he says, somehow knowing without being told that things have gone terribly amiss. "What do you need?"

He listens intently, patiently, as we recount every miserable detail of our ill-fated departure. Leaning forward, he nods sympathetically as we relate the trauma of this morning, our fears for Ali and Essie's safety. His eyes take in the frightened children, and he smiles at them encouragingly.

"Don't worry," he says, soothingly, putting his arm around my shoulder. "We've seen this before. We'll get them out. I'll make a few calls."

However, our actual reception at the Zurich airport departs significantly from this script. Gregory Peck has been unavoidably detained, but his stand-in is there, at the bottom of the escalator. I know without being told that he is from the consulate because there is a small group of travelers circling him, vying—mostly unsuccessfully—for his attention.

He is fairly young, about thirty years old, with a desk-bound flabbiness that strains his rumpled suit and encourages the collar of his shirt to curl upward. He takes his hands out of his pockets only to sweep his lank, sandy hair from his moist forehead or to gesture toward one of the gates.

I take advantage of what looks like a break in the action.

"Hello," I say. "I'm Ellen Estilai. My friend and her children are coming in on the next flight from Tehran. Our husbands have been...."

"Just a minute," he says, his eyes closed, his hand upraised. "I have to finish with these people first."

He resumes his conversation with an American woman and her Iranian husband who were on our flight. Their dual citizenship entitles them to emergency financial assistance, and the American Embassy is repatriating them.

"Your plane leaves in half an hour," he says, handing them their tickets to the States.

"Oh, no, you don't understand," the woman says. "We thought we'd spend a week here in Zurich, maybe take a train into the countryside...."

"Well, think again, Madam," he says, not bothering to hide the touch of irritation in his voice. "This is one of the most expensive cities in the world. If the United States government is paying for your ticket, you're getting on the next plane."

Having efficiently dispatched the would-be tourists, he turns to me with a look that asks, "Jeez, can you believe these people?"

"Yeah, OK," he says. "What's up?"

I explain what is up.

He is impassive as I tell him about the airport police station, about Ali and Essie's passports, their letters from the Prime Minister's office, their need for green cards. I assure him our husbands have done nothing wrong. I try to make eye contact with him as I tell him that we are very frightened. I can tell by the way his eyes dart about the airport that he is anxious to check this encounter off his to-do list and be on his way. He motions for us to move out of the way of foot traffic and stands listening with arms folded.

I make a mental note not to cry in front of this man.

"So, you already have your tickets to the States?" he asks.

I assure him that not only do Julie, the girls and I have our own tickets, we have Essie and Ali's tickets as well. We have more tickets than we need. We're OK with the tickets.

"Look, can you help us get our husbands out?" I ask, moving slightly to get in his line of vision.

"Well, probably not," he replies blandly.

"What are you saying?" I ask incredulously. "You can't do anything?"

He reaches in his pocket and hands me his card. "I'd advise you to go to your hotel," he says. "Get some rest. Then you and your friend can come and see me tomorrow at the consulate."

He turns and walks across the marble concourse and disappears down a long corridor.

For the second time in 24 hours, I am standing in the middle of an airport concourse with two children, watching a man with no answers disappear into a crowd, having absolutely no idea what I should do next.

Samira and Sarah have witnessed both these encounters intently. They look at me now, silently with tired, tear-stained faces—all brown eyes and grim little mouths pressed into horizontal lines. They are expecting some sign that things are progressing normally, some reassurance that I am in control.

It occurs to me that today, July 29, 1980, right here in the middle of the Zurich airport, my children have crossed a line. Their minds are opening to accommodate an essential truth that will eventually propel them out of childhood. They are now beginning to accept what before they may have only suspected: there are things that Mommy doesn't know how to do, important things—like getting their father out of Iran.

"Look, sweeties, we'll wait here for Julie and Mona and Ayda," I explain reassuringly. "They'll be here any minute. Then we'll go to our hotel and have a nice bath and a nap."

Samira sees Julie first, heading toward us with a baggage cart, Mona and Ayda following sleepily behind. Nearly six feet tall, Julie towers above the other exiting passengers. I am so relieved to see her.

She has been my stalwart friend for the last nine years—my Tehran survival guru, my life coach, and my thesis advisor. I could ask her anything—how to calm a colicky baby (warm mineral oil massaged on the stomach), where to get interesting furniture that isn't trying to look like it came from the shah's palace (the antique stores on Manouchehri Street), or which topic I should choose for my Master's thesis.

"How about all those Byronic heroes you've been finding in those Joyce Carol Oates novels?" she asked me one day. "You ought to do something with that."

"Yeah, right, how about *The Evolution of the Byronic Hero in the Novels of Joyce Carol Oates?*" I said, collapsing into laughter. But she was serious. And I began to see that she was right, as usual. Although it was several years before I could tell people the title of my thesis without laughing, I took the research very seriously. Happily, largely due to Julie's patience, our friendship survived the eighteen months it took to finish the job.

I am so grateful she is here.

"Well, happy birthday anyway, Julie," I say.

She gives me a wry smile and asks me if I've seen anyone from the consulate. I fill her in on my disappointing first encounter with the US diplomatic mission. It is early afternoon. We find a taxi and head for our hotel. Originally, we had booked two rooms, but we decided that the circumstances warranted that we stay together. We opt instead for a suite of two very large rooms, separated by French doors, with four beds and a bath. All plans for baths abandoned, we collapse on these beds and sleep fitfully until it is time for dinner.

Several times in my life, I have dreamt about forgotten or unknown rooms. These are extremely satisfying dreams—ones that I enjoy revisiting over and over in my mind, relishing the discovery of old treasures, of new opportunities.

Before we were married, Ali appeared in one of these dreams. In it, I was living in an old bungalow, much like the house on C Street in Davis, where I lived before I met him. I opened the kitchen door and found a room I had forgotten about. It was a utility room piled high with discarded stuff, old cardboard boxes, dusty jars—the

detritus of life. In the laundry sink, in a shallow glass bowl filigreed with rings of calcium deposits, was a large black fish sitting
in about half an inch of water, its body curved to fit the contours of
the vessel it has outgrown. The fish had a hole in its back where, in
desperation, it had reached around to gnaw on itself.

I screamed. The sight of the fish's gaping mouth was horrific. Overcome with guilt at my neglect for this living creature,
I grabbed the bowl and ran into the kitchen. Ali appeared and,
without asking any questions, calmly took the bowl out to the front
steps and sat down in the morning sunlight. Deep in concentra-
tion, his head of dark, curly hair bent over the bowl in his lap, he
silently, patiently set about repairing my fish.

That rescue was completely in character for Ali. He is a fixer. For
the last ten years, he has made things work. He has been my guide,
not only interpreting Iranian society for me but also helping me to
be part of it. And he is methodical. He is the kind of person who,
when he wanted to learn to play the piano, took the theory book to
bed with him and read it cover to cover before ever putting his fingers on the keyboard. He did the same thing with the instruction
manual for my new Husqvarna sewing machine—yes, because he
was curious, but also because he knew I would never do it. You see,
that groundwork would bore me to tears. My strategy, if you could
call it that, is to jump right in with my hands on the ivories or the
bobbin winder and then cry for help.

Ali is a chess player, a strategist, and an astute judge of character.
But somewhere there has been a miscalculation, an oversight, some
unknown algorithm, some lapse that we haven't identified. The
question is, where? Whom had we misjudged? What obvious slight
had we sloughed off? Who could hate us that much? And of what
is he being accused?

I have always had confidence in Ali's ability to put everything right, to fix whatever is broken. But there is no instruction manual for this problem. Now, here in Zurich, I can only wonder if he will be able to get us out of this one, to make things right again.

4

....

SAINT SEBASTIAN AND HAJJ AGHA

Tehran: 1975

We lived in a modest apartment on a quiet street about two miles from Tehran University, where I was a graduate student in the English department. A plant geneticist, Ali was a founding faculty member and deputy director of the university's Institute of Biochemistry and Biophysics (IBB).

That apartment was the first home we ever owned. We had to get a loan from the university for the down payment and another loan for the mortgage. It was not the home I had wanted. I preferred the old-fashioned, thick-walled Tehrani houses with alcoves and passageways and high-ceilinged rooms opening onto a central courtyard. But the university's home loan program didn't include old houses full of history, character and questionable plumbing.

Instead, we found a small, newly built three-bedroom apartment that was, as Iranians would say, *me'mar saz*, designed by a contractor, not an architect. And it was strictly *besaz-befroush*, built with minimal amenities for a quick sale.

We left the modern, architect-designed apartment we had been renting in Kooye Gisha and moved into this much smaller second-floor flat near the Parkway with gaudy floor-to-ceiling pink and white tiles lining the kitchen and bathroom walls. Instead of that artful arrangement of rooms flowing over three levels and winding around an atrium, we settled for a stodgily predictable floor plan, with three small bedrooms arranged in a row, all opening onto a large common room, the space defined only by a couple of columns, just I-beams sheathed in plaster and covered with wallpaper. One of the bedrooms was built—in violation of code, we later learned—directly over the furnace room in the garage below. With the furnace providing the building's hot water, that bedroom was bearable in winter but almost uninhabitable in summer.

We made this non-descript apartment our own with a hodgepodge of Iranian handicrafts and antique store bargains, eschewing the gilded Louis XIV furniture favored by middle-class Tehranis in favor of a funkier eclecticism.

We filled the living room with antiques from dusty shops on Manouchehri Avenue. We found folding wooden chairs with hand-woven tribal fabric and old coins instead of washers securing their joints. "That's money, Khanum," the antique dealer told me, jabbing his finger at the little metal discs. "Money, you understand?" He had already made the sale, but he wanted me to know the value of what I had just bought.

I did know their value.

I loved the old inlaid wooden chests with drawers that jammed, the cheap bisque-fired terra cotta water jugs, and the daybeds made to order at the local carpenter shop. I was content with the gray and brown carpets with geometric designs we bought when we couldn't afford the more colorful floral ones. To me, these things were soulful, unique, and Iranian. I loved them all the more because they weren't knockoffs of hackneyed European designs from some fancy shop on Pahlavi Avenue.

On the walls, we hung original artwork—either my own or that of my fellow art students at the University of California, Davis.

And of course, there was Saint Sebastian.

Saint Sebastian had been with me since the summer after my junior year in high school, when I was vacationing in Santa Cruz, California, with my family. I ran into him at the Oblates of St. Joseph's yard sale on West Cliff Drive. I was looking for picture frames, not pictures of saints. I certainly wasn't looking for a mediocre charcoal copy of a 17th-century painting by Guido Reni. This drawing depicted Saint Sebastian's first martyrdom, circa 288 C.E., when, as punishment for secretly being a Christian, he was tied to a tree and shot with arrows. Nursed back to health by St. Irene, he survived that attack and returned to Rome to openly preach Christianity, only to be bludgeoned to death at the behest of Emperor Diocletian.

But I knew nothing of his story at the time. I didn't know much about any of the saints, my biblical education being limited to intermittent Sunday school classes at friends' churches and college art history courses. I certainly didn't know that St. Sebastian was the patron saint of lace makers, police officers, diseased cattle, plague victims, and, munificently, even archers.

This Saint Sebastian had none of the gravitas of other iterations—not the muscular intensity of an El Greco, the solidity of a Piero Della Francesca, or the exquisite agony of a Mantegna. He didn't even have the rib cage of Reni's original. My Saint Sebastian was a pudgy, flabby, phlegmatic martyr. His arms did not bear the weight of his body. His bound hands were raised above his head as if he were idly stretching, not hanging from a tree. Throughout the centuries, artists have depicted him as a nearly naked youth, sometimes sinewy, sometimes effeminate, sometimes with several quivers' full of arrows sticking out of his bloody wounds. This portrayal of Saint Sebastian's martyrdom stopped primly at the waist. His naked torso was pristinely pierced with only two arrows. Calm and contemplative, his eyes looked heavenward for solace and his full lips were parted as if to say to God, "I gladly endure this in Your name."

I took St. Sebastian back to my family's vacation rental that summer, fully intending to replace him in the frame with a drawing of my own. Somehow, I never did. After all, he had a certain campy appeal. Perhaps I wanted to feel superior to this anonymous artist's aesthetic, but I was drawn to it at the same time, the way I was taken with the excesses of the Pre-Raphaelites, those overwrought Victorian esthetes. When I was an art student at UC Davis, masters of Bay Area Funk had schooled me in irony, but they hadn't totally eradicated my secret fondness for the pretty and sentimental.

So Saint Sebastian traveled from California to Iran and took up residence over the antique chest with the stubborn drawers, serving as my only visible nod to my haphazard Christian upbringing. Saint Sebastian, the patron saint of the hip and flippant.

Shortly after we moved in, the contractor who built our apartment building came to hand over his set of keys. A gray-bearded man in his sixties, he was wearing a dusty jacket and the kind of woven skullcap favored by Muslim villagers. He sat on the couch, making no apologies for his dirty workpants. He took an orange from the proffered fruit bowl, but refused a plate and fruit knife. Ali and I watched in disbelief as Hajj Agha tore apart the orange, oblivious to the juice dripping on the carpet.

"So, what are you going to do with your profits, Hajj Agha?" Ali asked him, trying not to notice the juice stains.

"I'm going on a pilgrimage to Karbala," he answered, barely looking at us as he dried his hands on his pants. With that, he handed Ali the keys and left.

Hajj Agha had not come to make our acquaintance or to get a

mental picture of the people who were living in the house he had built. He had not come to receive kudos for his work. What we thought about his finished product was irrelevant. The only responsibility he had toward us was to give us the keys. He had no curiosity about us, no expectations, but his disdain for us was palpable.

"So, he's going to Karbala," Ali said, after he left, shaking his head and smiling.

Karbala is the city in Iraq revered by Shia Muslims as the site of the martyrdom of Imam Hussain and his family nearly thirteen hundred years before. I knew only a little more about Imam Hussain than I knew about Saint Sebastian. I knew that his death was commemorated in passion plays called *ta'ziyeh*. I knew that on the tenth day of Moharram (the first month of the Islamic calendar), known as Ashura, the commemoration of Imam Hussain's martyrdom, masses of devout men proceed through the streets of south Tehran, flagellating themselves with chains to the insistent beat of drums until their chests and backs are bloodied. I knew that Hussain was the grandson of the Prophet Mohammad, the child of Fatemeh and Ali, who, next to Mohammad, is the most venerated figure in Shia Islam.

What I didn't know was that, according to Shia belief, it was the rift over Mohammad's successor and the Shias' backing of Ali, the proponent of equality among all true believers, which eventually led to the massacre of Hussain and his family at Karbala. According to the Shias, Ali had fought against the elitist and authoritarian Umayyad, the Islamic establishment in Mecca. After his death, Ali's son Hussain continued to oppose the injustices of the Umayyad. In 680 C.E., the Umayyad army, numbering in the thousands, surrounded the seventy-two members of Hussain's relatives and loyalists on a desolate plain south of what is now Baghdad, a place that Shia Muslims have come to call the Plain of Sorrow and Misfortune. Knowing he was outnumbered, Hussain refused to back down, preferring death to compromise. The Ummayad massacred almost all of them—men, women, and children—thus giving the Shias a role model for the struggle of the oppressed against the establishment.[4]

What did Hajj Agha know about us? What had he seen when he entered our apartment? Clearly, he saw an Iranian man married to a foreign woman. He saw that the woman was unapologetically without hijab (a chador or a headscarf and manteau), defying his standards of modesty, and brazenly joining in the conversation with a stranger instead of retreating to the kitchen. He also saw foreign-looking artwork—an etching of nude women and a charcoal drawing of a pudgy, slightly androgynous man with his hands tied above his head.

He saw a household that, to him, was very likely *najes*, unclean. In Islam, "people of the book"—whether it's the Bible, the Torah or the Avesta—are technically not *kaafar*, or infidels, if they are true believers. But if a person does not seem to be a true believer, he would be considered an infidel, and therefore unclean. Many uneducated Muslims assume that, whatever their beliefs, all non-Muslims are unclean. In the most stringently devout families, the tea glass that a non-Muslim uses must be washed three times to purify it. Perhaps that is why, not wanting to take any chances, Hajj Agha preferred to eat his orange without benefit of a knife or a plate.

However, it was fine to take our money. The money from the sale of the apartment building would enable him to make a pilgrimage that would help assure his place in heaven. Ali and I, who

---

4. For a comprehensive discourse on the influence of Islam on Iranian history and politics, see Sandra Mackey, *The Iranians: Persia, Islam, and the Soul of a Nation* (New York: Dutton, 1996).

SAINT SEBASTIAN AND HAJJ AGHA

were far less actively preoccupied with thoughts of the afterlife, were amused by his answer. From time to time, whenever we found fault with something in the apartment—cement clogging the bathroom's floor drain, the overheated room above the furnace, or the garish pink tiles, we thought of Hajj Agha running off to Karbala with our money and we laughed. We thought his decision to spend his money on a pilgrimage was the result of a lack of imagination, of a villager's insular mentality.

However, just as I failed to see beyond the amateurish charcoal drawing to the profound agony and faith of the real Saint Sebastian, Ali and I failed to see the resolve behind Hajj Agha's decision to pay tribute to the martyr on the Plain of Sorrow and Misfortune. That myopia would come back to haunt us.

Ellen and Samira (circa 1977) in the living room of their Tehran apartment, built by Hajj Agha. On the wall is the charcoal drawing of Saint Sebastian.

5
....

THE NAKED BRIDE

Tehran: 1975-1980

Like most apartments in the city, ours was sited north/ south in order to take full advantage of the sun's trajectory. The kitchen and living room looked north, onto the *koocheh*, or narrow street, and the Alborz Mountains in the distance. The three bedrooms faced south, overlooking the walled garden and the neighbors' living rooms in the buildings behind us.

The bank of kitchen windows, as wide as the room and reaching almost to the ceiling, afforded a panoramic view of our section of the *koocheh*. Convenience food being in short supply, I spent a lot of time in the kitchen, chopping, caramelizing, braising...and watching.

Down in the *koocheh*, there was the raspy symphony of the itinerant street vendors wending their way through the neighborhood, loudly announcing themselves.

Coat shalvari e! It's the coats and pants man!

Hendevaneh—man o bebor, man o bebar! Watermelon—cut me, take me!

Zarf e booloori e.... It's crystal dishes!

Their chants were interrupted only by the appearance of their customers—usually the ladies of the house who had set aside old clothes, pieces of dried bread for a vendor's donkey, or other goods with which to barter. Nothing went to waste.

In my kitchen, in every kitchen on the block, there was an insistent counterpoint to the cacophonous melodies in the *koocheh*. With our pressure cooker gauges rattling softly, our knives crunching into bundles of parsley and cilantro, and, always, our samovars bubbling, we each became part of the daily rhythm of the neighborhood.

Every weekday at about 10 a.m., after the *koocheh's* children left for school, after the women's visits to the greengrocer or butcher around the corner, there arose the most tantalizing aroma of fried onions. That was the signal that we had begun preparing our midday meals. Soon the fragrance of sautéed meats and fried herbs drifted upward, followed a few hours later by the soft, smoky scent of rice as it steamed on the stove. Although I didn't know my neighbors, I felt connected to them by this common effort.

Years before I ever saw Hitchcock's *Rear Window*, I was living it. To be sure, I wasn't confined, like Jimmy Stewart's character, by a wheel chair or a cast, but I was hooked on the little dramas that played out daily in the courtyards and on the balconies.

I knew when someone's mother was recuperating from an operation, when someone else's son brought his new bride home to live on the second floor. Each spring, for a month prior to *Nowruz*, the Persian New Year, I was treated to lessons in good housekeeping as my neighbors dragged their carpets out to be scrubbed in the front courtyards or emptied their pillow casings, washed the feathers, and spread them to dry on sheets. I would watch as the *panbe zan*, the cotton beater, came to empty the heavy comforters and mattresses, disgorging sluggish piles of compacted white cotton into the courtyard. He would then free the cotton from its accumulated dust, using a bowed instrument to beat it into frothy peaks before carefully stuffing it back into the bedding for another year.

Those high garden walls were traditional protections against prying eyes. But given the proximity of the surrounding multistory apartments, they were more a convention than a real barrier. People seemed to think that because they were inside their own gates, they were granted a kind of immunity. That's why the old woman across the street and two doors down felt she could shed her chador and sit in her garden naked from the waist up, her back to the garden's front wall, sunning her surgery scar.

One summer morning I got up at daybreak to bake a cake before it got too hot to have the oven on. It was a Friday, the Muslim Sabbath, and everyone was sleeping in. Some of the neighbors had taken their mattresses out on their balconies to escape the heat. I went into the kitchen to put on the tea, savoring the time to myself. As I stood at the window, surveying the empty *koocheh*, I noticed a slight movement in the pile of comforters on the balcony across from me. Suddenly, the young bride who had come to live on the second floor emerged from the bedding where her husband still slept and darted into her bedroom—completely naked.

When we bought our apartment, two of Ali's colleagues bought the other two apartments above us. One of them was Ashkan, a Tehran University professor who had served fourteen months in the shah's prisons. After being held for several months without being charged, he was finally accused of reading politically subversive material. However, the government may have been after something else.

Ashkan's brother was a leftist student who was arrested and tortured by the SAVAK, the shah's secret police. The story goes that when his captors asked him to name the members of his leftist group, he told them that if they would take him to a location in the south of Tehran he would provide the necessary documents. But just when they arrived at the destination, a crowded truck stop in a very poor section of town, he threw himself in the path of an oncoming truck. The SAVAK hoped that Ashkan could provide the names that his brother had taken to his grave.

Like us, Ashkan and his wife Ladan were not unhappy to see the shah go, but they were intent on ferreting out monarchists and other counterrevolutionaries in their midst. In the fall of 1979, when we returned to Tehran after Ali's sabbatical at Davis, we had to decide where to enroll the girls—a public school or one of the remaining English-language private schools favored by foreigners. Ladan was sure that she could secure Samira a place in one of the English schools. She knew of a colleague's child whom she felt should be expelled from the school because of her family's monarchist leanings. Ladan offered to make this happen. We declined her offer and enrolled Samira in a first-grade class in a public school and Sarah in a Persian-language preschool.

Over the next few months, Ladan, who had become active in the leftist Tudeh party, became more militant and reactionary. One morning, as we were leaving for work, we almost tripped over her young son's pedal car parked squarely at the foot of the stairs on the ground floor entry. Ladan had written "Death to America" with a felt pen on its hood, next to the decal of an American flag, and left it there for us to see.

She did this in spite of the fact that, during the shah's regime, Ali had intervened on her husband's behalf when he was in prison. Ali attended both his trial and his appeal and petitioned Houshang Nahavandi, Chancellor of Tehran University, and, through influential colleagues, the empress. Against the advice of cautious friends, Ali persevered and got Ashkan transferred to a prison that would allow his wife to visit him.

He did this by making sure that Ladan got some face time with the chancellor during a university reception. The three of us arrived at the University Club with the sole purpose of introducing Ladan to the chancellor. The Club was packed with professors and their spouses, all elegantly dressed and talking at the top of their voices. We made our way to the large crowd that had formed near the receiving line, waiting to speak to the Chancellor. We weathered a good ten minutes of being jostled and stepped on before the three of us advanced to the front of the line. In his haste to accomplish his mission, Ali single-mindedly propelled Ladan in front of him.

"How do you do, Mrs. Estilai?" said the Chancellor, nodding at Ladan.

A flustered Ali explained that Ladan was actually the wife of the professor who was in jail, the one he had told the Chancellor about a few days before. The Chancellor promised to meet with her the following week.

"Oh, and, actually, this is my wife," Ali added, gesturing toward me.

Eager to forget the awkwardness of that encounter, we tried make our way to the buffet but were turned back by a phalanx of women in evening gowns, their gold jewelry dangling over the remains of the food, jockeying for the last morsels clinging to the skeletons of poached salmon.

"Well, our work here is done," I said. "Let's go home."

"Oh, no," Ladan replied, with just a trace of a whine. "I paid a lot of money for this blouse, and I want it to be seen. Let's go have dinner at the Hotel Intercontinental."

Ashkan was allowed to have people monitor his trial and subsequent appeal, but Ali was the only colleague present. Others did not want to be involved, even as spectators. One friend who was supposed to accompany Ali to the court bowed out the morning of the trial, so nervous about attending that his bowels rebelled.

The charges against Ashkan were vague, but his defense was lackluster. He was found guilty of having connections to a leftist organization and sentenced to two years in prison. He lost his appeal, but was released some months later, apparently because of the letters of colleagues in the States and the intervention of the Empress's Special Office, as well as Ali's advocacy with university officials.

We looked forward to his return, but after he came home, Ashkan and Ladan's demeanor toward us was decidedly chilly. We chalked it up to the stresses of his being in prison for so long—the uncertainty, the loneliness, the mental exhaustion they both experienced. Or perhaps they were uncomfortable being indebted to Ali. However, we soon saw that it was much more than that. Ashkan and Ladan may have been grateful for Ali's intervention, but they were now suspicious of him all the same. *How was Ali able to help secure Ladan's visits if he was not connected to the establishment? Whom did he talk to and why did they listen to him? Why did Ali think he could attend the trial without arousing the regime's suspicion unless he himself was part of the regime?*

After the revolution, distrust was pervasive. The university that had once been my haven was now an unfriendly place, and I wasn't used to feeling ill at ease in that setting. There is usually something about a university—any university anywhere in the world—that seems familiar to me, even if I have never been there before. Its geography is logical and dependable. Pulled to the center of its energy by the vortex of the library, the student cafeteria, the bookstore, the art gallery, I feel immediately at home.

I especially loved Tehran University in the fall, in the evenings when the air was smoky and gravid with the promise of a new academic year. Autumnal sunsets had a special electricity accentuated by the melancholy call to prayer emanating from the campus mosque.

As the days grew shorter and the tall plane trees became lacier, the tiny, brightly lit bookstores across from the university on Shah Reza Avenue came alive with students stocking up on Cliff's Notes, cheap English editions of Russian novels, and the poems of Hafiz, Sa'di, Rumi, Nima Yushij and Forugh Farrokhzad. On the uneven sidewalks, pedestrians jockeyed for position with vendors offering golden dates still on their branches, pungent grilled liver on skewers, and mounds of fat, shiny, garnet-colored beets on round trays simmering in their own bubbling sugar.

By the fall of 1979, the university itself had become difficult to navigate. While many students still wanted to study, some used their classes as launching pads for small demonstrations against the decadent West's culture and philosophy. One afternoon, I walked into my modern English poetry class only to be given a friendly heads-up that there would be a campus-wide demonstration called sometime during the class, and all the students would be leaving to attend.

"That's fine," I said. "Let's just get started and see how far we get with today's assigned reading."

Surprised that I hadn't opposed their plan to close down my class, the twenty-five students settled in for the lecture with a measure of enthusiasm. Things went fine for the next fifteen minutes or so, until I began reading aloud William Butler Yeats's poem "The

Second Coming."

"'Turning and turning in the widening gyre,'" I began. A slight rustle came from the center row of seats.

"'The falcon cannot hear the falconer,'" I continued, reading over the murmurs.

When I got to the line, "Things fall apart, the centre cannot hold," five bearded young men in army fatigues—their hour come round at last—got up and without a word, slouched out.

The remaining students, suddenly in no hurry to leave, smiled encouragingly. "Go on, Khanum," one of them said.

So I did.

Mere anarchy is loosed upon the world,
The blood-dimmed tide is loosed, and everywhere
The ceremony of innocence is drowned;
The best lack all conviction, while the worst
Are full of passionate intensity.

It was that passionate intensity that was worrying us. We watched as the university became more openly conservative. Headscarves and worry beads appeared; neckties disappeared. *Agha* and *Khanum* gave way to *baradar* and *khahar* (brother and sister). Veteran professors were edged out in favor of young Islamic fundamentalists; a research assistant with a master's degree could become head of a department. Everyone was scrutinized, this time by the SAVAMA, the Islamic Republic's version of SAVAK.

Even I, a lowly adjunct instructor at the Faculty of Literature, did not escape scrutiny. When I came into the English Department office one morning at the start of the fall semester, the secretary greeted me with a worried look. "Before you go to your office, you need to stop in there," she whispered, nodding toward the conference room. "There's someone waiting to see you."

"Who?"

"Someone from the government. He's interviewing all the faculty."

I entered the room to find a slightly built young man, about the age of my sophomore students, seated at one end of the large conference table, pouring over a stack of file folders. When he looked up and motioned for me to sit, I chose a chair at the other end, as far away as possible. He seemed nervous, as if this were his first job.

"Name?"

"Ellen Estilai."

"Identity card number?"

I gave him the number I had memorized. Hunching over the table, he carefully recorded it.

"Birthplace?"

"Actually," I said, anxious to be out of there so I could prepare for my lecture, "all that information is in my SAVAK file."

Startled, he stared at me for a second, unsure what to do next. Perhaps he, too, was anxious to leave, because he closed the file and thanked me for my time.

I assumed I'd had a SAVAK file since my first teaching stint at National University, eight years before, because everyone in education had a file. A more experienced operative would have insisted on gathering his own information. Instead, the young questioner only confirmed my suspicions that the SAVAMA was interchangeable with its predecessor. A more circumspect interviewee would have kept her mouth shut and let the scene play out. I was lucky

CHAPTER 5   63 that my interrogator was as green as I was incautious.

I may have avoided interrogation by the SAVAMA, but just entering the university grounds each day was a gut-churning challenge. After we made it past the ostentatiously suspicious guard at the side gate on Anatole France Avenue, the one who asked to see our faculty ID cards every day, Julie and I would sometimes split a Valium with our morning coffee. I suspect many women developed an interest in Valium after the revolution. In a letter to the editor of the English-language newspaper *Iran Times*, an Iranian woman complained that Roche Laboratories had begun to dump inferior drugs in Iran. She was certain because she had been taking Valium for several months, but lately it had no effect on her.

Neither Valium nor vodka lime, our drug of choice, proved to be an adequate buffer. Ali and I were always on edge, always uncertain. To be sure, we were often uncertain about our bootleg vodka supply. Agha-ye G., our trusted Armenian supplier, was the only person in Tehran who was ever on time. If he said he would come at 3:30 in the afternoon, that's exactly when he would be on our doorstep, with 12 unlabeled vodka bottles in a discreet cardboard box. One afternoon, Agha-ye G. was a half hour late, and we were afraid the authorities had apprehended him. After the revolution, the possession of alcohol was a serious offense for both purveyor and customer, punishable by lashing. But sure enough, he arrived safely.

"Traffic," he explained before darting back into his car.

The high quality of Iranian vodka was one of the casualties of the revolution. Our supplier increased the price of his vodka, but its quality deteriorated along with the political situation. After a while, it tasted so bad that no amount of imported Country Time lemonade powder could improve it. Our neighbor Ashkan was certain that the distiller was neglecting to remove the stems from the raisins and turning out methanol, which could cause blindness. "I think this vodka is causing me to lose my voice," he rasped one day. "It may even be affecting my DNA."

Ali and I were getting a bit frayed as well. We slept fitfully, neglected to floss, and even challenged our own DNA with that vodka. The constant stress had caused our gums to bleed and the roots of our hair to hurt, and soon there was no vodka at all. But still, we didn't want to leave. This was our home, our country, and we refused to be forced out just yet.

Were we being too paranoid? Were we not paranoid enough? It was difficult to decide just when enough was too much. Essie, Ali's close friend and colleague at the Institute, at first refused to be concerned. "As long as we can teach and do our research," he said, "we should stay here." But I had read an article in *Harper's Magazine* about German Jewish scientists in the 1930s and 40s who, despite all the warning signs, remained at their university posts because they thought they could still do their research, only to perish in Nazi death camps.

Ali and I decided that if the government forced women to wear the veil, we would leave—not only because we didn't want to raise our daughters in that system but also because the mandatory veil would be symptomatic of so many other forms of oppression—for both men and women. Essie and Julie agreed. We began making contingency plans.

During the 1979–80 academic year, the university was the scene of much social and political debate, and women were finding their own voices. In fact, the whole country was struggling to find its voice after thirty-seven years of Mohammad Reza Pahlavi's regime. Under his rule, women certainly had achieved a measure of freedom. His father, Reza Shah, had outlawed hijab in 1936 as part of his campaign to modernize the country. Early in his reign, Mohammad Reza Shah stopped enforcing his father's ban on the chador, but gradually, women made their own choices about how best to express their modesty. That sartorial freedom paved the way for the freedom to vote, attend university, become a doctor, ride a bike, or hike in the mountains with male classmates. However, all of these freedoms were superficial and inadequate when no one, man or woman, had the freedom to challenge the system.

After the shah was deposed in 1979, many Iranian women wanted not only to keep the rights and privileges they had gained but also to help create a truly democratic society in which open debate would be encouraged, not stifled. They watched as the SAVAK, the shah's dreaded secret police, were replaced by Khomeini's SAVAMA. The name had changed, but it was still the same deadly game.

Earlier in the year, I had attended a rally for women's rights at Tehran University that was coordinated and facilitated by women, with sympathetic male students running interference, protecting the women from the thugs that were waiting outside the doors. We had heard that goon squads on motorcycles frequently attacked women, pulling up on sidewalks and slashing them with knives or dousing them with acid, and then speeding away. At one point during the rally, the power went off, but when male colleagues produced flashlights, lanterns, and bullhorns, the program went on. It was exhilarating to hear women using their voices in this new way and to see so many male students supporting them.

But that exhilaration was short-lived.

In March 1980, the government had decreed that women had to

wear hijab—either a chador, the floor-length veil, or a long scarf with a manteau, or knee-length coat, and pants. Women who resisted were considered whores and enemies of Islam. American activist Kate Millet joined hundreds of Iranian women in a protest at Tehran University, and the government backed down for a while.

But in June 1980, the government closed all universities across the country, eliminating the primary gathering place for debate. Soon after, they announced on television that women working in government institutions—schools, universities, banks, hospitals— must observe Islamic hijab. This time they meant it. The announcement conveniently included illustrations, complete with the allowable colors: gray, brown, navy, maroon, and the ever-versatile black. The next morning, we contacted the American Interest Section of the Swiss Embassy.

Most of our friends had already left for Europe or the States. But our close friends Essie and Julie were as stubbornly entrenched as we were. We had led parallel lives in Tehran, sharing gossip in the same faculty lounges, trading our stair-step daughters' hand-me-down clothes, celebrating Thanksgiving and Christmas together. Now we were leaving Iran together.

Ali and I told ourselves we would be back when things calmed down. We gave power of attorney to Ali's older brother Reza. We left our furniture and put our books, clothes, and other personal items in the storeroom so Reza could rent out the apartment until we returned.

Part of me wanted to be free of all this factionalism and uncertainty; part of me wanted to stay. I wanted to escape, but I wanted to belong.

It was this need to belong that had driven me to learn Persian. I prided myself on my command of the idiom. The secret to my steep learning curve was pretending. Make-believe was my major strategy. I was not content to merely memorize verb conjugations and the uses of the subjunctive. My tactic early on was to convince myself that I was Iranian. Even before I had the vocabulary, I had mastered the cadence of a Persian sentence. I watched other women carefully and adopted their subtle body language. That first month in Tehran, I willed myself to dream in Persian. I willed myself to become Iranian. Now that I had become Iranian, I had to leave.

PART II: *Sharqzadeh*, East-Toxified

6

PREPARING FOR IRAN

Davis: Summer 1970

That day in 1969, when the tall handsome foreign student with dark curly hair and molten brown eyes walked up to my table in the UC Davis student commons and introduced himself, he got right to the point. A few minutes into our conversation he announced, "I plan to go back to my home country."

This abrupt non sequitur did not make sense to me at the time. But years later, Ali explained that before he met me, he had seen me walking across campus and told his friend Mohsen, "I wouldn't mind marrying that girl." In the interest of full disclosure, he wanted to make sure that I knew his future was in Iran—even if I didn't yet know that I would be part of it.

A few months after our first date, Ali asked me to marry him.

I said yes, without any hesitation.

That was the easy decision. Deciding what kind of wedding to have was the hard part. We knew what kind of wedding we didn't want—stuffy, extravagant and overly formal—but we didn't want a flowerchild ceremony, either. When nearly a year passed without firm wedding plans, Ali's good friend, Farrokh Khalaf, gave us an ultimatum. "I'm leaving for Iran in three months," he announced one day. "If you want me to organize your wedding, you'll need to get married in July."

He made us an offer we couldn't refuse. One day we were our dillydallying, procrastinating selves, blissfully ignorant of all the work we would have to do to make a wedding happen. The next, we had a wedding planner (Farrokh), a caterer (that same Farrokh) and a best man (Farrokh, yet again).

Our friend was used to cloning himself. The father of two little girls, Farrokh was finishing his Ph.D. thesis while waiting tables at a fancy restaurant in Sacramento frequented by state lawmakers. He took the knowledge he'd gained there and started the only Persian restaurant in Yolo County—and he still found time to play on the university's soccer team. Farrokh mobilized our wedding troops like some can-do go-getter from a 1940s Hollywood musical. *Hey kids, let's put on a wedding!*

That wedding became our friends' summer project. We reserved the gazebo in the UC Davis Botanical Gardens for the ceremony and the Rec Pool Lodge for the reception. My friend Katie sewed my dress, a caftan made from a gold-on-white silk sari, and when the dry cleaner accidentally shredded it, she quickly and graciously offered to make another one. Ali and I silk-screened our invitations, with our names in Persian script. Bijan supplied flowers he grew in a university greenhouse. Abdi solicited empty milk cartons to hold the flowers for the centerpieces. Farrokh found a large caldron at a nearby Campbell's Soup cannery to make the stew for *lubia polow*, rice pilaf with green beans. Parviz and Reza made kebabs. Parviz's brother, Jahangir, spent several nights peeling potatoes for the crispy *tahdig*, literally, "the bottom of the pot." Farrokh and my bridesmaid Anne made the three-tier cake, with layers of custard and strawberries. Ali's former roommate Khosrow played Persian dance music on his accordion, and Abdi's cousin Farzin kept the glasses of Ali's major professor and 130 other guests filled with Champagne.

After the wedding, my mother, ever careful to dissociate herself from the deadly sins, announced, "I don't envy anybody. But if I did, I would envy you your friends." I think such envy would have been easily forgiven. Each time I look at our wedding photos (taken by my former roommate Kathy Silva), I am humbled by the generosity of this cross-cultural collaboration that made the day so memorable. I knew I would be sad to leave my American friends, but I sensed that, if these new Iranian friends were any indication, I would feel welcome in Iran.

At this point, one might ask how, if at all, I prepared myself for a life in Iran. Did I read up on the history? Peruse the highlights of a thousand years of Persian literature? Study the current politics? I did some of that, with a characteristically scattershot approach. Finishing my bachelors' degree and planning for the wedding didn't leave a great deal of time for systematic cultural immersion, and in those days, I was anything but systematic.

With only a few months to prepare and so much culture to learn about, I quickly found my comfort zone. I played to my strengths and concentrated on words and food.

What did I know about Iran before I got there?

I knew how important poetry is to Iranians. I, who had never been asked to memorize anything more challenging than "Evangeline" or "The Jabberwocky," marveled at how Ali and his friends (all of them science, engineering, or economics students) traded poetic references, laughing as they called up entire poems by Hafiz and Sa'di and Khayyam. After dinner or a poker session or a pick-up soccer match, they would challenge each other with a game called *mosha'ereh*, a contest in which a person recites lines of a poem and the next person answers with another line, beginning with the last letter of the previous verse.

It was easy for them. They had libraries in their heads, but their literary agility was not an aberration. *Mosha'ereh* was a popular game played in many Iranian families, from the unschooled to the highly educated. Ali's family, too, had libraries in their heads, because in Iran, poetry is truly an oral tradition that spans all social classes. Beloved Iranian singers and composers have for generations put classical Persian poetry to music that emanates from taxi cab radios to concert halls, from humble *kahgeli* (adobe) huts to marble-clad mansions in north Tehran. "Reading," "reciting" and "singing" may be translated by the same word: *khaandan*. When an illiterate Iranian "reads" poetry by reciting it from memory, singing it from his soul, he is in fact far more culturally literate than many educated Westerners.

Seeing that the poetry shelf of my own mental library was empty, Ali set about introducing me to his favorite poets, Rumi, Hafiz, Ferdowsi, Sa'di. He knew that classical Persian poetry, with its unfamiliar vocabulary and convoluted sentence structure, would be rough going for me, so he settled on the work of Forough Farrokhzad, an iconic and iconoclastic poet who died in a car crash in 1967 at the age of 32. A proponent of the New Poetry (*sher e now*), Forough was bound neither by social conventions nor literary ones.

Ali would read Forough's poems to me, painstakingly translating them and explaining the cultural and literary references. We started with *Tavallodi Digar* (*Another Birth*) a collection published in 1964 and *Iman Biyavarim be Aghaz e Fasl e Sard* (*Let Us Believe in the Beginning of a Cold Season*) published posthumously in 1967. Her poetry was a revelation to me. It was accessible not just because of its free verse and conversational, confidential tone, but also because the voice was intensely sensual and feminine. At first, we read the spare, deceptively simple poems, like "Couple."

Night falls
and after night, darkness
and after darkness
eyes
hands
and breathing, breathing, breathing...
and the sound of water
dripping from the faucet drop by drop by drop

Then two red glows
of two lit cigarettes
tick-tock of the clock
and two hearts
and two solitudes[5]

Of course, in choosing these poems, Ali was interested in more than just my literary education. Forugh's poetry was the perfect choice for two young lovers. If you were going to introduce your bride to the Bible, you might as well start with the Songs of Solomon. The passion Forugh wrote about was not the idealized, courtly love of Persian classical poets; instead, it was raw and private. It was daring because hers was a strong and vibrant woman's voice, unflinching, uninhibited, and disillusioned.

You can cry out
in a voice utterly false and strange
"I love—"

---

5. Forugh Farrokhzad. *Another Birth*, trans. Hasan Javadi and Susan Sallée (Washington, DC: Mage Publishers, updated and revised edition, 2010), p. 89

You can, in the over-powering arms of a man,
be a wholesome and beautiful female
with a body like a chamois spread
with large firm breasts
You can, in the bed of a drunk, a vagrant, a fool
defile the chastity of a love.
[....]
You can be just like a mechanical doll
and view your world with two glass eyes.
You can sleep in a cloth-lined box for years
with a body stuffed with straw
in the folds of lace and sequins
You can cry out and say for no reason at all
with every lascivious squeeze of a hand:
"Ah, how lucky I am!"[6]

Just as provocative as the poems' overt sensuality was their implied criticism of contemporary politics and social mores. I appreciated Forugh's acknowledgement of her sexuality. I understood
the jaded resignation of one who has been disappointed by love and
by a woman's role in the social order, but I was even more drawn to
the political sentiments in "Someone Who Is Like No One," with
its scathing denunciation of the political establishment and a moribund society. The poem recounts the earnest, hopeful dreams of a
little girl who yearns for "someone new/someone better/someone
who is like no one," a brilliant, honest savior to put things right, to
create a more just society.

6. Farrokhzad, "Mechanical Doll" pp. 65 and 67.

Why am I so small

that I get lost in the streets?

Why doesn't father—who isn't small,

and doesn't get lost in the streets—

not do something to hurry the arrival

of the one I've dreamed of?

Or the folks who live in the slaughterhouse district,

whose garden soil is blood-soaked,

whose pond water is blood-streaked,

and whose shoes trace blood....

Why don't they do something?

Why don't they do something?[7]

Years before I saw the films of post-revolution Iranian directors who invite us to see society's imperfections through the eyes of children, I saw how an artist must sometimes adopt the persona of a child to tell a profound truth. In a repressive society, this persona can be both a clever conceit and a vital means of self-preservation.

Of course, my appreciation of Persian poetry was greatly hampered by my unfamiliarity with anything more than the rudiments of the language. UC Davis had no Persian language courses, so Ali's former roommate and close friend, Mohsen, volunteered to hold free classes for the wives and girlfriends of Iranian students. This generosity was characteristic of Mohsen. He often volunteered to help fellow students with their research and dissertations, and his home was always open for impromptu dinner parties and poker

---

7. Forugh Farrokhzad, *Sin: Selected Poems of Forugh Farrokhzad*, translated by Sholeh Wolpé (Fayetteville: University of Arkansas Press, 2007), p. 106.

games. Mohsen was a natural teacher, patient and methodical, and imbued with confidence in his students' capabilities.

Six of us took him up on his offer. Our reasons for learning the language varied. Some just wanted to have a familiarity with their husband or boyfriend's language; others, like me, were preparing to move to Iran and needed to be able to converse.

Our textbook was the classic *Persian Grammar* by Ann K. S. Lambton, a professor of Persian at the University of London. This book was not for the timid. First published by Cambridge University Press in 1953, its approach has remained scholarly and left-brained through all its subsequent editions, giving no quarter to the shiftless and uncommitted. *You think that learning one new alphabet is enough? Well, I'm sorry, but you'll also need to know the phonetic alphabet to decipher those little squiggles. You don't feel like tackling the present subjunctive just yet? Too bad. Turn to Lesson Two, page 11. Oh, you say you're confused by the discrepancy between the colloquial Persian that your boyfriends are speaking and the Persian in my textbook? Not my problem.*

On a good day, reading a sentence in an unfamiliar alphabet is like opening the tiny windows on an advent calendar; the little treasures of meaning reveal themselves slowly. Yet there are days when, no matter how much body English you apply to wrench the windows open, the meaning of those squiggles remains hidden.

Like Arabic, from whence its alphabet came, Persian is written from right to left. There are thirty-two letters, with a few phonetic redundancies, a surfeit bestowed on the Avestan-speaking, cuneiform-reading Sassanid Persians by their Arab conquerors. (Some of these letters are redundant in modern Persian, but not in Arabic, where they are pronounced differently.) Persian has three letters that correspond to the English letter *s*, as well as two *t*'s, four *z*'s, two *h*'s, and two *a*'s. Even with this embarrassment of phonetic riches, the ancient Persians had to create four letters, *cheh, pe, je* and *gaf,* to accommodate sounds not present in the language of the invaders.

Depending on where they fall in a word, most of the thirty-two letters have four forms: initial, medial, final joined and final unjoined. Some letters remain relatively unchanged and easily recognizable wherever they fall. Others, shift their shapes, so the student must learn to recognize many more than thirty-two characters.

To further challenge the new student, short vowels are usually not written unless they come at the beginning of a word. Sometimes, a written word is just a tight little fistful of consonants, and the reader has to use the context to pry open its pronunciation. A word spelled with the Persian equivalent of k-r-m could mean *kerm* (worm) or *karam* ("bounty" or "generosity), as well as the English borrowings (*kerem*) (cream) or *kerome* (chrome). T-r-k could mean *tarak* (break), *tork* (Turk), or tark (abandon). This ambiguity doesn't faze native speakers, who breeze through the text buoyed by their syntactic expectations, but it's daunting for the stumbling beginner who has little sense of what's coming next.

As a class, we stuck it out for a semester and got through the first five chapters or so, petering out somewhere after the passive voice. Still, the classes gave me a head start. By the time we arrived in Tehran, I could read just enough Persian to distract myself from the insane traffic by reading billboards and neon signs, sometimes laboriously puzzling out the letters until I realized that they were merely advertising *hambairgair* or *saandoveech.*

With food, I was on firmer ground. Ali taught me the three or four dishes he knew how to cook, and I set about adding to our repertoire. Before we went to Iran, I told an American friend who was dating an Iranian man about a cookbook I had just bought, *In a Persian Kitchen: Favorite Recipes from the Near East*, by Maideh Mazda. My friend already knew about it. She said that when she moved into her rental house, she found an abandoned copy in the middle of the living room floor. It was the only thing the previous occupant had left behind. "There's a story there," she said wryly. We both laughed as we imagined a disillusioned American woman who had bought the cookbook with high hopes of pleasing her Iranian boyfriend. Perhaps the cookbook had scared her off.

I didn't have the good sense to be scared. I was fearlessly in love. If only I had read more carefully, more dispassionately, I might have had an inkling of how radically my life was going to change.

"Our house was always full of people," Mazda remembers lovingly, "and we had company for lunch, tea and dinner, and often, guests stayed on for weeks or months."[8] *Weeks. Months.* What did I not understand about that sentence?

Iranians believe that a guest is God's friend, or, as Mazda says, "God's gift," a gift that apparently cannot be turned away.

> Because a Persian house is always open to an unexpected guest, a Persian man would never hesitate to bring four or five guests for lunch without informing his wife in advance. The Persian housewife has solved the problem in her own way. She knows that it isn't right for her to tell her husband or her son that she prefers to know beforehand whom he is bringing for lunch or dinner. She knows that this is a national custom and

---

8. M. Mazda, (1960) *In a Persian Kitchen: Favorite Recipes from the Near East.* Tokyo: Charles E. Tuttle Co., p. 12.

that she is not going to be able to train her family to do otherwise. She has solved this problem by learning how to keep the necessary food on hand."[9]

If I was at all alarmed by this national mindset, I might have been mollified by Mazda's assurances that Persian dishes can be easily expanded to accommodate the unexpected guest. But instead of worrying about such sleight of hand, or the responsibilities that required it, I focused on the exotic pairings—ground beef, split peas, and quince; pomegranates and walnuts; carrots and candied orange peel; eggplants, whey, caramelized onions, and mint. In a few months, I would realize that I would need to do more than stock my pantry or adjust ingredients to accommodate the guest. I would need an attitude adjustment as well.

Ali and Ellen at Lake Berryessa, near Davis, California, 1969.

9. Mazda, p. 96-97.

Ali and Ellen's wedding, in the gazebo of the UC Davis botanic garden, July 1970.
Photo Credit: Kathryn Silva

7
....

WESTITIS, EASTITIS

Davis: Fall 1970

Two of the first Persian words I learned in Davis were *gharbzadegi* and SAVAK. In those days, it was impossible to be in a gathering of Iranian students without hearing these words. In the minds of many Iranians, SAVAK and gharbzadegi were subtly intertwined and threatening, each in their own way.

Gharbzadegi, the title of a 1962 polemic by the revered Iranian writer Jalal Al-e Ahmad, has been variously translated as "Westitis," "Weststruckedness," "West-toxification," or "Westomania." Al-e Ahmad wrote, "I speak of being afflicted with 'Westitis' the way I would speak of being afflicted with cholera."[10] The root of the sickness, "this disease imported from abroad," is the East's dependence on the mechanized culture of the West.[11] His basic point was that Iranians had not been able to "preserve [their] 'cultural-historical' personality in the face of the machine and its unavoidable onslaught."[12] While acknowledging that machines are here to stay, that "the world is caught up in the machine of historical determinism," he was more interested in the way Iranian society

10. Jalal Al-e Ahmad, *Plagued by the West* (Gharbzadegi), Caravan Books, Del Mar, New York, 1982, Paul Sprachman, trans., p. 3.
11. Al-e Ahmad, p. 3.
12. Al-e Ahmad., p. 7.

would deal with machines and technology.[13] "As long as we are solely consumers," he said, "as long as we do not manufacture machines, we shall be afflicted by the West. And the ironic thing is that as soon as we are able to make machines, we shall become machine-stricken!"[14] That was the bind in which developing nations found themselves. However, for Ali and his fellow Iranian students, gaining their expertise in the heart of the mechanized world, gharbzadegi was a condition that didn't apply to them.

Ali and his friends frequently used gharbzadegi or the adjective gharbzadeh to denote someone or something that was westernized to a fault, that had sold out to or been corrupted by the West. But even though they were being educated in the West, they didn't think of themselves as west-stricken. That epithet was for those who had lost their culture, who put on foreign airs. Their "cultural-historical personality" was intact. When they read Al-e Ahmad's description of the "western-stricken man"—opportunistic, bereft of ideology, without belief in God or humanity, nihilistic, and empty, "like a dust particle floating in space or a straw floating on water"—they did not see themselves.[15] What they saw was a call to action.

They agreed with Al-e Ahmad that Iran needed an appropriate infrastructure in which to manufacture and operate machines—education, methodology, skilled workers, factories, and markets[16]—and they saw themselves as the people to make this happen.

And they were exactly the people who could make this happen. But Al-e Ahmad had misgivings about sending students abroad

---

13. Al-e Ahmad, p. 6.

14. Al-e Ahmad, p. 7.

15. Al-e Ahmad, pp. 67-69.

16. Al-e Ahmad, p. 56.

and then expecting them to succeed in their homeland, with its own moribund institutions invaded by western advisors controlling everything to their own countries' advantage. He likened Iran's foreign-trained graduates to hothouse plants in need of tending, each transplanted from a different environment—English, American, French, or German—only to wilt in that unfriendly climate.[17]

Al-e Ahmad had even less faith in marriages with foreign spouses. Marrying a foreigner was "one of the most vivid symptoms of Westitis." This type of "incompatible" marriage and the "domestic problems of mixed households" would only get in the way of solving the pressing problems of Iranian society. He was certain that marrying a foreigner, "a souvenir spouse," was also indicative of a deep-seated sense of being inferior to the West.[18]

Ali had read *Gharbzadegi* eight years before we got married. If he remembered the passages about Western-educated Iranians marrying foreign wives, he kept that to himself. Very likely, he had forgotten about them. They were irrelevant to the matter at hand. He had long ago taken from *Gharbzadegi* what he needed, a deeper understanding of the need for Iran to chart its own course in the world, without the interference of foreign powers. What he rejected was Al-e Ahmad's view of the role of the clergy. The author felt that if they could just stop arguing about the "minutiae of religious life" and adhere to the principles of Shi'ism, the clergy could be the "last barricade against west-strickenness."[19] But Ali felt that Al-e Ahmad had ignored the damage that the clergy had inflicted on the nation by helping to keep people ignorant and full of superstition.

---

17. Al-e Ahmad, p. 93.

18. Al-e Ahmad, pp. 93-94

19. Al-e Ahmad, footnote, p. 36.

Beyond the definition of *Gharbzadegi*, I knew nothing of Al-e Ahmad's philosophy, of his prejudice toward foreign wives and his insistence on the "traditional Iranian family (a wife and husband who are of the same blood, compatible, and familiar with each other)".[20] I was blissfully unaware of that viewpoint. Nor did I know that he felt that teaching of foreign languages in universities only served to supplant the teaching of Persian. Looking forward to teaching English in Iran, I was oblivious to the threat I might pose to Persian language and literature. I was sure that our life in Iran, whatever it was going to be, would be authentic and purposeful, and that I would not be a culturally insensitive American. And I didn't feel like a souvenir.

And besides, I was fast becoming hopelessly *sharqzadeh*, east-toxified.

But it would have been helpful in 1970 if I had understood the implication of Al-e Ahmad's views—namely the role of the clergy. We might have assumed that *Gharbzadegi* made an argument for secular nationalism, yet we would later see how it set the stage for the Islamic Republic. It wouldn't be the first time we saw what we wanted to see.

I was far less worried about who was West-stricken than I was about who was stricken by the SAVAK, the shah's secret police. Early on in our relationship, Ali wanted me to know about Iran's political situation so that I could decide for myself if I wanted to live under that oppressive regime. This knowledge was easy to come by because political debate was all around us.

UC Davis was home to a large community of Iranian students of all political persuasions, the most vocal of which were the Islamic

20. Al-e Ahmad, p. 94.

fundamentalists and the left-leaning nationalists. Ali and most of his friends belonged to the latter group. Although these two factions were at odds politically, each was against the shah for different reasons. Whenever two or more Iranians got together—in the student union, after a poker game, at Persian Club events—a political discussion was inevitable. They even argued over the organization's name, eventually changing it to the Iranian Students Association, to denote an active political group rather than a mere social club.

The leftist students were nationalists who wanted Iran to be free of Western influences and adopt an Iranian-style democracy on Iran's own terms. If there was to be a monarchy, they wanted it to be the constitutional monarchy defined by the existing Iranian constitution. They blamed the shah's cozy relationship with the United States for Iran's lack of political freedom. It was, after all, the CIA-led coup in 1953 that, with the support of the British, overthrew the democratically elected prime minister, Mohammad Mossadegh, and brought the young shah back from a few day's exile in Italy.

For over half a century, the British had been meddling in Iran's affairs. They had always had their eyes on Iran's rich trove of natural resources and proximity to the Soviet Union, but now their major concern was Iran's oil industry, which Mossadegh had nationalized. Had I known the details of Ann K. S. Lambton's career, I might have been even less enthusiastic about her grammar book. A former cultural attaché at the British Embassy in Tehran during World War II, Lambton became a renowned authority on Iranian society and helped shape Britain's policies concerning Iran. The British Foreign secretary recruited her to suggest strategies for undermining Mossadegh's regime.[21, 22]

The British tried to enlist the help of the U. S. in overthrowing Mossadegh. The CIA failed to convince President Harry Truman to depose a constitutionally elected leader purely to allow the British to continue their dominance over Iran's resources. However, when Truman's successor, Dwight Eisenhower, became president, the CIA changed their tack. They convinced Eisenhower that Mossadegh would allow Iran to become communist.

Pledging never to allow Iran to become "Iranistan," that is, to never let it fall into the hands of the Soviets, the shah silenced debate by imprisoning or executing political prisoners and muzzling the press. While from time to time, Washington signaled to the shah that he needed to institute more democratic reforms, the U. S. was willing to let him run the country his way, as long as he was an effective bulwark against Communism.

The Islamic fundamentalists hated the shah for what they viewed as hypocritical displays of Islamic piety, his marginalization and imprisonment of Muslim clerics, his dogged attempts at replacing traditional society with Western mores and values, all in the name of progress. Alcohol, gambling, western cinema, women without hijab, and men and women dating without benefit of temporary marriage (*sigheh*)—all these and much more were seen as subverting Islamic principles.

I learned about the Shia' tradition of *sigheh* firsthand in 1970 at an Iranian Student Association meeting in Davis. Morteza, one of the leaders of the Islamic students, was there with an American

21. Stephen Kinzer, *All the Shah's Men: An American Coup and the Roots of Middle East Terror*, p. 114. Hoboken, NJ: John Wiley & Sons, Inc., 2003.

22. Abbas Milani, *The Shah*, p. 83. New York: Palgrave MacMillan, 2011. Kinzer refers to Lambton as a press attaché, but Milani identifies her as a cultural attaché.

woman we hadn't met before.

"Hello," she said, "I'm Janet, Morteza's temporary wife." She was a university student in her mid-twenties and Jewish. She didn't seem at all distressed that her status was only temporary, that her relationship would very likely end when her temporary husband returned to his homeland and entered into to an arranged marriage with a devoutly Muslim girl.

Morteza, who would go on to become a high government official in the Islamic Republic, was certainly living his beliefs. As ardent and vocal as the Islamic students were, I didn't take them seriously. How could such backward thinking ever have primacy in Iran? However, I took very seriously both the Islamists and the leftists' arguments against the shah's violations of human rights.

Before I met Ali, all I knew about the Shah of Iran was what I read in *Life* magazine. As a child, I sympathized with the beautiful, sad-eyed Soraya Esfandiari-Bakhtiari, the shah's second wife, whom he divorced in 1958 after she failed to produce an heir. A year later, I followed the dashing monarch's engagement and marriage to the luminescent Farah Diba with the same awe and reverence I reserved for the British royal family and later for the Kennedys. Devouring *Life* magazine's December 7, 1959, cover story, "A Big To-Do for a Shah's Bride-to-Be," I poured over childhood snapshots of the future empress from her family album showing glimpses of what the writer described as "something very like an American middle-class life"—Farah on a Girl Scout hiking trip, with her school basketball team, as a fifteen-year-old flag bearer parading past the shah's royal box, poignantly unaware that six years later she would be on view in quite a different way.

Like any girl who grew up on fairytales and Hollywood movies, I was entranced by the black and white photos of a royal party at one of the shah's eight palaces—the ornate chandeliers, gilded brocade furniture, sparkling designer dresses, elaborate makeup, and beehive hairdos. But while I was admiring all that opulence, it didn't occur to my twelve-year-old self that, except for the carpets, there was nothing even vaguely Iranian about the palace's décor or the women's attire. This could have been a party in any palace in any European country. It was positively *gharbzadeh*. Twenty years later, the Pahlavi family's ostentatiously Eurocentric orientation would prove to be one of many black marks against them and their cohorts.

The shah's foreign life-style was emblematic of his dependence on the West, and in turn, his dependence on the SAVAK to maintain that relationship. During the Iranian revolution, the clergy, and the religious right, finally becoming the barricade against westitis that Al-e Ahmad hoped they would become, would paint the shah as the quintessential western-stricken man, opportunistic and hollow, a dust particle floating in space. However, it was not the foreign spouse but the SAVAK that was the most vivid symptom of Westitis. The shah, like his predecessors, had made many concessions to stay in power and one of them was to keep his country from going communist. He had made a foreign marriage of sorts, with a bride price of US-made F-16s and other military toys. In return he brought a dowry of censorship, prison cells and torture racks. He had made his bed, and we all would have to lie in it.

Al-e Ahmad himself was a victim of this foreign marriage. From 1962 to 1964, he published several versions of *Gharbzadegi*, only to have them suppressed by Iranian censors. The book circulated clandestinely until, in 1979, ten years after his death, the Iranian Revolution made it possible for it to be read openly. And why not? It helped set the stage for the Islamic Republic's attack on Western-influenced intellectuals in Iranian universities. I had just left one of these intellectuals behind in Mehrabad airport.

PART III: Adoption and Adaptation

8
....

SWEEPING CHANGES

Tehran: September 1971

That first month in Tehran, we were relatively alone, except for Ali's good friends, Mahmoud and Mahin Fadaei. When they picked us up at Mehrabad Airport, they promptly installed us in an empty apartment on the second floor of their house in northeast Tehran. Luckily for us, their tenants had just vacated; otherwise, Ali would have had to look for lodgings as well as a job.

Like Ali, Mahmoud and Mahin were from Kerman, a city in southeast Iran over 600 miles from Tehran. Mahmoud, who had been a leftist activist in his student days, had settled down to become a successful construction contractor. Mahin was the elder sister of Ali's best friend Farzin. The two boys had been inseparable during high school in Kerman—playing chess, studying for exams, and dreaming of their academic careers. Together, they left their hometown to spend their senior year of high school in the capital. They remained close while at Tehran University—Farzin at the College of Medicine and Ali at the College of Agriculture, twenty-five miles away in Karaj. The two boys had spent many happy hours as guests in each other's homes, and Mahin and Mahmoud were part of Ali's extended family.

They told us the apartment was ours for as long as we wanted it, and we could pay them the modest rent whenever Ali found a job.

The two-bedroom apartment was identical to theirs on the ground floor, but empty, except for a bed, two nightstands, and a dining room table and chairs—all lent by our generous hosts.

Our meager belongings, four small wooden crates with a motley assortment of textbooks and household goods, were stuck at the Port of San Francisco, hostages of a dock strike, and would not arrive for three more months.

The hollow rooms echoed with recriminations. *You're not ready for company*, they seemed to say. *You're not ready to be grownups.* The bare floors were an intimidating expanse of gray terrazzo tiles that seemed to need daily sweeping and mopping. I was used to the funky, comfortable, bohemian clutter of our student cottage in Davis, and this emptiness made me melancholy.

During the day, I would wander downstairs to visit with Mahin and either attempt to help her or try to stay out of her way as she performed her daily chores. In her mid-thirties, she had three young children and a deeply ingrained work ethic. Barely five feet tall, she was constantly in motion, stopping only to gently swat her diabetic husband's hands away from the dates and pastries or help one of the children with homework.

Mahin's decor reflected the prevailing Iranian middle-class aesthetic: floor to ceiling windows festooned with layers of fringed, velvet draperies; vibrant Kermani carpets; floral wallpaper; elaborate crystal chandeliers; kitschy imported china figurines of graceful European ladies; and doily-covered coffee tables arrayed with crystal bowls of nuts, small plates and fruit knives awaiting the inevitable drop-in guest.

Our first full day in Tehran began with a traditional Iranian breakfast downstairs in Mahin's sunny, immaculate kitchen. The room was filled with the aroma of *sangak* flatbread that Mahin's son had retrieved from the bakery just down the block, baked in an oven filled with red-hot pebbles. We slathered the bread with sweet butter and homemade sour cherry preserves; we wrapped it around boiled eggs or feta cheese and walnuts. We drank glass after glass of fragrant tea.

Thus fortified, Ali prepared for his initial visit to Tehran University in search of employment, leaving me alone with Mahin. I was apprehensive. She spoke no English, and my Persian was pretty much limited to the names of body parts and food and an uneasy acquaintance with the subjunctive mood.

"What will we do all day? How will we communicate?" I asked Ali, an edge creeping into my voice. "How soon will you be back?"

"You'll be fine," Ali said as he grabbed his briefcase, gave me a quick kiss, and made for the door.

As I watched him disappear confidently down the walkway and out the gate, I felt a small wave of panic sweep over me. I had known that I would eventually be on my own in Iran, but not on my first day. I cursed my laziness. *Why didn't I spend more time learning Persian?* I remembered last night's traffic on the way home from the airport. *What if he has an accident?* I imagined shattered glass scattered like diamonds over his lifeless body slumped in the back seat of the crumpled taxi. I saw the crowds of curious passers-by staring helplessly at the smoking wreckage. I imagined myself, in widow's weeds, accepting the condolences of friends and family....

I was jolted out of my miserable reverie by the cheerful sound of Mahin's radio playing "Ameneh," the song everyone was singing, the song I had already heard three times since we arrived. *Ameneh, cheshm e tow,*.... Ameneh, your eyes.... I turned and went inside.

Alone in the house, Mahin and I smiled at each other. I helped her clear the breakfast dishes. I watched, still smiling, as she straightened up the living room, stopping now and then to ask me if I wanted anything. I ate fruit on dainty dishes. I drank tea in tiny glasses. I continued to smile. Soon my cheeks began to ache.

Suddenly, the awkward silence was broken by the cries of a passing street vendor.

"*Jaru, Jaru e, Jaruuuu.*"

"*Jaru?*" I asked, nodding toward the street.

Laughing, Mahin ran to the kitchen and brought back a broom. "*Jaru,*" she said, with a triumphant grin, happy to have made this breakthrough.

Our conversations that day were extremely simple and direct—slow and deliberate on her part, monosyllabic on mine. She often had to put down her broom to look up a word in a Persian-English dictionary, which she then handed to me, her plump hand pointing to the English definition. But mostly she just showed me, punctuating her carefully enunciated running monologue with an expressively didactic pantomime or running into the kitchen to fetch tangible examples: a cup, a sheaf of fresh herbs, or a thermometer.

At one point, eager to hold up my end of the conversation, I searched my tiny trove of Persian vocabulary for some nouns to wrap around my basic verbs. I had decided that, when in doubt, I should use a French word. So many French words had made their way into the everyday speech of middle-class Iranians that it was a safe bet that—even with my rudimentary French—one or two would hit their mark.

"*Regle e?*" I asked, wanting to know if something was the rule, a regular occurrence.

Mahin froze and just stared at me.

That evening, when Ali came home, I told him about the exchange.

"Oh," he said, "you asked if someone was menstruating."

It was then that I adopted the motto "cringe and move on."

By lunchtime on that first day, I knew the Persian words for diapers, hard-boiled and soft-boiled eggs, feta cheese, butter, jam, and all the fresh herbs I had helped her clean and chop for lunch, as well as the chorus of a song in praise of Imam Ali that was playing on the radio. *Ali jaanam, Ali jaanam, Ali noor e dow chesmanam.* (Ali dear, Ali dear, Ali the light of my eyes.)

When you learn a word like "broom" at the age of twenty-four, you remember where you learned it. It was fitting that Mahin introduced me to the *jaru*, because her own was never far away from her. This over-sized whisk broom—a thick, three-foot-long sheaf of straw bound at the top to form a handle—was pressed into service from the front gate of the house to the back wall of the garden every day, not just in her house, but in every house on the street, in every street in Tehran—or Kerman or Isfahan or anywhere there was dust. And there was so much dust.

But dust never had a chance to settle for long in the Fadaei household.

Bent at a 45-degree angle, her straight brown bob falling across her heart-shaped face, Mahin would flick her *jaru* across the surface of the large Kermani carpets, coaxing piles of debris onto the mosaic tile margins that surrounded them. Oh, sure, you could buy vacuum cleaners in Tehran, but Mahin, like many other Iranian women, was convinced that a broom was the best tool for the job—and far less likely than a Hoover upright's beater bar to damage her hand-knotted treasures.

In the kitchen, she would pour water on the tiles and use the *jaru* to hurry the puddles into the large drain in the center of the gently sloping floor. Under her sure and practiced hand, the *jaru* would zigzag down two flights of stairs and skip out the front door, delivering a little pile of brown powder to the dustbin, a tangible testament to its lowly yet pivotal place in the household.

The first house gift I received was a broom—that, too, compliments of Mahin. It was a thoughtful, practical gift that came just a day or so after our arrival. It was also a clear signal that I needed to begin my life as an Iranian housewife.

Of course, I had done housework before. Reluctantly. I grew up in a household in which cleanliness was prized but clutter reigned. I had acquired my mother's sullen, desultory attitude toward "women's work." During World War II, Mother had been a reporter for the *Washington Post*. The city desk had rarely had a woman on staff, and when the city editor came back from vacation, he told her plainly, "If I had been here, you wouldn't have been hired."

Despite that misogynistic sentiment, she stuck it out and proved herself, but after the soldiers came home to marry their sweethearts and take up their "men's work," she dutifully assumed the role of housewife and mother—and martyr to the cause.

Soon after I was born, my parents moved from Washington, D.C. back to their hometown, Ellwood City, Pennsylvania. Taking advantage of the GI Bill, they set up housekeeping in a tiny, shingle-covered log cabin on Wiley Hill, just a few doors down from the house my father grew up in, within shouting distance of the orderly homes of three of his siblings.

My mother thus found herself in close proximity to a work ethic she admired but did not aspire to. Housework was something to be endured between visits to the library. She could see Aunt Shirley's wash on the line across the street, but she resisted the concept, espoused by her sisters-in-law down the road, that Monday is always washday. Washday should be whenever she got around to it, after she finished reading her book.

Perhaps that's why the *jaru* never really felt comfortable in my hand. All that bending over hurt my back. Negotiating the stairs, backwards, at a 45-degree angle challenged my already shaky sense of balance. The expanse of the bare floors seemed so vast, the challenge so insurmountable, the task so unrewarding. *The floor will be just as dusty again tomorrow. And besides, I'd rather read my book.*

So more often than not, the *jaru* was relegated to a corner of the kitchen, out of sight, waiting for someone more agile and motivated than I.

As the dust settled on our empty apartment, it soon became apparent to Mahin that my agenda—if indeed I had one—was different from hers. She was at first amused by my lack of housewifely skills, but slowly she came to realize that I lacked sufficient direction and gumption. To her, my days seemed free form, my schedule haphazard, my life unfocused. One afternoon, after a lengthy nap, I went downstairs to pick up the mail. After a brief chat with Mahin, I announced that I was going back upstairs to start doing some housecleaning. "That's good," she said, "because it's already half-past four."

The ubiquitous *jaru* came to symbolize for me my ineptitude and uncertainty and, yes, my total lack of preparation to run an Iranian household. The *jaru* mocked my innate laziness. It laughed at my foreigner's awkwardness and resisted my clumsy attempts to befriend it. I began to question what I was doing in Tehran, whether I was up to the task, whether I could ever achieve the high standards set by Mahin.

9

YOUR FOOTSTEP UPON MY EYE

Tehran: October 1971

After a month in Tehran, it wasn't just the housekeeping that I found daunting. I was intimidated by pretty much everything. The simplest act seemed to take so much energy. Making small talk with strangers, crossing streets, negotiating crowds, even passing through doorways—all required a new set of skills, not just linguistic but also social and athletic.

First, there was the issue of *taarof.*

Taarof is an Iranian national pastime. I once heard American TV talk show host Bill Maher define *taarof* as "lying." That's misleading. It's not exactly lying, but it's not the absolute truth, either. At best, *taarof* is the offering of niceties, compliments, and ceremonial courtesies. At worst, it's the gray area of white lies, low on the color spectrum but high on the list of necessary social skills. *Taarof* underscores the relationship between two parties: elder and younger, superior and subordinate, host and guest, power broker and supplicant.

There are several classes of *taarof.* The most ubiquitous of all is the doorway *taarof:*

"Please, after you."

"No, absolutely not. I beg of you, after you."

"No, I beg of you, *jaan e shoma* (upon your soul), after you."

This will continue until one of the parties has exhausted his supply of *taarof*, or a bystander says, "For God's sake, please close the door and come in." (Unfortunately, the doorway *taarof* has no counterpart on Tehran streets. Motorists abandon all *taarof* as soon as they get behind the wheel.)

Once you get through the door, there is *khosh o besh*, the greetings *taarof*:

"Salaam. How is your health? Is it good, God willing?"

"From your kindness, thank you, I'm well, praise be to God."

Tehranis are highly adept at the greetings *taarof*, but Kermanis are champions. A meeting of two Kermanis unleashes a rapid barrage of *khosh o besh taarof*, pleasantries mumbled under the breath, one on top of the other, each volley punctuated by smiling, nodding, bowing, head tilting and placing of hands on the heart.

The two parties, talking at the same time, will say, "*Salaam, ghorban (*master for whom I would sacrifice myself*)—You are well, God willing?—Thank you. I am your inferior—I beg of you, I am under your shadow—God willing, may your Excellency's shadow never lessen over my head—How is your mother?—Your father?—Praise be to God—Your sister?—Your sister's husband?—Your children?—Praise be to God—Please bring your honored presence (to my house)—Oh, I don't want to trouble you—Not at all, consider it your own home. Your footstep upon my eye.*"

When a guest does bring her honored presence, her host immediately launches into the hospitality *taarof*:

"Please have some *shirini* (pastries)."

"I couldn't possibly—no, upon your soul."

"You must take some—are you *taarof*-ing with me?"

"No, upon the souls of my children, I don't know how to *taarof*—oh well, if you insist—maybe just one."

"No, that's so little—please take more. More! Are you on some kind of diet?"

"Thank you, may your hand not hurt. These are excellent!"

"I beg of you, may your *head* not hurt. They are unworthy of you."

I was no match for such linguistic marathons. My simple, tongue-tied *salaams* sidelined me immediately. During my first year in Iran, my sister-in-law Sakineh actually felt the need to apologize for my pitiful attempts at *taarof*. "She doesn't know how to do that," she explained. *Yet…. She doesn't know how to do that yet.* Her smile implied that I would get it eventually. I would have to.

My problem wasn't just linguistic. I was used to American directness. These endless streams of pleasantries took so much valuable time. And they were full of pitfalls. I soon learned the folly of openly admiring something that could easily be detached from its owner. No sooner had I complimented the baby lambskin hat of a friend's teenaged daughter than her mother cried, "*Pish kesh!*" Take it. It's yours. If the young girl was reluctant to part with her hat, she didn't show it. Whisking it off her head and plopping it onto mine, she joined the chorus protesting my protestations. Iranians' largesse is exceeded only by their capacity for insistence. I lost that contest every time.

I was equally unarmed when it came to deflecting the inquiries of the friendly but curious strangers at dinner parties:

"So, you've been married 14 months and you aren't pregnant? Why not? Can't you get pregnant? How old are you?"

"Your husband just got a job? Congratulations, God willing.

How much does a professor make these days?"

"I like your dress. How much did that cost?"

"Are you Muslim?"

I used up so much energy struggling to understand a question and then finding an answer that I had little left for deft dissembling.

In spite of everyone's kindness, I felt cut adrift. I had always been proud of the fact that I was an Italian/Welsh-American, but in Iran, I soon understood that I was not even an unhyphenated American but instead a *khareji*, a foreigner—a generic, undifferentiated, non-specific Outsider.

That otherness was magnified when I went out shopping. I dressed conservatively, but like many Iranian women in this cosmopolitan capital, I was uncovered—*bi hijab*. In neighborhoods in the north part of town, being *bi hijab* was not a problem, but the farther south we went, the more stares I attracted. I could sometimes feel the action slow down as I passed. In more traditional neighborhoods, young Muslim men, whose mothers, wives, and sisters wouldn't think of running out of the house to get a pint of milk without their chadors, felt that they could stare at me, gapemouthed, with impunity.

It wasn't just my lack of hijab that set me apart in these neighborhoods. Most of the time, I could pass for an Iranian—that is, if no one was paying too much attention. But my confident stride or my long swinging hair must have branded me as a foreigner, and therefore, fair game. Sometimes, young men would use the crowded thoroughfares as an excuse to jostle unsuspecting women—a furtive touch, a flutter of fingers against a skirt. By the time I realized what had happened, the culprit would be half a block away.

If Ali was with me, I was careful not to tell him about these encounters until we were safely home. I was afraid that he would feel the need to defend my honor. But he was aware of how easily I got tired and anxious on these outings. One day, after several hours of enduring the stares and negotiating the crowds on Manouchehri and Islambol streets, he could see I was flagging.

"Let's take a break," Ali said. "You need some hot chocolate. Let me take you to a café I used to go to when I was a student. Café Naderi. It's just around the corner on Naderi, near Lalezar."

Naderi, Islambol and Lalezar streets formed an old, weathered neighborhood that had once been the center of town, full of cinemas, theaters, cafés, and high-quality grocery and butcher shops that catered to the affluent households in the northern part of the city. This old quarter, a maze of narrow passageways and shops with carved wooden doors and windows, had a European feel to it, and indeed, the transliterations on old shop windows and weathered street signs, like "*Chah*" instead of "*Shah*," were vestiges of the days when French and not English was the most prevalent foreign language spoken in Tehran.

The aroma of fresh-baked pastries and coffee beckoned us even before we saw the café. Once we were inside, the din of the street vanished. The café was filled with men, all quietly reading, their cigarette smoke filling the large room with a soft blue haze.

We found a table in the center of the café and Ali went to the counter to place our order. Alone at the table, I was aware that something was very different about my surroundings, but I couldn't quite define it. Ali returned with our hot chocolate and we sat in companionable silence.

"I really like this place," I said. "I don't know why, but I feel so comfortable here."

"Well, it has an illustrious history," he said. "Lots of poets, novelists, and intellectuals would come here to write."

As I surveyed the room, hoping to see a writer at work, I realized what made this place so appealing. No one was staring at me. No one was even glancing at me. I was invisible. My eyes traveled from table to table, taking note of each man, his head down, engrossed in his book or newspaper. Some of the newspapers were Persian; others had what looked like strings of rounded n's and u's and upside down m's. Slowly it dawned on me that these were Armenian newspapers. These men were oblivious to me because they were Armenian Christians whose wives, daughters and sisters also went without hijab. But all of the men were far too busy reading to notice a *bi hijab* foreigner.

Places like Café Naderi insulated me. I could withstand the stares if I could find little enclaves of indifference like this one. I could live in Iran if I chose my surroundings carefully—the university, the museums, the shops in the north part of town, the homes of family members and like-minded friends, both Iranian and expatriate. There I could ignore the fact that more than thirty-five years after Reza Shah banned the chador, underneath the veneer of modernity applied by his son's regime, there was still a significant segment of this predominantly Muslim country that believed women should be covered, and those women who were not covered were immoral. The chador had been optional for the last 30 years, and because so many women in this cosmopolitan capital went without hijab, it was easy to think that hijab was no longer an issue, that it was merely a matter of personal preference. It was easy to think everyone accepted that a woman's morality did not necessarily depend on a piece of cloth. Nine years later, I would understand how wrong I had been.

Beyond the curious stares and furtive jostling, our forays down-town were fraught with other perils. Even with Ali beside me, I was terrified by the traffic, both as a passenger and as a pedestrian. The free-form crush was unfathomable to me. There were lane divisions, but drivers ignored them. If a driver did not tailgate, he risked having another car wedge itself in front of him. Taxis disgorged their passengers in the middle of the street. There were crosswalks, but pedestrians did not have right of way, and they crossed at their own peril. Pedestrians with children in tow and laden with packages ignored crosswalks altogether and dodged be-tween passing cars with astounding impunity.

Then there were the *joobs*, or street gutters, some of them as much as four or five feet wide, that lined both broad avenues and narrow *koochehs*. On Pahlavi Avenue, a major thoroughfare lined with stately plane trees that ran from the suburb of Shemiran in the north to the train station in the south, the *joobs* were formi-dable channels of rushing mountain water that skipped over piles of leaves and twigs and eddied around the detritus of gum wrap-pers, plastic bags, lottery tickets, and hapless children's canvas shoes.

Leaping over a *joob* was easy for the sure-footed natives, but a daily terror for me. With the cars whizzing past me, the blaring of horns in my ears, the fist of exhaust fumes in my chest, I would stand frozen at the edge of the *joob*, unable to screw up my courage to jump, opting to walk several yards out of my way to find a foot bridge.

I began to feel that life was cheap in Iran. At least, my life was cheap. Rather than make things safer, people left things up to God. They didn't use seatbelts. They didn't wear motorcycle hel-mets. They crossed against the light. They said, "I'll see you tomorrow, *insha'allah*, God willing." They said "I'll get my bachelor's degree in June, *agar khoda bekhad*, if God wills it."

There was also the prevailing understanding that what God wants is already set, that everyone has his or her *ghesmat*—kismet, one's allotted portion or fate. That fatalistic worldview—comforting to so many believers—only served to make me feel more helpless in this new environment.

I was more than ready for a brief escape. When Ali had definitely secured his position at Tehran University, I was happy to head for Kerman and leave behind, for the time being, the quiet apartment and the spare, empty, unstructured days.

As we boarded the bus for Isfahan, the first major city on our journey, I was unaware how crowded my life would soon become.

10

GET ON THE BUS

Isfahan: October 1971

Our plan was to travel by bus to Isfahan, six or seven hours south of Tehran, and stay overnight at the Shah Abbas hotel. Ali's younger brother Ahmad would meet us there the next day and we would drive directly to Kerman, another 12 hours away.

Our friend Mahin would postpone her usual sweeping that morning until she was sure that we had crossed over water, so that our essence would not be swept away. Any body of water would suffice—a river, a stream, a pond. Mahin knew the road well and could estimate how long it would take us to fulfill the requirement. Because I was sure she was anxious to get on with her chores, I wondered if she might let a running *joob* on a nearby street count as a body of water.

Mahmoud drove us to the TBT bus station on Fisherabad Avenue. He helped us with our bags, keeping up a steady stream of cheerful suggestions to counter my obvious nervousness.

"You'll love it, Ellen Khanum," he said. "There's no place like Kerman. Make sure Ali takes you to see my sister Aghdas, you know, the one who's a seamstress. She'll make you a dress. Ali Jaan, give our best to everyone in your family. And don't forget to take Ellen to Mahan to see the *Bagh e Shazdeh* (the Prince's Garden)."

"Which one is the driver?" I asked, eyeing the small group of bedraggled-looking men leaning against the front of the bus, smoking. "They look tired. Do you think they've had enough sleep?"

"Ellen Khanum, you worry too much," Mahmoud replied, smiling reassuringly. "People take this road all the time. You'll enjoy the trip, *insha'allah*."

In the crowded parking lot, among chador-clad women with their bags full of sweets and plastic sandals, bearded men with calloused hands and sweater vests warped from too many washings, and scruffy students memorizing their mimeographed class notes, we found our bus, stowed our suitcases, and settled into our seats. We waved goodbye to Mahmoud, who stood watching to make sure we got off safely.

As the driver pulled out, deftly navigating around the throngs of travelers and well-wishers still crowding the station, we looked at each other and laughed, relieved to be on our way.

We were finally going to see Ali's family.

Ali had waited for this day since he left Iran six years ago. Actually, he'd waited most of his life. All those years of study, no matter how effortless they had seemed to others, had led him to this point. He had channeled his talents and diverged from the path taken by his father and brothers. He had been first student throughout middle school and high school, winning a full scholarship to Tehran University, and another one to study abroad. While family pressures and tradition intervened to divert his older siblings, he had remained resolved to not just finish his studies but excel at them. He had chosen an academic life, a foreign wife, and a home in Tehran, far from his family.

At 18, Ali left Kerman for Tehran to attend twelfth grade at the rigorous Hadaf High School, the better to position himself for the *concours*, the university entrance exams. With the help of his brother Reza and sister Fatemeh, he scraped together the tuition and rented a room in a house with no indoor plumbing. His elderly, penurious landlady carefully monitored his use of electricity and forbade him to study in his room late at night, so he and his friend Farzin would meet at the corner of Pahlavi and Pasteur avenues, and benefiting from the generous electricity illuminating the neighborhood of the Marble Palace, they would study under the light of the streetlamps.

As often as they could, Reza, Ahmad, Ali's brother-in-law Asghar Agha, and other truck-driving relatives, would visit Ali in Tehran. Ali was very lonely, and looked forward to these visits, but his circumstances made it difficult for him to play host. Late one cold winter evening, a group of relatives arrived, tired from their long journey. Ali made them tea and, oblivious to his student's schedule, they stayed up talking late into the night.

The next morning, while his guests were still asleep, Ali got up and stumbled out to the courtyard to wash the tea glasses for breakfast. But to his dismay, the courtyard pool had frozen over. He was not given to fits of self-pity, but on this morning, as he hacked away at the barrier of ice, Ali wept, asking himself why he hadn't stayed in Kerman like the rest of his classmates.

He survived that rigorous senior year of high school and went on to study at Tehran University's College of Agriculture in Karaj. There he excelled and upon graduation was awarded a first student scholarship to study abroad.

Ali was always a good student, blessed with a photographic and auditory memory, critical thinking skills, and a love of learning. He could read a passage or hear a lecture once and the material was his, so he had plenty of time to tutor classmates, play chess with friends after school, or read to his parents late into the night.

He was the only one of his school-aged siblings who was actively pursuing an academic career. While his sisters Sakineh, Fatemeh and Naazi were certainly intelligent and talented, their parents encouraged them to be thinking about finding husbands. They saw no value in educating a girl if she was only going to be married at 17. His brothers Reza and Ahmad were more interested in going into the family trucking business than studying math and science. While they loved to take apart their father's truck engines, Ali hated the feel of axle grease on his hands. He was much more interested in the poetry of mathematical patterns than in how a carburetor works.

Both Ali's parents were illiterate, and their evening entertainment was limited to listening to their battery-run Grundig radio or nightly readings by one of their seven children. Ali was usually the one pressed into service, as he was the most accommodating and never seemed to have any homework. Therefore, most nights, after dinner, they would sit together, Ali's father cross-legged on the floor, leaning on pillows piled against the wall, and Ali positioned next to him beside the kerosene lamp, reading from classics of popular Persian literature.

Despite those late nights, Ali was consistently the top student in his class. In high school he majored in mathematics—the most demanding course of study in the Iranian education system. Every year, from seventh grade on, he had received the first student prize in his grade level—usually a crystal bowl or a silver vase paid for by the Ministry of Education. But when he finished 10th grade, the principal, Agha-ye Haeri, had other ideas.

A few days before the end of the school year, the principal called him into his office, where he was met by six of his teachers, all smiling broadly as they sipped their tea. As he greeted each of the men, Ali noticed a bicycle leaning against the wall—not just any old bicycle, but a shiny, green Robin Hood bike. He couldn't take his eyes off it.

"Go ahead, it's yours," said the principal.

Attached to the bike was a letter written on school stationery that read:

> *Whereas during your years of study in this high school, you have ranked First Student, both in your studies and in your behavior, and whereas in this current year, you have ranked first in your examinations, therefore you are presented with a Robin Hood bicycle, obtained by admirers, as an award. It is hoped that you will continue the same performance during your future studies.*

Flushed with excitement, Ali thanked his admirers, secured his books to the back of his new bike, and pedaled his way home through the dusty streets of Kerman. Breathless and exhilarated, he opened the gate and carefully carried his bike down the steps to the courtyard. His father was already at home, tending to the fruit trees, when Ali rolled the bike in and flipped down the kickstand.

"What's this?" his father asked gruffly.

"It's a new Robin Hood bike," Ali replied. "The school gave it to me for being first student for so many years."

Ali was trying not to appear too prideful, but his shining eyes and glowing face betrayed his absolute joy in his new acquisition. He waited for his father's congratulations.

The old man put down his pruning shears. His eyes slowly traveled from Ali's dusty shoes up to his close-cropped head. He looked Ali in the eye and said, "I piss on the school that made you First Student."

Ali felt a familiar sting behind his eyes.

"But Baba," he protested, "I really am a good student."

"How could you be? I never see you study."

Ali's heart sank. Yet he knew that his father wasn't really insulting him, just questioning the wisdom of a school system that would give such an expensive prize to someone who seemed to put forth so little effort.

Baba's reaction to the bicycle may have been caused in part by his unfamiliarity with education, but it also may have been the result of the prevailing parenting style. Baba's generation never let children get too full of themselves or tarry too long in the spotlight, lest they become obnoxious and self-centered or *por roo* (cheeky).

Ali referred to the bicycle story many times, so many that his father's assessment became a frequent punch line among his university friends and colleagues any time one of them received an honor. *I piss on the Persian Club that elected you president.* When Ali finished his Ph.D., he was looking forward to telling his father. His friends congratulated him, but cautioned him: "Of course, you know what your father will say."

The two of us might not have been together on this bus without the Robin Hood bike. Ali sold it to pay for most of his senior year tuition in Tehran. It is what propelled him forward to Karaj, to Davis, and to me.

Now, 13 years after that shiny Robin Hood bike appeared in the Estilai courtyard, I was preparing to meet Ali's father, the very man who might be inclined to relieve himself on the University of California, Davis. If he was skeptical about Ali's academic achievements, might he also be skeptical about a foreign bride? And unfortunately, his wife was not there to advocate for me.

Ali's mother had died of cancer in 1965, just a few months before he left for America. Even though she had no education, she had vision.

"You have a gift," she had told him. "You can't do anything for us if you stay here. You must go abroad to study."

She was also pragmatically resigned about any future marital plans. "And you'll probably marry a foreigner," she said, matter-of-factly, letting him know, with a smile and her bright, steady gaze, that it would be all right with her.

As the first person in his family to graduate from anywhere, he was now coming home with a Master's and Ph.D. from a prestigious American university. In spite of his full scholarship, his family had made many sacrifices on his behalf, and he was finally making good on his promise to return to them.

Ali's brother Reza and his sister Fatemeh, who had modest incomes and families of their own, had not only contributed to his expenses when he was a senior in high school in Tehran but also when he was a student at the College of Agriculture. When Ali left Iran to study on a government scholarship, his father was required to put the family home up as collateral to ensure his son's return and subsequent service to the country. But his biggest obligation was to his mother's vision of his success—a success he could now share with all of them.

I had been waiting for this day, as well. Early in our relationship, Ali began to regale me with tales of his family—the uncle's wife who made the bootleg vodka the family fondly referred to as *eau de cologne;* the senile grandmother, Nan Jaan, who knew the entire Qur'an by heart, who railed at being left behind "like a dog" when the family went out; his brilliant, mercurial brother Reza, two years his senior, who quit school in the 8th grade over a fight with another student, became a truck driver, got married at seventeen and now had five children.

By my meager standards, his family was huge—three sisters, three brothers, 18 nieces and nephews, uncles, aunts, hundreds of cousins and their families, almost all living in the same town, and all involved in each other's lives. Having grown up with just a younger brother, three thousand miles away from my first cousins, I was intrigued by the sheer mass of the Estilai clan.

I had seen only the few old black and white photographs Ali had brought with him to the States. Some were stiff formal portraits, others tiny snapshots of family groups, old and young, standing in the garden, staring seriously at the camera. The studio portraits were taken in the early 1950s, but they looked much older. Ali's sisters had bobbed hair in French waves, bright red, bee-stung lips, and mid-calf dresses made of delicately patterned silk or velvet that my Italian grandmother might have worn in the twenties or thirties.

In one full-length portrait, his sister Fatemeh and her husband, Asghar Agha, stand squarely side by side, gravely facing the camera, just to the right of an electrical cord the photographer forgot to hide—she in her dark brocade dress, shimmering white stockings and ankle strap pumps, he in a light, double-breasted pin-striped suit, his pant legs grazing dusty, scuffed shoes. Underneath his suit jacket, his tie lay atop his sweater vest—an oddly endearing sartorial touch. Asghar's Chaplinesque moustache and shock of wild black hair were the only intimations of the sense of humor he was reputed to have. Then there were the photographs of Baba, Ali's father, with his white stubble and high cheekbones, an older, sterner version of his son.

Yes, I too had been waiting for this day, but not without some apprehension—and not only about the bus trip, and traffic, and *ghesmat*. To be sure, I was nervous about meeting his family. *What will they think of me? Do they really not mind that I'm not Iranian, not Muslim? Before we married, did they have someone else in mind for him, someone more suitable? Will we have anything to say to one another? Will I be an embarrassment?*

I thought about the vision that Ali's mother had for him—that he would study in the States and probably marry a foreigner. Grateful for her open-mindedness, I was sorry that I had never had the chance to meet her, but I was sure that I would have loved her.

I was less sure about Ali's father.

"Do you think your family will like me?" I asked Ali, for what must have been the twentieth time.

"Trust me, they'll love you," he said, as he always did.

"What about your father?"

"Get some rest," he said.

11

....

ISFAHAN IS HALF THE WORLD

Isfahan: October 1971

As the bus sped down the road, I decided to put aside my traffic fears and enjoy the scenery. I rested my forehead against the window and watched as the vibrant colors and clamor of Tehran gradually gave way to the surrounding desert. I was mesmerized by the dun-colored landscape dotted with scruffy desert plants, its barrenness interrupted now and then by small, blue-domed adobe structures, some with minarets, most in ruins.

"What is that building in the distance?" I asked Ali. "This is the fourth one like this I've seen. It looks like some kind of mosque, but it's in the middle of nowhere."

"It's another *imam zaadeh*," he explained. "These are the tombs of people who are said to be descendants of the Shiite imams. Villagers go there to pray. They tie pieces of cloth to the tomb's grill-work so that their wishes will come true. They might make a kind of contract, a *nazr*, or vow. They might say, 'if my wish is granted, I will light so many candles there…or donate money to the poor…or make food for the village.'"

How convenient, I thought. *A spiritual reststop.*

I imagined the shrine's cool, dark, musty interior, the bits of faded, tattered fabric like so many forgotten hopes, left there to turn to dust. *What would I wish for, what prayer would I tie to the grill if I had the chance?*

I would probably just wish to get to Kerman in one piece.

The bus arrived in Isfahan that afternoon. Along the tree-lined streets, shopkeepers were readying for the onslaught of last-minute evening shopping. The air was filled with the scent of charcoal and grilled lamb. We turned onto a broad avenue and saw the Zayandeh Rud, the Lifegiving River, which winds through the city. The lights of the Khaju Bridge, one of twelve that span the river, would soon struggle for prominence with the setting sun.

We took a taxi from the bus station to the Shah Abbas Hotel. One of the finest hotels in the country, it was built in the 17th century by the last Safavid king as a caravanserai for the *Madrasseh ye Madar e Shah*, the King's Mother's Theological School, which stood next door. Now a modern hotel, it was a tribute to both the Safavid aesthetic and Isfahani hospitality. Everywhere were rich carpets, colorful ceramic tiles, and intricately carved jalousie screens. The bellboys and waiters were dressed in Safafid-style uniforms—long, brocaded tunics, loose-fitting pants and dome-shaped felt hats fashionable in the 17th Century court of Shah Abbas.

With the bellboy's help, we took our bags to our room, which happened to have two double beds. We didn't bother to unpack, because we were expecting to leave early in the morning. We went downstairs and, within sight of the Madrasseh's dome and minarets, had tea in the caravanserai's courtyard, enveloped by the thick, heady scent of roses and honeysuckle.

Ali's brother Ahmad was to meet us the next morning to take us to Kerman, but since we had the whole evening to ourselves, we decided to take a quick turn around the ancient bazaar and the Naqsh e Jahan (Image of the World) Square. In the Safavid era, the square was a polo field, and the shah watched matches from the balcony of the Ali Qapou palace.

The old saying, *"Isfahan—nesf e jahan,"* (Isfahan is half the world) reflects Iranians' reverence for this ancient cultural center and former capital. As we strolled through the broad, tree-lined avenues, I began to see why this motto had survived for hundreds of years. Since the reign of the Safavid king Shah Abbas (1588-1629 C. E.), the former capital has been a center of art and design. This was the same Shah Abbas who, to assure his long reign, had one of his own sons killed and two others blinded. He may have been a merciless, murdering despot, but he knew how to inspire artists, artisans, architects, and city planners for both the greater glory of God and his own kingship. Flanked by the bazaar, the palace and two mosques, Naghsh e Jahan Square presents an image of the world that is a tightly woven tapestry of the sacred and profane, art and commerce, the particular and the universal.

Isfahan is bound together by interlocking patterns. Each of its components is exquisite, sublime, and ethereal, so much so that if the city were not anchored by a wise, underlying structure, it might fly away, buoyed by its own audacity. Nearly every surface is embellished. Even the rare surface that is not decorated with repeated designs is itself repeated to form a larger design—like the arches and supports of bridges reflected in the river or like a small clay dome that is reiterated over and over on neighboring roofs, joining with other domes to form a sprawling but orderly collection of adobe goose bumps for the amusement of passing birds.

Earthbound, I couldn't take in all these patterns at once. I had to savor them individually. As we walked the labyrinth that is the old bazaar, Ali and I were treated to a visual symphony of designs, a tactile lyric poem with recurring motifs. Pierced brick windows cast ever changing circles of light on dusty stone floors. A waiter's jacket was echoed in the towering bolts of brocade stacked in the fabric shop. Delicate tendrils of vines radiating from the center of a tiny enameled plate emerged again as silver filigree against a wooden door and recombined yet again on the domed ceilings of a mosque or a palace. The mark of the Qur'an was everywhere—embedded in the delicate tangle of plasterwork calligraphy over a doorway or hidden in the tile-work puzzle of chunky, geometric script that even a devout student of the holy text might have difficulty deciphering.

You would think that this constant reverberation of patterns would be exhausting, a Stendhal syndrome-inducing assault on the senses, but I found it comforting. The rhythm of these designs teased my eyes back and forth between the particular and the general, the personal and the public. I could become intoxicated with the roses in a corner of the hotel garden, then look down on those same roses from the second floor balcony and see how they fit into the logic of that garden, a garden which like all classical Iranian gardens is a blueprint for paradise. I could lean in to examine the tiny star-shaped ivory inlays on a wooden picture frame, then step back to see the same designs overhead on the domes-within-a-dome ceiling of the Madrassah. I could imagine that ceiling itself as the heavens and the tiny stars as players in the universe.

Caught up in the rhythm of these patterns, I forgot all my apprehensions. I forgot to be self-conscious. Isfahan is half the world, and in this half of the world, for a few hours at least, I could find comfort in a larger pattern, a higher order.

We returned to the hotel for a leisurely dinner and then, at about 10 p.m., we went up to our room, hoping to rest up for the long trip the following day. Exhausted, we fell into one of the beds and drifted off to sleep.

Suddenly there was a knock at the door.

"Ali," I whispered, "don't open the door until you know who it is."

My heart was racing. I had heard too many stories about midnight visits from the SAVAK. The knocking got louder, and there was a muffled voice—no, two voices—in the corridor.

"Just a minute," he shouted, in the direction of the door. Struggling into his trousers, he hobbled across the room and peered through the spy hole. He smiled and unlocked the door.

In the hallway stood two men grinning broadly—familiar grins, Estilai grins.

"Bah, bah! Ahmad Jaan, Hossein Jaan. Come in," Ali said, embracing them both.

Drawing the blankets around me, I searched their faces for the family traits—the liquid-chocolate brown eyes, full lips, wavy dark hair. Our photo album was beginning to come to life. Ali introduced me, and I climbed out of bed for another round of kissing and more grinning.

Uncomfortable meeting relatives in my nightgown, I crawled back under the covers while Ahmad and Hossein sat on the other bed. Hossein was Fatemeh's oldest child. He was still in high school but had taken time off to accompany his uncle Ahmad on this trip. They had decided to get an early start from Kerman that day, and even though they knew we might be asleep when they arrived, they woke us because they couldn't wait to see us.

I had already met Ahmad over the telephone, shortly after we arrived in Tehran. It was on one of those mornings when Ali was off making the rounds of university departments looking for a job, and I was left to my own devices in the empty apartment. When the phone rang, I was happy at the prospect of hearing a human voice but terrified when I realized I would have to speak Persian.

"*Allo,*" I shouted into the mouthpiece—the only word I had much confidence in getting right. *So far so good.*

I heard a man's voice on the other end of the faint connection unleashing a string of words that included Ali's name.

"*Baleh,*" I answered...yes. That seemed like a safe reply. Yes, go on.

Then I heard something that sounded like Kerman and Ahmad.

I knew then it was Ali's younger brother, Ahmad. I had seen a snapshot of him sitting in the cab of his truck somewhere in a grove of palm trees, gazing moodily into the distance, his collar turned up like a 1940's B-movie actor posing for a publicity still.

"*Ali neest,*" I said. Ali isn't here. "*Ali raft,*" I continued, bravely nudging my monosyllables from the present tense into the past tense. Ali left.

"*Ali neest?*" he said, then something that must have been "Where is he? When will he be back?" I could hear him smiling. Even with the bad connection and unfamiliar words, I was sure he was smiling. I knew I sounded like a first-grade primer.

"*Ali neest,*" I repeated, not knowing how to say, *He's gone off to find work and left me alone for hours in this apartment without furniture or a* Time *magazine or a translator.* I decided to change the subject with the only other verb construction I was sure of. "*Baba khoob e?*" I asked. Is your father well?

"*Baleh, Baba khoob e,*" Ahmad replied, laughing now, not even trying to contain his amusement.

A month or so having passed since that telephone call, I was happy that I had progressed enough to follow their conversation and chime in now and then. After a few minutes, Ahmad looked at me and said, *"Ali neest. Ali raft. Baba khoob e?"* This was to be the first of many times that Ahmad would gleefully quote my early attempts at Persian conversation.

I was really enchanted with the spontaneity of Ahmad and Hossein's arrival and the easy rapport they had with Ali—even after so many years apart. They quickly got him caught up on family gossip—who was getting married, who was having trouble finding work, who was buying a house. There was the inventory of family ailments, of new babies, of lost opportunities. I tried to follow along, nudging a translation out of Ali now and then. But mostly, I just basked in the warmth of this meeting—this impromptu slumber party. We stayed up talking until about 3 a.m., when Ahmad and Hossein, installed in the second bed, decided to turn out the lights and go to sleep.

The next morning, with surprisingly little difficulty, we woke up and went down to breakfast in the hotel restaurant. When it was time to check out, we all accompanied Ali to the registration desk. The hotel clerk eyed the four of us icily. His cold, disapproving gaze lingered on me a bit longer.

"Agah-ye Estilai," he said, with studied formality, "It has come to my attention that you had two extra people in your room last night."

"Well, yes," Ali replied. "My brother and my nephew came from Kerman to take us home. I just returned from the States, and I haven't seen them in six years."

"Be that as it may," the clerk said, "they should have paid for their own room. I'm sorry, but you'll have to pay extra for them."

"Really, they didn't intend to stay overnight," Ali explained. "We just got to talking and before we knew it, it was very late. They just fell asleep."

"I am sorry sir," the clerk insisted. "But those are the rules. You'll have to pay for them."

As Ali, still protesting, reached in his pocket for his wallet, the manager came over to see what the fuss was about. He looked down at the register and then up at Ali. His eyes narrowed as he asked, "Are you the same Ali Estilai who spent sixth grade in Shahr Babak?"

"Yes, that's me," Ali replied, smiling faintly. Ali had spent his last year of elementary school with his sister Fatemeh and her family. Because she was homesick for Kerman, she had asked their parents to let Ali live with her for a year.

"I know you," said the manager. "I'm Jafar Jafarzadeh. You might remember me. We were classmates. You were a very good student."

"Jafar, of course I remember you," Ali shouted.

There was kissing on both cheeks and hugging and slapping of backs.

"Welcome back," Jafar said. "Needless to say, I won't charge you for the extra guests."

How easily the matter was resolved before Ali had a chance to argue his case with the manager. It was no longer important who was right—only that there was a connection between these two men. They may not have been best friends that year in Shahr Babak, but they had known each other, and that was enough. Once that connection had been made, once that past relationship had been acknowledged, it was understood that the infraction would be overlooked.

We packed up the car and headed for Kerman. We were an hour or so out of Isfahan, heading south toward Na'in, when Ali got an idea.

"Where did you say Ghasem's village is?" he asked Ahmad.

"It's about three hours northeast of here," Ahmad replied. "We'd have to turn around—and probably lose half a day."

"Let's do it," Ali said.

12

THE VILLAGE OF PENART

Isfahan Province: October 1971

Laughing at his brother's spontaneity, Ahmad dutifully spun the car around and set off for Ardestan and the village of Penart where their brother Ghasem was performing his compulsory military service in the shah's Literacy Corps. He turned up the radio and resumed his normal driving position, hunched purposefully over the old Volvo's steering wheel. I was safely in the back, with Hussain, where I was less likely to obsess about the oncoming traffic. Ali, prone to carsickness when he wasn't driving, was upfront in the passenger's seat.

Ali came from a family of truckers, all of whom prided themselves on their driving skills. Ali's father and uncle were the first to establish a trucking business in Kerman in the 1930's, and Ali's brothers Reza and Ahmad and several cousins and brothers-in-law had all been at one time or another part of that enterprise. They loved to drive and jumped at any excuse to be on the open highway.

With popular Persian songs blaring from the radio and a string of garish colored lights twinkling from underneath the car's dashboard, we headed off across the expanse of desert to bring cheer to a lonely literacy corpsman.

"What if Ghasem isn't home?" I asked, worried that this detour would be for nothing.

"Where else would he be?" Ahmad replied. "He's miles away from nowhere, with very little money and only a motor scooter for transportation. He'll be there."

"And he'll be really happy to see us," added Hossein, idly twirling his worry beads.

More than a year before, Ghasem had received his diploma from a technical high school in Kerman, where he was studying to be an electrician. Like all male high school graduates, he was faced with two years of compulsory military service, so he opted for *Sepah e Danesh*, the Literacy Corps.

In 1963, persuaded by the Kennedy administration, the shah set in motion the *Enghelab e sefid* (White Revolution), which included the establishment of the Literacy Corps, a joint project of the Army and the Ministry of Education. This war on illiteracy was a major component of the shah's campaign to modernize the country and one of the requirements for receiving US aid. From 1963 to the end of the Pahlavi regime in 1979, 200,000 young men and women served in this "army of knowledge." Traveling from cities and towns to remote villages, these young middle-class men and women taught a total of 2.2 million boys and girls between the ages of 6 and 12, as well as another one million adults. In this polyglot country, their job was not just to make villagers literate but literate in Persian, the official language. They also were charged with inculcating good hygiene and social behavior, as well as a sense of national identity. In addition, they advocated for co-educational schools.[23]

In the mid-1970's, sensing growing discontent and cynicism with his regime as a whole, the shah changed the name of his White

---

23. Seyed Farian Sabahi, The Literacy Corps in Pahlavi Iran (1963 – 1979): Political, Social and Literary Implications. *Cahiers d'etudes sur la Mediterranée orientale et le monde turco-iranien.* No. 31, janvier-juin 2001.

Revolution to the Revolution of the Shah and the People (*enghelab e shah va mardom*). But not all the people were persuaded, especially the mullahs. From its very inception, the Literacy Corps and other modernizing initiatives were targets of hardline Muslim clerics who were certain that government meddling in the lives of villagers would only increase the country's dependence on imperialist powers and subvert strict adherence to Islamic values. They were unmoved by the promise of linguistic homogeneity, especially if it came at the expense of traditional social mores. Of course, the mullahs also feared that their own power over the villagers would be diminished.

Ghasem had served his six months of teacher training and had been working in his assigned village for five or six months. He still had one more year away from family and friends before he could be discharged.

Ghasem was the youngest of Ali's six brothers and sisters. Only twelve when his mother died, he was still the baby of the family at nineteen. I had seen his pictures in our photo album—the dark, wavy Estilai hair, a round face with just a trace of adolescent baby fat—a sweet, open face with a ready smile. I was looking forward to meeting him—and to getting my first glimpse of an Iranian village.

As we neared Ardestan, we saw a double rainbow arching across the desert. We all agreed that this was a good omen for our visit. Little by little, I relaxed, forgetting to be vigilant about oncoming trucks, forgetting to be apprehensive about meeting new people. Instead, I drifted off to sleep with the songs of popular female singers Haideh and Pouran on the radio and the easy banter of the men in my ears, the hum of the engine, the swoosh of the passing cars....

"Ellen Khanum, wake up," Ahmad said, looking at me in the rearview mirror. "That's Penart," he said, pointing to dun-colored roofs about half a mile away. "We're almost there."

We had turned off the highway and were making our way to the village on a narrow, bumpy dirt road. On a small hill in the distance, we could see Ghasem's village, a rough collection of adobe huts and trees. As we approached, we saw a young man at the top of the hill staring at the road. Suddenly, he started running down the hill, waving his arms wildly. Ahmad and Hussain burst into laughter.

"That's Ghasem," Hussain explained. "He's spotted us."

Ghasem careened toward us, almost running into our car. Giddy at the sight of us, his voice choked with laughter, he opened Ali's door, pulled him out and enveloped him in a bear hug. There were kisses all around, punctuated by lots of *masha'allahs* (praise be to God) to ward off any evil spirits.

Ghasem was even more handsome than his pictures, more like a very young Elvis Presley. He was wearing a khaki wool uniform, a size too small and two inches too short. He must have grown considerably in the year since it was first issued to him.

Taking my hand, Ghasem helped me scale the hill, cross the *joobs* and negotiate the uneven steps to his one-room hut. He moved quickly and effortlessly, springing up and down the uneven terrain and balancing on the edges of rocks, as I did my best to keep up. The tiny village was a hodge-podge collection of adobe huts and narrow, winding passageways that appeared to be sculpted out of the earth by some lost, crazed disciple of Antonio Gaudi.

"*Khosh amadid*, welcome," he said, proudly waving us inside. We made ourselves comfortable on the floor while Ghasem happily set about making tea. The whitewashed room was bare except for a worn red and blue flowered Kermani carpet on the dirt floor, some cushions set against the wall, and a bedroll tied up in a plaid cloth. There was no electricity, but our host soon had the kettle boiling on the Primus stove.

"I can't believe you're here," Ghasem said, beaming. "I didn't think you'd have time to come to visit me, with your schedule and all."

Outside the open door, shy little girls in flowered dresses and headscarves had gathered to get a peek at their teacher's visitors. Behind them, old women sauntered past, covering their toothless grins with corners of their chadors. Some stopped to stare at me, and sensing my discomfort, Ghasem good-naturedly shooed them away.

"So, Ghasem, what's it like here?" asked Ali. "Have you settled in?"

"It's not too bad," he replied. "I've made some friends, and the *kadkhoda* is a good person."

The *kadkhoda* (literally the god of the garden) was the village lord or headman to whom all the villagers deferred. It was necessary for the corpsmen to have the *kadkhoda's* support in order to gain the trust of the villagers. Ghasem did have their trust. Parents were eager to have their children educated. Several of his eighteen students came to class on foot from neighboring villages.

"Are you making a difference?" Ali asked.

"I'm doing what I can," his brother replied, shrugging his shoulders.

"What tools did they give you?"

"We have a teacher's manual and some textbooks."

In good weather, his classroom was outdoors. Children sat on the ground in a circle around him and recited their lessons. I closed my eyes and imagined the chanted rhythms of the first-grade Persian reader and the exploits of Dara and Sara, the Iranian Dick and Jane. I could hear the spare, insistent syllables bouncing off the dry earth, harkening back 2000 years to the Parthian and Pahlavi languages, to Persian's pre-Islamic roots.

Baba nan dad.... Baba ab dad.... Emrooz baran barid.... Sara va Dara be madar komak mikonand. (Father gave bread.... Father gave water.... Today it rained.... Sara and Dara help mother.)

While we rested, Ghasem jumped on his motor scooter and headed for the nearest grocery store several miles away to buy food for dinner. I could see that Ali had his doubts about Ghasem's situation, so with his brother out of the room, I asked him what was bothering him.

"Well, I just really wonder if this Literacy Corps is all it's cracked up to be," Ali explained, helping himself to more tea. "First, there's the lack of resources. Ghasem is going to need more than just a set of textbooks. Second, there's his limited training. Six months of boot camp? How is he going to teach these kids?"

"But with such widespread illiteracy," I said, "every effort is admirable. It's a start."

Fresh from the States, Ali had high expectations, and perhaps it was unfair to compare the Literacy Corps' approach with that of the standard American elementary school. But Ali was also skeptical about the government's dedication to the cause. If the shah was so intent on eradicating illiteracy and modernizing the country, he wondered, why didn't he put more resources behind the project? How about some desks?

Ghasem returned and, from the back of the scooter, unloaded a crate of soft drinks, a flat of eggs, a packet of Indian tea wrapped in mauve paper, a block of feta cheese, and a package of frankfurters (*saucisse*)—all unscathed from their perilous journey over the rutted dirt road.

Ghasem busied himself with the dinner preparations but wouldn't let anyone help. He was clearly enjoying having company. As the *saucisse* for the omelet sizzled in the frying pan, he retrieved some village *taftoon*, a large oval of perforated flatbread, from a bread box and washed a handful of fresh herbs in a basin. He spread a plastic tablecloth on the floor, and within minutes we had a feast.

"*Nush-e jaan*," Ghasem said. Nectar for your soul. The simple meal, the clean air of the village, the sheer joy of being with family was indeed nectar.

Ever the perfect host, Ghasem volunteered to shepherd me to the outhouse, or what passed for one in the village. Outhouse is too grand a word. It was a sort of rock enclosure with a hole in the ground, carved out of the hillside. I never really saw it clearly, because Ghasem kept himself and his kerosene lamp at a discrete distance. *This is pathetic*, I thought as I groped around the privy with a small flashlight. *I'm 24 years old, and I still have to be taken to the bathroom.* I could see the headlines in the English edition of *Kayhan*: American Bride Dies from Fall into Pit Toilet.

All too soon, it was time to get back on the road. As we gathered our belongings, Ghasem's sunny mood clouded over. It was as if he couldn't bear the thought of our leaving without him. He thanked us for coming and told us he would try to get to Kerman in a few days. Then he stopped for a moment, excused himself and went outside.

Within minutes, he was back, grinning, hurriedly stuffing clothes into his rucksack.

"I told the *kadkhoda* that my brother and his American wife are here from the States, and I have to go to Kerman to be with them," he said, laughing. "You have another traveling companion."

Ali's brother Ghasem, with friend, in the village of Penart, Isfahan Province, where he served in the Literacy Corps, October 1971.

Ghasem teaching students in Penart.

13

GOING WITH THE GRAIN

Kerman: 1971

Kerman was at once sunny and chilly—like drinking hot tea and eating ice cream at the same time. As our car wound around the Meidoon e Bagh e Melli (The People's Garden Square), down tree-lined boulevards and through narrow *koochehs*, we saw the angle of the autumnal desert light throw our surroundings into high relief. Our exhaustion accentuated the play of shadows on the rough bricks, domes, and archways. We gave ourselves over to the contrasts of this sharp, electric clarity, the crisp air and the spongy, smooth, numbing exhaustion that had rounded off all our edges.

We had left Ghasem's village at 10 p.m., and Ahmad had driven all night. At sunrise, we had a flat tire. Ali and I sat by the side of the road while our three companions cheerfully wrestled with the spare.

"Shouldn't you offer to help them?" I asked Ali.

"They know I don't know how to do anything," he explained. "Why pretend I can?"

As we rolled into town at mid-morning on that bright, clear November day, the five of us were lost in our own thoughts, each with our own mix of excitement and apprehension. Ahmad, Ghasem, and Hussain were smiling to themselves, proud and relieved to have delivered us safely to Kerman and eager to see the family's reaction to us.

Our first stop would be the home of Ali's older brother Reza, his wife Pouran, and their five children. Ali's father lived there most of the time, as did Ahmad, and even Ghasem, when he was on leave from the Literacy Corps.

I sensed Ali's tense anticipation and tried to imagine what he must be thinking. With every block, every familiar bookstore, greengrocer and shoe repair shop, his smile became wider, his eyes brighter. I could see in his face traces of the proud Ali of the Robin Hood bike, the sleepy young boy who had stayed up late reading to his father, the high school senior who left his lonely rented room to study by the light of the streetlamps.

Yet he wasn't that boy anymore.

He was now the Ali who had learned English in San Francisco, got his Master's and Ph.D. at UC Davis, lost money at blackjack in Tahoe and Reno, played on the chess team, arm wrestled in a Paris café, and married an American.

And what, exactly would his family think of this American?

I knew what I thought.

What am I doing here, anyway? I can barely speak Persian. Can't ta-arof. Useless with a broom. Definitely not a Muslim. No, just a hopeless impostor. These people won't be fooled for long. And I wish I could wash my face before I meet anyone.

"Ali, what should I call your father?"

"Just call him Baba," Ali answered with a smile.

The old Volvo lurched over the uneven pavement, rumbled down a narrow lane and jerked to a stop in front of a house that looked like all the houses we had just passed—a modest stretch of nondescript whitewashed adobe, interrupted only by a blue metal door and a few tiny, randomly spaced windows set high on the wall.

Ahmad rang the bell and pushed open the door, stepping aside to let us through. We entered a short, dark passageway that opened onto a bright, sunny courtyard.

And there he was, alone in the middle of the courtyard, Ali's father—moving toward us, arms outstretched, worry beads hanging from one hand, his lips moving in silent prayer.

"*Masha'allah*," he said, as he enveloped Ali in his long arms, kissing him, not in that dainty Tehrani two-cheeks way, but full on the mouth. "*Masha'allah*," he said again as he turned to kiss me in the same way, not waiting for an introduction. "*Khosh amadid.*" Welcome.

He looked as I thought he would. I had memorized his picture from the photo album—his white hair, his tanned, lined face, high forehead, and strong, square jaw—Ali's features, only heavier, more rugged.

A beaming Reza and Pouran were right behind him—Reza, two years older than Ali, dark and thin, with a wavy pompadour, and Pouran, with her long, brown hair and dancing eyes full of laughter.

Soon the courtyard was filled with shouts and laughter and more *masha'allahs*.

Ali agha, welcome. You made our eyes bright. Welcome. You've brought happiness.

"Do we look older, Ali Agha?" teased Pouran, her pretty, round face breaking into a wide smile.

There was a brief discussion with nods in my direction, and then Ghasem appeared with metal chairs. Apparently, Baba felt that I would be more comfortable in a chair than on the carpeted courtyard tiles.

Small brown finches chirped busily in a cage in the chilly shade of the corner—"Ahmad's children," Reza explained, to everyone's amusement—everyone's except Ahmad, who did his best to look forlorn.

Suddenly, Pouran appeared beside me, grabbed my hand and, giggling, shoved two delicate gold bangles on my arm—a present for the new bride. She disappeared into a room off to the side of the courtyard and returned with a tray of tea and Yazdi pastries. We sat in the bright sunlight and drank the tea from *estekans*, little glasses encased in filigreed stainless steel holders set with fake turquoise stones. The tea was bitter, and the tiny spoon kept sliding around and hitting my nose.

Everyone watched me intently as I drank. They observed how many sugar lumps I took (not enough, they said) and noted that I drank my tea *shireen*, with the sugar cube stirred in, not tucked in the side of my mouth. I had tried to drink it the other way, but I always ended up with too much sugar in my mouth and only bitter dregs in the bottom of my glass.

Ali took a photograph of Baba sitting stiffly on a metal chair in the middle of Reza's courtyard, smiling gamely, his hands on his knees, his neck disappearing into the puffy goose down jacket my parents had sent along with us to give to him.

"Does it get cold in Kerman?" my mother had asked Ali before we left for Iran. "I'd like to get something for your father. Perhaps we could give him a warm jacket."

"Kerman is in a desert, and it can get very cold at night," he told her. "In the winter, it sometimes snows."

My mother had gone alone to the sporting goods store and had come back with a bright red parka, a magnificent true red that could be visible for miles in a blizzard. Ali took one look at it and began to draw upon his considerable reserve of tact. He explained how most Iranian people, especially older men, dressed conservatively and favored dark colors, and that, beautiful though the jacket was, his father had never worn that color in his life.

My mother immediately exchanged the red down jacket for a navy blue one. That version was still too flashy for Baba. Its downhill-racing bravado proved incongruous with his quiet demeanor. Yet he graciously submitted to the photograph. Then, with a smile, he stood and took off the jacket. "It's too warm in the sun," he explained.

While Ali and his family caught up with one another, their endless questions and answers punctuated by laughter, I drifted in and out of the conversation, catching only a few words and phrases, names of relatives and towns. As I sipped my tea, I took in my new surroundings—the three rooms opening out onto the spare, yellow brick courtyard; a small raised pool with scalloped edges off to one side, a plastic water pitcher and washbasin leaning against it; children's clothes hanging on the line above; four small rosebushes offering the only greenery; the promising smell of rice pilaf slowly steaming and something simmering in tomato sauce.

My eye caught the flash of a samovar in the corner of a dark room that had to be the kitchen. Leaning forward, I could barely make out the shape of a large gaping hole in a corner near the door.

Pouran, noticing my curiosity, jumped up and took my hand, beckoning Ali to come along to translate. As we stepped up into the dark kitchen, a small room with a sink, a counter, and a few shelves, I saw that the hole in the wall was actually the mouth of a *tanoor*, a floor-to-ceiling, cylindrical clay oven used for baking bread. It was cold now, filled only with ash.

"A woman comes once a week to bake," Pouran explained, gesturing toward the bundles piled in a corner. She unwrapped one of the plastic tablecloths to reveal a stack of large brown discs—*noon e khoonegi*, the Kermani version of homemade flatbread. She broke off a piece and offered it to me. It was slightly hard but chewy, made of whole-wheat flour and laced with cumin and turmeric—much earthier and hardier than the white flatbreads I had become used to in Tehran.

While in college, I had read Henry Miller's "Staff of Life," a diatribe against Wonder Bread culture. "You can travel fifty-thousand miles in America," Miller groused, "without once tasting a piece of good bread." San Francisco sourdough notwithstanding, he was right. Paling in comparison to the crusty Parisian baguettes of his expatriate experience, the gluey, machine-made loaves of 1940s America were a metaphor for all that was inauthentic, tasteless, and culturally isolationist about his homeland. If our bread defines us, I thought, Kermanis are definitely a force to be reckoned with.

Before resuming our tour, Pouran checked the pots of rice and stew sitting on top of the two Primus stoves. We went back out into the courtyard and into the hall, not a corridor but a kind of all-purpose room, where the family ate on a tablecloth spread on the carpet, slept on bedrolls brought in every night from the storeroom, and watched television, leaning on thick cushions propped against the wall. The *mehman khaneh*, or formal living room, was furnished with a very good Kermani carpet and small Western-style sofas.

At one point, Pouran insisted that we all go up on the flat roof, the better to see the neighborhood. However, I soon realized why we were up there. Reza and Pouran had bought a sheep to be sacrificed in gratitude for our safe arrival. Pouran guessed that I would be upset to see an animal slaughtered in front of me, so she made sure it was killed out of my line of sight. Only after the deed had been done did I look down into the courtyard below to see the butcher intently hovering over his work, carefully separating the fluffy skin from the still warm body.

All the rooms in the house opened onto the walled courtyard, the center of the family's activities. Unlike American homes—or even some modern Iranian ones—with picture windows that visually connect the inhabitants with the outside world, traditional Iranian houses turn in upon themselves, enveloping and protecting against the harsh winds of the desert and prying eyes of neighbors.

By comparison, the Pomona, California tract houses I grew up in seemed far more welcoming to the outside world. The always-prominent driveway was a tacit invitation to turn in off the street, the porch light a promise of safe haven, the picture window and half-drawn drapes a teasing frame for a tableau of domestic order.

Yet we rarely had company. Our house looked outward, but our family turned inward upon itself. My parents rarely entertained. Their neighbors were simply people to wave to. Their own parents and siblings were 3,000 miles away, and my mother was separated from her family by old grudges as well as geography.

While my father was outgoing, my mother was a "convivorphobe," afraid of the guest at the feast—specifically, the feast she was obliged to prepare. A rare visit from a relative or, even more rarely, one of my father's colleagues, was anticipated by stomach-churning anxiety and a last-minute cleaning marathon. The Hoover upright's track marks were still visible in the shag carpet when the dreaded guest arrived.

Like many children, I looked forward to company as a respite from the unrelieved monotony of our daily routine. I loved visitors. I relished their stories, their idioms, their mannerisms, their otherness. But with my mother's anxiety and feelings of inadequacy, getting ready for these infrequent visits was like preparing for war.

Mother took a slash and burn approach to tidying up. With cold resolve, she stripped from the living room piles of magazines and newspapers, baskets of unfolded laundry, and remnants of other unfinished projects and banished them to a back bedroom. Armed with a crevice tool, she attacked the vestiges of neglect lurking between the sofa cushions and along the baseboards.

"Go with the grain," she would cry, as someone cleaned the dining room table—oblivious to the fact that this grain was Formica.

We soldiered on in silence broken only by the occasional command from our leader.

By the time the doorbell pierced the tense hush, I, too, had come to fear the guest at the feast.

"They're here," someone would hiss, and we would take our battle stations. I braced myself. I was sure the visitor would see through our feeble line of defense, our little sham of *ad hoc* tidiness, and that we would be unmasked—paper tigers in the campaign against clutter and disorder.

All this drama was squandered on a relatively small number, for we never had more than two or three guests at a time. For an Iranian housewife, however, two or three guests are par for the course. Two or three guests are what her husband or children might bring along at the last minute to any family lunch or dinner. The Iranian housewife learns to expect the unexpected. She spends most of her mornings cleaning or, if she is fortunate, making sure a servant cleans. She shops strategically and cooks defensively. Whatever else she might not have, she always has fresh herbs and cheese and flatbread from the corner bakery and enough eggs for an omelet. She makes expandable meals. No one is ever turned away.

"Just add a little water to the stew," Ali's mother would say over her shoulder as she hurried to welcome the unanticipated guest.

An Iranian friend liked to tell how his mother, on hearing a guest's approaching footsteps, would hurriedly snatch food from the family's plates—an eggplant here, a kebab there, a spatula of rice—so that there would be enough for new arrivals. His family had frequent visitors, and having been the victim of his mother's largesse too often, as soon as he was served, he would gobble up his meat before any guest could appropriate it.

While the Iranian housewife is adept at improvisation, if she is actually going to invite three extra people, she might as well invite thirty and make a lot of people happy in one fell swoop. A guest is, after all, *habib e khoda*, dear to God, someone who should be accepted without question. The word for receiving guests or entertaining, *pazirai*, can also be translated as "acceptance" or "admission." *Your footstep on my eye. This is your own home.*

Reza and Pouran's courtyard began to fill up again with the laughter and shouts of more of the Estilai clan, a swirl of flowered chadors and a blur of blue and gray school uniforms. First came Reza and Pouran's three eldest, Mohammad Reza and Minoo and Mehdi, returning from school; then Ali's sister Sakineh and her children, Habib and Teymoor and Batoul and Fakhri; followed closely by another sister, Naazi, holding her youngest, Farzad; her husband Ahmad, and their children, Mansour and Nasser and Mansoureh and Manijeh and Mojgan and Mozaffar, all adding their shoes to the piles collecting in front of the sitting room doorway.

I was giddy with the sheer numbers of them.

How am I going to remember all their names? How will I communicate with them? What if Ali's not around to translate?

Even though I was overwhelmed, I was buoyed by the family's positive energy. I immediately saw the easy camaraderie they had with one another, that effortless interaction that comes with always being in and out of one another's homes. With my limited Persian, I may have missed some subtleties, but it seemed as if they communicated among themselves with an economy of words, an elliptical way of speaking—or even wordlessly, with nothing more than an eyebrow raised, a chin lifted, or a head slightly cocked.

The sugar bowl is empty? A glance from father to daughter is enough to get it refilled. Out of sodas? A nod in the direction of the car keys and a few minutes later, a case of Pepsi appears. A child is misbehaving? A mother's stern gaze as she bites into her knuckle will restore order.

That is not to say the Estilais were a quiet family. Not at all. Conversation intended for general consumption was boisterous and lively, punctuated with raucous laughter. No, it was just that they were adept at private communication in the middle of a crowd, a necessary survival skill in large families.

That first night, after a late dinner and conversation, Pouran went to the *anbari*, the storeroom, to get the bedding, heavy cotton mattresses, about eight inches thick, and sturdy cotton comforters covered in shiny satin or damask material. A white bed sheet—washed in a nearby stream and bleached by the relentless Kerman sun—was sewn or pinned onto each comforter and mattress. Each set weighed about 40 or 50 pounds. Every morning, the bedrolls were folded and tied up into large squares of red plaid fabric. Pouran lugged six or eight of these to and from the *anbari* every day.

For three nights, Ali and I had the sitting room to ourselves. But on the fourth night, Pouran told us that her eight-year-old daughter Minoo had begged to be allowed to sleep with us. "She won't take up much room," Pouran said, "and she promises not to bother you."

With her spindly legs and arms and thick mane of dark hair, tiny Minoo could have stepped out of a John Tenniel drawing, an Iranian version of Alice in Wonderland. She certainly didn't take up much room, nor did she bother us. She entered the room silently, and looking neither to the left nor to the right, she crept under the comforter, settled in between us, and went to sleep, too shy to say a word.

Far from being upset at having an intruder in our bed, I was flattered. I lay awake in the darkness thinking how, in less than a week, I had gone from the barrenness of our Tehran apartment to the abundance of this family. I thought of how Ahmad and Hussain had knocked on our hotel room in the middle of the night because they couldn't wait until morning to see us—how sad Ghasem had been at the prospect of being left behind in the village—how everyone had rearranged their lives so that Ali and I would be well-fed, entertained, and comfortable. This trip was nectar for the soul. It was what every family reunion aspires to be—a celebration of connectedness, of old roots and new growth.

My life was crowded now with more personalities than I had

ever had to deal with at one time—and deal with in an unfamiliar language while trying to sit cross-legged on the floor. But the Estilais were warm and welcoming people who were prepared to like me. This time, I was the guest at the feast, and I was going to take full advantage of this hospitality.

The next night, Ali and I decided that we had had enough of the sitting room's solitude. To everyone's delight, we dragged our bedrolls into the hall and slept with the rest of the family.

Ali's father Baba, the day Ellen first met him, in Kerman, October 1971. He is wearing the blue jacket her mother sent him.

14

....

THE LOW HOUSE

Kerman: October 1971

When Ali was about to enter sixth grade, he left Kerman
for Shahr Babak, about two hundred inconsistently paved miles
away, to keep his homesick sister Fatemeh company. The house
he left, his family's home for sixteen years, was a large, rambling
U-shaped structure of smooth, light reddish brown brick, with
fifteen rooms and a veranda with several loggias, all overlooking
an expansive courtyard. Baba had designed it himself and over-
seen the construction. The courtyard had a large pool in the center
surrounded by fruit trees and vegetable plots carefully tended by a
gardener. The domed entrance gate, decorated with plaster friezes,
had stairs leading to the roof above one of the wings. In the back,
the compound was separated from their neighbors in the Jewish
quarter by an ancient adobe wall about 15 feet high and about five
feet thick, perhaps the vestiges of an old moat that had encircled a
much smaller Kerman hundreds of years before.

As a teenager, Ali's sister Naazi, dangling her feet in the irrigation ditch, would read popular Persian epic stories to the gardener while he trimmed the trees or weeded the sweet basil and
dill. Once in a while, on school days, the gardener would harvest
bundles of lettuce or other vegetables and send them along with
Naazi so that she could share the family's prosperity and ingratiate

herself with her teachers.

That was the house of Ali's childhood, but the house to which he returned from Shahr Babak ten months later was very different.

This new house, five doors down the vestigial moat from their former home, was one-half the size of the old one and made not of brick but of whitewashed adobe. Two rooms looked out onto a small, unpaved courtyard, with only a few fruit trees. Instead of a pool for washing up, there was a spigot under a tree. A flowered chintz curtain separated the small kitchen from the adjoining sitting room. In a corner of the courtyard was a passageway that led to an *anbari* with a dirt floor. Above that, primitive steps provided access to three unfinished rooms, open to the elements except for their domed roofs. Behind the main house, out of sight, like an afterthought, lay two other small rooms.

The family called this new home *Khooneh-ye jar*—in Kermani dialect, the Low House, so named because it was almost 15 feet below street level, accessible by rough stone steps. But the name Low House reflected more than just its elevation. It also evoked the family's reduced circumstances.

Ali's father and his uncle, Agha Amoo, the first people in Kerman to have a trucking business, once had a partnership that lasted for twenty-eight years, beginning in the early 1920s. Evading potholes and highwaymen, the two brothers traveled all over the country's then primitive roads, bringing eggplants and oranges from Bam and Jiroft; dried fish and shrimp, Indian tea, and colorful fabric from the Persian Gulf port of Bandar Abbas; dates from Khuzestan and Bam; and prayer rugs and melons from the holy city of Mashhad.

After ascending the throne in 1925, Reza Shah began developing a system of narrow dirt roads linking provincial capitals like Kerman with outlying towns and villages. When the unpaved road between Kerman and Jiroft was first built in 1942, it took Baba and Agha Amoo seven days to travel 143 miles. They hauled sugar, ghee, whey, and petroleum to Jiroft and returned with charcoal, wool, oranges, and lemons. The road was so narrow that if they wanted to make a U-turn, they had to unload all their freight, jack up the truck, pivot it around, and reload it again.

Theirs was the first truck ever to roll into Jiroft. It came without warning. The villagers, who had never seen a truck before, lined the road and cheered as they approached. They thought the truck was some kind of miracle or a perhaps a mobile *imam zadeh* shrine. When Baba and Agha Amoo climbed out of the cab, the villagers rushed to pay tribute to them, pressing five rial coins into their hands and loading the truck's hood with boxes of dates.

With all this hard work, the brothers' business thrived, but their relationship did not. Baba loved and trusted his younger brother. During all those years, they had had no formal contract, and all the profits from the business were put in one pot and drawn on as needed for the construction and furnishing of their homes. Although Baba was the one to mete out the money, he had always directed his wife and daughters to make sure that Agha Amoo's house was well appointed, that he had the best carpets and silver, that his garden was full of sturdy fruit trees.

He thought they would be partners forever.

Family members differ on just how it happened, but sometime in 1948 the two brothers had a falling out. Everyone agrees that their wives couldn't get along—but of course, not everyone agrees whose wife was at fault. What is clear is that one day Ali's father just gave up. Tired of the bickering, he ceded everything to his younger brother—the four trucks, the customers, the money they had amassed—and retreated to his garden.

"Velesh kon," he had said, with an upward tilt of his chin. *Let it go.* The rift left him disappointed but not bitter. Baba and his brother remained friends. But financially, Baba never recovered his bearings. Oh, he tried to make a go of it in business, opening first one shop, then another, selling gasoline and motor oil to other truckers. But his record keeping was indifferent, and he would extend credit to his customers, many of them old friends, and then be bashful about asking for payment.

To make sure that unmarried daughters would have sufficient dowries, Ali's mother, Bibi Robabeh,[24] found work in a factory that made wool yarn. Her husband would have forbidden it if he had known; he would have seen it as a rebuke to his ability to provide for his family. So several days a week, as soon as he was safely out of the house, she would leave the midday meal preparation in the hands of one of her daughters and steal off to the factory, a few blocks away. There, seated on the carpeted floor of a huge, dark warehouse of a room with thirty or forty other women, the ends of their chadors tied behind their necks *khaleh suskeh,* or Auntie Cockroach-style, she would tame the huge, dusty mounds of sheep's wool set in front of her with her carder, separating the debris from the wool destined for fine Kermani carpets.

None of the children, who all knew about this clandestine activity, were happy to see their mother working in a factory. Certainly, they were concerned that she was working too hard, but some of the children were embarrassed to see her occupied in a task they believed to be below her station. They avoided going anywhere near the factory, so it often fell to Ali to take lunch to his mother after he got home from school. On those days he would sit with her and help her card the wool, listening to the women's

---

24. Bibi is an honorific bestowed on respected elderly women.

conversations, their songs, savoring their camaraderie.

The factory manager was a woman who had once worked as a maid in Bibi's house. They had a cordial relationship, and the woman was eager to help her former employer.

"Khanum Estilai, you don't have to come all the way here to work," she said one day, after Bibi had been employed there for a couple of months. "We'll bring the wool to you."

So, several days a week, as soon as the coast was clear, Bibi, through one of the children, would send word to the factory that it was safe to deliver the sacks of wool. She would store them out of sight in one of the unused rooms, tackling them in between her other chores.

In spite of Bibi's clandestine income, Ali's father had to take out a loan on the house to pay for day-to-day expenses. Little by little, he was forced to sell silver and carpets so that he could make the monthly payments. However, few in the community knew about the family's straits. The Estilais were still regarded as relatively well to do. People had expectations.

When Baba took Reza to the bazaar to have his old watch re-plated, the goldsmith laughed and said, "I would think the son of Mohammad Estilai would have a solid gold watch."

Every spring at *Nowruz*, the Persian New Year, teachers asked their students to contribute to gratuities for the school's janitorial staff. "Mr. Jahanbakhsh, one toman," the teacher would say as he recorded the students' pledges in his ledger. "Mr. Habibi, two tomans. And Mr. Estilai?" he asked, looking hopefully at Ali.

"I'm sorry, sir," answered Ali, his face reddening. "I don't think I can contribute this year. We just don't have…."

"Nonsense! Mr. Estilai, 10 tomans."

Ten tomans! It was impossible. Ten tomans could buy two and a half kilos of lamb, or three liters of cooking oil, or five kilos of rice. Ten tomans was who knows how many hours spent carding wool.

After a week of enduring his teacher's reminders, a tearful Ali beseeched his mother, who in turn listed all the ways that money had already been spent.

"But Bibi," Ali pleaded, "my teacher will be angry, and we'll lose face. Everyone is expecting us to contribute."

Maybe it was the tears, maybe the thought of losing face, maybe the hours Ali had put in carding wool at her side, but Bibi finally retired to the storeroom and rummaged in an old trunk where she had hidden her secret stash of money—husbanded from her factory wages and tied up in an old scarf. "Here, my dear," she said, pressing the coins into his hand. "Here are two tomans." The family honor was saved, frayed but intact.

Even with Bibi's thrift and spunk and resourcefulness, Baba could no longer make the loan payments. Four years after he and Agha Amoo parted ways, Baba was forced to sell the house he had built. He quickly found a buyer across the old wall in the Jewish quarter. For many years, Jewish community leaders, eager to expand their current school, had been eyeing the property. Jewish friends had repeatedly approached Baba, telling him how much it would mean to them to have such a fine house for their students. Baba had resisted but finally, he had no recourse. He sold the house to the school, and as part of the deal, he received the Low House in exchange. In the years that followed, it was some consolation to him that the house he had designed, built, and lost had found a new life as a Jewish school, *Madrasseh-ye Ganj-e Danesh*, the Trove of Knowledge School.

On our second day in Kerman, we all were invited to lunch at the Low House, where Ali's eldest sister, Sakineh, lived with four of her five children. Baba had gone ahead to help Sakineh get ready for us. When we arrived, he was waiting for us in the garden, the same garden in which he had so gruffly received the news of Ali's Robin Hood bike fourteen years earlier.

A beaming Sakineh greeted us, thrilled to be welcoming Ali back to the family home. The atmosphere was festive as, one by one, the relatives arrived—the same people who had been at Reza and Pouran's house the day before. Chadors were flung aside, kisses and *taarofs* were exchanged, and children were released to the garden.

Pouran made sure her little boys peeled off their good "outside" trousers to reveal their *pijameh* underneath—the simple drawstring house pants men and boys would change into as soon as they got home. Habib, Sakineh's eldest son, ran to get a pair for Ali so that he, too, could be comfortable sitting cross-legged on the floor.

We sat down on the Kermani carpet, leaning against stacks of embroidered cushions that protected us from the chill of the thick adobe walls. With someone's chador thrown over my legs, I struggled to sit cross-legged but soon gave that up.

Tea appeared immediately, a tray of tiny *estekans* in delicate silver holders. The *sofreh*, or tablecloth, spread on the sitting room floor held platters heaped with fresh fruit, bowls of roasted seeds and nuts, and *masqati*, or Turkish delight—squares of sweet gelatin candies laden with pistachios and dusted with powdered sugar.

There were dates from Bam, in the southern part of Kerman province, and homemade *kolompeh*, a local delicacy. This small, round pastry was made with wheat malt and whole wheat flour, filled with a paste of dates, walnuts, and spices, and stamped with a floral design.

After tea, Ali and I took a walk around the garden. From his descriptions, the house appeared to have changed little in the eighteen years since the family had moved there. The three upper rooms remained unfinished. The courtyard was still without a pool, the house without indoor plumbing. Before making the trek up the stone steps to the outdoor privy at the far end of the courtyard, it was wise to make sure that the plastic water pitcher was full.

In the middle of the garden, Batoul and Fakhri, Sakineh's teenage daughters, crouched near the only spigot, washing dishes in a basin with a handful of date palm fibers—"A Kermani dishrag," Batoul explained with a wry laugh.

In the shade of a pomegranate tree, hugging the courtyard wall, stood a weathered wooden bed with sturdy planks surrounded on three sides by a smooth, gently undulating railing. It was the kind of bed I had seen at old teahouses in the villages north of Tehran, with carpets and cushions and water pipes, but this one was unadorned. It was half of what had been, until seven years before, Baba and Bibi's bed. Baba's half of the bed remained inside the house, where he slept.

I stood by the bed, my hands on the silky wood of the railing, my mind filled with half-formed imaginings of Ali's mother, of the children she had given birth to there, what her last moments might have been like, who would have been with her.

Suddenly Baba appeared beside me and motioned for me to come with him. Ali and I followed as he disappeared into the *anbari*. Standing in the doorway, we watched as he poked around, weaving in and out of the single shaft of sunlight that cut diagonally across the dark, fusty room. Finally, he found what he was looking for, a large bulky object wrapped in a burlap sack. Baba stepped out into the sunlight and handed the sack to me.

"*Baraye shoma*," he said. For you.

The sack slipped away to reveal a heavy brass samovar, dulled with age, but solidly elegant. Its surface had long ago relinquished its sheen to a light brown patina.

"Ahhh," Ali exclaimed softly, a smile of recognition spreading across his face.

Resting on a square, footed base, the samovar was about eighteen inches tall and about as big around at the widest part of its twelve-faceted bowl. The top of its lid formed a pierced socket where a china teapot would nestle, warmed by a cylinder full of hot charcoal inside. All the samovars I had seen in Tehran and Kerman were shiny chrome, electric imports from Germany or Japan. Clearly this one was special.

"It's very old," said Ali. "Look at the date on the lid."

Leaning closer, I was able to make out tiny Cyrillic letters and a date: 1870.

"It's been in the family for as long as I can remember," explained Ali. "Baba must have brought this home in the 1920's or 30's after one of his trips to Mashhad." Not far from the Turkmenistan border, Mashhad was a source for many Russian imports—black wool shawls with fat red roses, Turkmen carpets, Moskva cameras and, of course, samovars.

Lifting the lid, I saw that Kerman's hard water had encrusted the samovar's innards with a stucco-like deposit of calcium.

"It's missing the spigot handle," Baba said apologetically.

"It doesn't matter," I said. "It's beautiful. Thank you. I'm honored to have it."

No one had ever given me anything like this before. No one had ever entrusted me with a family heirloom. I certainly hadn't grown up surrounded by heirlooms. I was raised in spare, pared-down, mid-century California tract homes far away from my parents' Pennsylvania roots. The occasional curlicues on a wooden fascia board or fake shutters on front windows were the only nods to an architectural past—more Early Disneyland than Early American.

In 1952, our family left the tiny, shingle-covered log cabin across the road from Aunt Shirley's house—where my father grew up— the house with the old oak furniture and the family Bible and Uncle Dan's wooden leg in the attic, down the road and around the corner from Aunt Mae's house with the patchwork quilts and the family china and the 200-year-old spinning wheel. When we left Ellwood City, all our meager belongings could fit into a small U-Haul trailer pulled cross-country by a Chevy coupe to Seattle, then two years later to inland Southern California.

We were isolated not just from relatives but from the comforting continuity of family objects passed down through generations. Ours was an acrylic-carpeted, melamined, Formica-ed, linoleumed existence. We amassed old newspapers and magazines, we squirreled away glass jars and plastic milk jugs, we made room for ungainly ceramic lamps from the thrift store, but not for family heirlooms.

All the wrong things piled up.

While my father had a suppressed appreciation for antiques and art, my mother's professed disdain for material possessions set the tone in our household. "*Things* are not important to me," she would declare. As for me—I liked *things*, especially those that had a story, those that resonated with the rhythms of past lives.

And this samovar resonated.

This samovar had chased the sleep from the family at thousands of breakfasts, offered solace on cold winter nights, welcomed hundreds upon hundreds of guests, broken the fast during Ramadan, sealed business deals and witnessed marriage contracts.

Now it was going to travel to a bare, modern apartment in Tehran and sit on a cold, uncarpeted floor until its new owners could afford to put furniture under it. But it wouldn't be lonely for long. Things would pile up, as they inevitably do, both the right things and the wrong things.

After Ali and I returned to Tehran, Baba worried about that spigot handle. He continued to rummage in the *anbari*, hefting decades' worth of vinegar jugs and pickle jars and spare machine parts until he uncovered it. He came to visit us in Tehran a few weeks later, and before even taking off his coat, he pulled from his pocket the errant handle—a tapered, filigreed stopper—and slipped it neatly into the spigot.

The samovar would eventually come to rest on a tall tambour chest from an antique store on Lalezar Avenue, surrounded by brass trays and terra cotta water jugs, Hamadani pottery, lush Kermani embroidery, and Turkmen cushions. But it was the samovar I loved best. It was my first tangible link to a past that I was hungry to know more about and to a family and culture that I yearned to be part of.

For you, Baba had said. And in saying that, he had said, *you are one of us.*

The family samovar that Ali's father gave to Ellen. The table cloth is an example of *pateh doozi*, traditional Kermani embroidery.
Photo Credit: Salimeh Estilai

15

WHAT'S IN A NAME?

Kerman: October 1971

I was indeed beginning to feel like one of the Estilai clan. Baba and the rest of the family accepted me without question. They didn't care whether I was a Muslim or not. They didn't care where I was born or who my parents were. They were happy that Ali was happy, but they cared about my happiness as well.

How does one account for this openness to a stranger from a faraway land and foreign culture? This was, after all, a traditional Muslim family, a provincial family, and, at the time, not well educated. They could have been impatient with my halting attempts to speak Persian. They could have criticized my lack of hijab. They could have slyly brought up the names of countless young girls— the daughters of friends, or friends of friends, or perhaps one of their own relatives—who might have made a more suitable bride. They could have scoffed at my insistence on finding a job instead of staying at home. They could have demanded that I become Muslim and shunned me when I didn't. They did none of those things.

Instead, they simply accepted that Ali and I were different, that because of my background and our educations and aspirations, our life together somehow required an odd set of solutions to unfamiliar problems—finding wood for canvas stretchers or collecting tree stumps to use as stools in our otherwise bare apartment. If our attempts at finding these solutions perplexed them, they kept that to themselves. Instead, they concentrated on helping us in any way they could.

Indeed, the Estilais' acceptance of me was all the more remarkable given their circumstances. A Tehrani friend of mine from an upper-middle class family remarked recently that Ali's family was very unusual in its wholehearted acceptance of me. One of her brothers had married an Italian doctor, and many members of their family were staunchly against the match. Even the family maid was involved in a scheme to have the Italian bride replaced with an Iranian one.

Personally, I had never witnessed that kind of underhanded treatment of a foreign bride. Most of my American friends who had Iranian husbands enjoyed warm relationships with their in-laws, but those in-laws were mainly upper-class Tehranis. I knew that the Estilais were special.

So what prepared Ali's family to welcome me with unconditional openness? A family's way of being in the world is often the result of choices made by generations before them. I can't say when the seeds of this Estilai openness were first gathered, but perhaps they were sown in a lush Kermani garden half a century before I arrived.

Baba was born in 1897, in the village of Badiz, in the gathering twilight of the Qajar dynasty, around the time that Mozaffaruddin Shah inherited the throne from his father, Nasseruddin Shah. Badiz was about a day's donkey ride from the city of Kerman, the provincial capital. Baba's people were farmers who, several generations before, had been Qashghai tribesmen, nomadic pastoralists from the area around Shiraz in Fars Province. Sometime in the late 18th century, they migrated to Badiz in search of grazing land for their sheep and goats.

By the turn of the century, Baba's grandfather, Mohsen, had amassed a good amount of land which he farmed successfully, in spite of the many challenges that farmers faced in those days— rocky soil, primitive irrigation systems, the difficulty of getting goods to market over poor roads, failed crops, famine and marauding bands of tribesman who thought nothing of usurping their lands or demanding extortion money in return for what passed for protection.

His success did not go unnoticed. One day, to his surprise, the Governor of Kerman Province invited himself to tea.

"I would love to have some land here," mused the governor.

"It would be a great honor to have you as a neighbor, Your Excellency" said Mohsen.

"Do you get on well with your neighbors?" asked the governor.

"Yes, Your Excellency, for the most part," said Mohsen. "But one must always be careful."

"Precisely," said the governor. "Precisely. I think we should become neighbors."

"I would be honored, Your Excellency," Mohsen said.

"But of course, I would need some land," the governor said. "Perhaps you have some land you might not need."

Whether from a desire to ingratiate himself with his powerful guest or from the perceived threat that if he didn't he would regret it, Mohsen agreed to make the governor a gift of a large tract of farmland.

The governor proved to be a good neighbor. He and Mohsen remained on cordial terms for many years, so much so that when the governor learned of the marriage of Mohsen's son to the woman who would become Baba's mother, he returned the land Mohsen had given him as a gift to the bride.

In 1914, when Baba was about 17, he left the village of Badiz in search of the larger world, which he found in a blacksmith's shop in the city of Rafsanjan. The blacksmith was also from Badiz, so eventually, the news of his apprenticeship traveled back to Baba's father, Ali. When he heard that his son was toiling in a hot, noisy blacksmith's shop instead of in the fresh, open air of Badiz, Baba's father made the day's trip to bring him back.

"All that red hot metal will melt your brain," he told him.

Baba dutifully returned home, but as soon as he received his draft notice, he was off again. His father or grandfather could have asked the governor to exempt him, but Baba was intent on joining the army and seeing the world. As it happened, he didn't get much farther than the Kerman office of that very governor, where he was assigned to be an *abdarchi*, or tea server.

The governor took a liking to the new recruit because he was tall and handsome and a reliable worker.

"Where are you from, soldier?" asked the governor.

"From Badiz, Your Excellency."

"Badiz? Who is your father?"

"Ali, son of Mohsen."

When the governor realized that Baba was the grandson of his old friend, he said, "When you finish your service, you must come to work for me."

That is how, two years later, Baba found himself in the governor's *bagh*, or walled garden, in Zarisf, a Zoroastrian enclave in the eastern part of Kerman. The governor hired Baba to be his *anbardar*, keeper of the storehouse. Baba didn't let the fact that he couldn't read or write stop him from assuming his new post.

His excellent memory allowed him to keep track of the governor's sacks of wheat and barley and sugar and rice, the boxes of nails and pipes, the baskets of pomegranates, the spools of wire and jugs of pickled eggplant, storing them neatly and doling them out to the household servants.

Baba soon became friends with members of the bustling household—the governor's son, the gardeners, and the other employees. When he wasn't parceling out supplies, he spent many hours with the khan's Armenian driver, learning about car engines and listening to stories of travels abroad on the open road.

While on a trip to Armenia, the governor had bought a Ford touring car. Because he didn't know how to drive, he hired the young Armenian to bring him home to Kerman. The driver had planned to return to his family immediately after delivering the car and its owner, but somehow, the governor had persuaded him to stay. Perhaps what kept him there was the lush, fragrant garden rimmed with roses and honeysuckle and the tall cypress trees reflected in the central pool. Perhaps it was the easy-going, languid pace of provincial life or the star-filled skies of Kerman that lulled him into staying. Whatever made him tarry, it was two years before the driver decided that maybe it was time to go back.

Baba was sorry to see the driver go. He would miss those chats about carburetors and European tours.

"Who will drive the khan, now?" Baba asked the driver.

"Who knows?" the driver said. "I promised him I would stay until he found someone. That's the least I can do. But he needs to find someone soon. I really want to see my family."

Baba was suddenly aware of a great opportunity.

"I might be able to help you," he said. "I have a brother, Akbar.

He's young, but he's a good worker and he's trustworthy."

"How old is he?"

"Twelve, but he's a fast learner."

"Can he drive?"

"No, but that's not a problem," Baba assured him. "You can teach him."

With the driver's help, Baba convinced the khan to hire his younger brother. The khan must certainly have been looking for an experienced driver, but when presented with the choice between the earnest relative of a trusted employee or an unknown driver with who-knows-what kind of scruples or work ethic, he decided to take his chances with Baba's brother.

Baba loved working for the governor. He learned from everyone he came in contact with—the gardeners, the Zoroastrian neighbors, the Armenian Christian driver. Like his own son, who would leave Iran for America some 40 years later, Baba had left Badiz for a larger sphere. The garden was Baba's university, one that would ultimately provide him with a career, a wife—and a new family name.

One day, after Baba had been working for the governor for several months, a carpet merchant named Mirza came to the house to measure the rooms for new carpets. The khan's house had many rooms, but even so, Mirza's task took longer than expected. Perhaps he had to wait while the family finished their midday meal or their afternoon nap, or perhaps Baba, hungry for news of the outside world, engaged the carpet dealer in conversation. Certainly, tea was involved, perhaps several *estekans* of tea, and very likely some pastries. At any rate, Mirza was so late that his mother and younger sister, Robabeh, came looking for him.

The moment Robabeh entered the garden, Baba knew he was in love. He immediately set about getting to know her brother Mirza and earning his friendship. During the next few days, the beautiful Robabeh, also smitten, found many excuses to come to the garden. However, Baba was growing increasingly concerned that the governor's son might want Robabeh for himself. He knew all too well that when the governor's family wanted something, they usually got it, so he asked Robabeh to stay away.

This separation proved too difficult to bear, so Baba soon found himself asking Mirza for his sister's hand. Mirza readily agreed to the match, with one stipulation, namely that Baba take his wife's family name, Estilai.

Iranian family names were a relatively new invention. In 1919, the Majles passed an act introducing the use of surnames. After Reza Pahlavi became shah in 1925, this suggestion became a mandate.

Before the government's intervention, people were known by their hometowns, their professions, or who their fathers were. For example, at birth, Baba's name was Mohammad e Ali—or Mohammad, the son of Ali. When they had to choose a surname, the family chose Mohseni, in honor of Baba's grandfather Mohsen.

Although family names were still a novelty in 1920's Iran, the prevailing understanding was that a man's children would have his family name and not his wife's. Legally, Iranian women have always kept their own family names. While the wife of Agha-ye Mansouri might be known by her neighbors in the *koocheh* as Khanum e Mansouri, in the rest of the world—her workplace, her doctor's office, the courthouse, the airline ticket counter—she is known by the name on her identity card, her maiden name.

When his future brother-in-law insisted that he take his bride's name, did Baba stomp out of the room in a huff, demanding to know why a perfectly good name like Mohseni wasn't good enough for his intended? Did he take the demand as a blow to his male dominance, a harbinger of marital trouble to come? He did not. Instead, he turned the name over and over in his head. He liked the sound of it. More than that, he liked its meaning. Estilai comes from the Arabic *estila*, meaning "having entire power or authority; predominance, conquest, ascendency, domination." Baba's family name paid tribute to his grandfather, but his bride's family name was a more profound statement. Perhaps it was because Roba-beh's maternal great-grandfather had been a Qur'anic scholar in Hamadan. Or perhaps it was because her mother was a *seyyedeh*, a female descendent of the Prophet Mohammad, who could recite long passages of the Qur'an by heart. Whatever it was, these Esti-lais had a sense of self that could not be denied.

Somehow, Baba's willingness to take his wife's family name was indicative of a larger openness and flexibility, an expansive spirit, maybe even a little adventurism. A man who would take his wife's family name, not worrying what anyone thought, might also be expected to be open to many other things, including a foreign daughter-in-law.

Of course, in the matter of the family's tolerance, Ali's father was only half of the equation. Ali's mother, Robabeh, had left her mark as well. After all, she was the one who had cheerfully, matter-of-factly assumed that Ali would marry a foreigner. Together, Baba and Robabeh formed a united front against discrimination. Ali and his brothers and sisters grew up in a household accepting of visitors with other customs and beliefs. They often heard their parents say, "To Jesus his religion, to Moses his religion. We all sleep in our own graves."

While other Muslim families might have expected a foreign daughter-in-law to convert to Islam, Ali's family felt no such compulsion. They were devout Muslims, but the Estilais had none of the "them vs. us" mentality of their more doctrinaire co-religionists. Their home and their hearts were open to people of many faiths. One of Baba's closest friends was a sun worshipper who lived with the family for several years. Then there was the handsome young Indian who asked for their daughter's hand. He was a serious contender until he was out-maneuvered by another suitor, a distant cousin, who threatened to kill himself if his intended didn't marry him.

And of course, there were the family's easy friendships with their Jewish neighbors—no small thing when many Muslims considered Jews to be unclean. Until the time of Reza Shah, Jews were confined to ghettos, and even after they were allowed to live among the general population, the distrust of most of their Muslim neighbors relegated Jews to their own enclaves. But Ali's family harbored no such distrust. "Of course we were friends with our Jewish neighbors," my sister-in-law Sakineh told me years later. "We even lent them our meat mallet."

Zoroastrians didn't fare much better in those days, even in Kerman, which still remains a center of Zoroastrian life centuries after the Arab invasion. Before Reza Shah's time, when it rained, both Jews and Zoroastrians were forbidden to come in physical contact with their Muslim neighbors for fear that the damp would transfer their imagined inherent impurity. Zoroastrians were also forced to wear special shawls on which they had to walk or sit during visits to a Muslim's house. But Baba's best friend Rostam was a Zoroastrian who frequently accompanied him on road trips—and never with a shawl. Ali's family was close friends with a Bahai man who made regular visits with his whole family and entertained them with his *tar*, a long-necked lute.

All those friends paved the way for me. When Ali brought me to Kerman, I was immediately accepted. Ali's family never quizzed me about my religious beliefs, never made me feel like an outsider. I was one of the beneficiaries of Baba's adventure in the governor's garden a half century before.

16

·············

WILD RUE

Kerman: October 1971

There are certain smells that, without fail, take me back to those first days in Kerman over fifty years ago: the tiny, dark brown seeds of *esfand*, or wild rue, scattered on smoldering embers, their pungently green, musky, acrid smoke rising and swirling and finding its way to the back of my throat; that and the fragrant ghosts of dust chased from stone tiles by a pail of water—or the perfume of a lump of opium, reduced to a burnt syrup by a piece of hot charcoal.

But most of all, it's the wild rue.

Each time Ali and I came back from a large dinner party or a trip to the bazaar, possibly exposed to a stranger's evil eye, one of my sisters-in-law would scurry to prepare hot coals in a brazier and toss in a handful of wild rue to protect us.

"*Cheshm nakhoreh, insha'allah,*" someone would explain with a knowing smile. "To ward off the evil eye, God willing."

Many Iranians, especially those in the provinces, believe that some people have an evil eye or variation thereof—a salty eye (*cheshm e shoor*), an envious eye, an eye that wounds (*cheshm zakhm*). If someone is *cheshm khordeh*, stricken by the evil eye, he is open to a multitude of woes.

New mothers and their children are believed to be especially vulnerable. Friends and family members are careful not to praise children of any age excessively for fear of inviting the evil eye. On seeing a newborn for the first time, it's common for a visitor to exclaim, "Praise be to God, what an ugly child!" The child's mother is unperturbed. She knows the code and is grateful for it.

Some Iranians believe it's possible for someone to have an evil eye and not know it. And it's highly likely that in a large crowd, at least one person will cast an evil eye, one person will be envious. That's why it's best never to draw attention to one's self. Showing off is not only obnoxious but also dangerous. Whether it's receiving a Robin Hood bike for being first student or bringing home a Ph.D. degree or even an American wife, you might be setting yourself up for sorrow if you flaunt these acquisitions.

In spite of myself, I was drawn to the wild rue's protective powers. Even when its appearance in the room signaled that I might be, however remotely, in some kind of danger, I found the soothing, enveloping smoke reassuring.

Intellectually, I knew that this age-old practice was just an old wives' tale, and I felt I had overcome my childhood superstitions. With only an occasional twinge, I allowed myself to step on sidewalk cracks or cross paths with black cats. I stopped knocking wood. If I didn't open an umbrella indoors, well, that was because there was no reason to, right? As I swept up the shards of a broken mirror, I would talk myself out of seven years of bad luck. You make your own luck, I reasoned. You vaccinate. You signal before changing lanes. You hope for the best.

But really, what did I know?

It's natural to want to feel some control over the vagaries of existence—the truck in the ditch, the barren womb, the infant dead from influenza. And after a month dodging Tehran traffic, boy, did I need a hedge against those vagaries. Whether I believed in evil eyes or not, the wild rue's gentle smoke was a comfort I never refused.

Cheshm nakhoreh, insha'allah, I would think, inhaling deeply. *Just to be on the safe side.*

17

SCHAUB-LORENZ IS THE WHOLE WORLD

Kerman: October 1971

Those first days in Kerman, I was continuously on display. At dinner parties, I was fussed over and coddled. Much was made of my attempts at rudimentary Persian (*"How cute"*) or my long hair (*"Just like Iranian women"*). The family, eager to know me and ensure my comfort, was genuinely interested in my reactions to even the most inconsequential occurrences, and Ali was kept busy translating my every response.

"Does Ellen like yogurt?.... Then why isn't she eating any?"

"Doesn't she like sugar with her tea?.... Then how come she takes only one cube?"

"What does she think of the chador?"

"How does she like [fill in the blank]: *sitting on the floor?....Iranian food?....sleeping on the floor in the same room with so many people?*

So, one afternoon after our siesta, yearning for some time out of the spotlight, I found a quiet place where I wouldn't have to have an opinion. I settled into some cushions at the back of the hall where all five of Reza and Pouran's children, aged four to nine, were watching cartoons on television.

Besides the few cushions, the room was bare, except for a red and blue flowered Kermani carpet that skirted the edges of the thick whitewashed walls and the television, a large console placed at the far end of the room, opposite the door leading to the courtyard. A single naked bulb hung from the vaulted ceiling. Sitting in a half-circle on the floor in front of me, the children shyly acknowledged my presence before returning their attention to the screen.

In 1971, television was still a novelty in the Estilai family. Reza and Pouran had purchased their first black and white set only a year before. Television had been introduced in Iran in 1958 with a parliamentary bill allowing Habibollah Sabet, a prominent Bahai and private entrepreneur, to develop Television of Iran, a broadcast center in Tehran. It was a lucrative, self-contained operation, with Sabet, RCA's local representative, producing the programs and selling the commercial airtime as well as the televisions themselves.

In 1966, the government established its own operation, National Iranian Television, the better to promote the modernization programs of the shah's White Revolution. Three years later, the government bought out Television of Iran and—with the exception of the US Armed Forces Television—gained direct control of all television programming in the country.[25]

Programming on the two state-run channels was limited to a few hours a day, mostly in the late afternoon and evening. Large portions of the daily newscasts were devoted to the comings and goings of the glamorous royal family. In addition to Iranian sitcoms and variety shows, the government imported American programs, like *Star Trek, Bonanza, Peyton Place, Perry Mason* and *Mission Impossible*. Milky black and white reruns of the soap opera *Days of*

---

25. Annabelle Sreberny-Mohammadi and Ali Mohammadi, *Small Media, Big Revolution: Communication, Culture and the Iranian Revolution*, University of Minnesota Press, Minneapolis, 1994. Chapter 4, "Dependent Development and the Rise of Television."

Our Lives, several years old and dubbed into Persian, were popular prime time fare.

As dull as it was, *Days of Our Lives* provided me with many random but potentially useful phrases, such as, *"Mickey aqim-e?"* (Mickey is sterile?), that I would mumble to myself until I got them right. But my favorite source for new Persian vocabulary was the endless stream of television commercials, to which I accorded the same respect and attention as the programs they were sponsoring.

Mine was a natural reaction to a compelling medium. In 1969, the creators of *Sesame Street* revolutionized children's programming when they adapted the format of television commercials to teach children letters and numbers. They recognized that commercials are the perfect vehicle for language acquisition. With their catchy, repetitive jingles and concentrated messages tailored to short attention spans, they engage the language learner—be it a preschooler just beginning to talk or an adult immigrant eager to master the idioms of her new language.

Hanging on every syllable, attuned to every nuance of intonation or gesture, I was the advertisers' ideal audience. Bic pens, Toshiba rice cookers, Pif Paf insect repellent, Bah Bah air freshener— I could have been a credible spokesperson for any one of them. Random bits of hype lodged in my brain and found their way into my conversations at odd moments.

"Ba sos e makhsoos e sandveech," I proudly announced one day as I handed Ali a sandwich slathered with Yek o Yek's "special sandwich sauce." When a clearly surprised Ali abandoned his sandwich to give me a congratulatory kiss, I knew I was on to something.

I found that television commercials were also great bellwethers of social change. As much as I loved Iranian art and history, folk culture and handicrafts, I was intrigued when I saw East and West bump up against one another: elaborate Louis XV furniture in the sitting room of an otherwise traditional home; melamine dishes with ancient designs; a portrait of John F. Kennedy rendered in a Persian carpet; and cabarets, featuring belly dancing and bottles of Johnnie Walker on the tables, frequented by families with women in Western-style dress as well as chadors.

Sometimes these cultural collisions had unsettling effects. Never was that more apparent than in the ubiquitous commercial for Schaub-Lorenz televisions. I had seen it several times a day in the few weeks we had been in Tehran, and there it was again that day in Reza and Pouran's living room. The children were as entranced as I was, even though they must have seen it hundreds of times.

The ad featured a middle-aged man and his attractive, much-younger wife. He was the classic *jahel,* a member of the urban lower classes and a staple of Iranian popular culture—a distant cousin of the rural American redneck.

While the word *jahel* translates as "ignorant," the *jahel* himself is frequently thought of as the salt of the earth, generous and friendly, an endearingly uncomplicated innocent.

The paunchy and mustachioed husband was dressed in a black suit, with a white shirt open at the collar and a too-small black hat perched on his balding head. His wife, clad not in the traditional chador but in a dressing gown, sported a bouffant hairdo and fashionably feline eye make-up. In a singsong rhyme with a heavy Isfahani accent, she berated her husband for not providing her with enough entertainment.

"Didn't you say that you would take me to the beach, take me here and there?"

Just as she said, "take me to the beach," she flung open her dressing gown to reveal a two-piece swimsuit.

Immediately, the five little heads in front of me whipped around, and five pairs of big brown eyes locked with mine. Those eyes told me that, once again, they wanted to know exactly what I thought. I smiled at them—surprised by this sudden attention. Seeing that I wasn't shocked, they just as quickly turned back to the TV. Still, I wasn't exactly sure what I thought about the commercial. I wasn't shocked, but I was perplexed.

Clearly, the husband had his hands full with this woman. Playing upon the time-honored, international stereotype of the materialistic, nagging wife, the ad seemed to suggest that buying her a television would make her forget all about an expensive trip to the seaside and skimpy swimwear. In fact, in his Isfahani accent, the husband tells her,

Somebody who has a husband,

Has children,

Doesn't go here and there,

Doesn't go to the beach....

If our Isfahan is half the world,

Schaub-Lorenz itself is the whole world.

But who was the audience for this message? What did the average Iranian think of it? And who was the average Iranian, anyway? Was this swimsuit really a sign that Iranians had become so westernized that this commercial was acceptable to the masses? Or were they scandalized by it? And did they really want the *whole* world?

The commercial had been airing for several months, but it was still provocative, especially to these children, who had never seen any of their relatives in a swimsuit. It had been almost thirty-six years since the late Reza Shah, the founder of the Pahlavi Dynasty and the current shah's father, had outlawed wearing the chador and headscarves in public.[26] This edict, brutally enforced by the police, was intended to speed the country's modernization. In the late 1930s, women venturing out wearing *hijab* were attacked and their offensive coverings were confiscated.

The chador was now optional. After the Allies engineered the abdication of his father in 1941, Mohammad Reza Shah allowed women to once again take up the chador. But 30 years later, my sister-in-law Pouran, like millions of Iranian women, would never leave the house without one—let alone wear a swimsuit, even at home. Certainly, most Iranian women did not aspire to be that woman in the skimpy suit. They may have wanted her television set, but not her swimwear.

The *jahel*, like millions of his traditionally minded countrymen, was caught in a conundrum. By allowing television into his living room, he was affording his family cheap entertainment within the safe confines of his home. But he was also opening the door to a host of foreign influences, both positive and negative, that undermined his control. He would forgo the seaside, only to be inundated by a tidal wave of unfamiliar attitudes, fashions, and moral ambiguities.

Iranians had a long history of adapting to foreign conquests and influences while maintaining ancient customs. Years later, with this in mind, one of Ali's colleagues at the Institute would point to an Iranian travel poster on the wall of the faculty lounge.

"Welcoming visitors for 2500 years," proclaimed the poster.

"Yes," the colleague laughingly agreed, "Alexander the Great,

26. Massoume Price, "Women's Movement: A Brief History 1850 – 2000," March 2000, The Iranian, www.Iranian.com.

Genghis Khan, the Arab hordes. We've welcomed them all."

And they had survived them all, in part because of an ability to live and let live, to embrace the positive aspects of a new culture and ignore the bad. Since the Industrial Revolution, Iranians had mimicked the West in commerce and education. Using sexy bathing suits to sell German televisions to conservative chadoris was just one more seemingly pragmatic accommodation.

I found the cross-cultural pollination of 1970s Iran a charming and reassuring sign of an inevitable surge toward modernity, but I was unaware of the depth of the growing discontent among traditional and devoutly religious conservatives. I brushed aside fleeting glimpses of social and religious resistance: *jahels* staring gape-mouthed at me because I dared to go without *hijab,* or the wife of my husband's friend who objected to paying for an American guest's wine at a restaurant. *This intransigence will work itself out,* I told myself. *It has nothing to do with me.*

But nine years later, the beaches at the Caspian seaside resorts would be segregated; on their side of long, dividing curtains, women would swim in street clothes and chadors. Bathing suits would become only one of many casualties of the culture wars that were just now escalating.

18

A (BATH)ROOM OF ONE'S OWN

Bandar Abbas: October 1971

"What do you mean: 'They're going to sacrifice another sheep'?"

I stared at Ali, who seemed relatively undisturbed at the prospect of another innocent animal slain on our behalf.

We had been on the road for about an hour, on our way from Kerman to Bandar Abbas to visit Ali's sister Fatemeh and her family. Ali, Ahmad, Ghasem and I had said our goodbyes to the Kerman contingent that morning. The other sisters and brothers and their families planned to make the six-hour trip in a few days, when school was out for the weekend.

In preparation for our journey, Pouran had prepared a tray with traditional items intended to protect us from the dangers of the road: a glass of lemon sherbet for a sweet journey, rosewater for freshness, some pastries for strength, and a copy of the Qur'an for divine intervention. Standing by the door, she held the brass tray above our heads as the four of us took turns passing under it, stopping to take a sip of sherbet and a bite of pastry, kissing the Qur'an, and touching it to our foreheads. Pouran murmured a prayer under her breath, softly blowing the words in our direction as we left the house. Then she took a pitcher of water and poured it in our wake to ensure our safe return. I wasn't a Muslim, but I felt protected by this act.

As we hurtled down the two-lane road, I stared at the rocky, brown hills dotted with the occasional stand of trees and tiny adobe huts.

"When are they going to kill it?" I persisted. "And where?"

"In front of the doorway, as soon as we get there," Ali explained, cheerfully.

"You're kidding."

"Oh, no. In fact, we're supposed to step over it when we enter the house."

Ali was clearly enjoying this too much. Never a big fan of animal sacrifice himself, he nevertheless found my anxiety amusing. Like Reza and Pouran, Fatemeh and Asghar were sacrificing the sheep to give thanks that Ali and I had safely arrived in Iran. In accordance with Islamic custom, they would also distribute most of the meat to the needy.

I knew this was a great honor, but until a few days ago in Kerman, no one had ever slaughtered an animal on my behalf. Like most city kids, I was isolated from the grim eventualities of animal husbandry. Occasionally, on summer visits to relatives in rural Pennsylvania, a hapless chicken or rabbit I had admired the day before was dispatched without fanfare, well out of my line of vision. I didn't ask questions about the provenance of the main dish. I didn't want to know.

Already slightly uneasy about meeting more new people, my apprehension was magnified by the prospect of stepping over a freshly slaughtered sheep writhing in its death throes. I imagined the poor animal struggling to free itself, the gleam of the sharp knife against its neck, its mournful cry, the blood spurting onto the threshold.

I worried about my own threshold. *Am I going to be able to keep my composure or am I going to embarrass Ali by running from the scene like a ninny?* I played the sound of the dying sheep over and over in my head. *Tragedy…from the Greek* tragōidia, *the goat song—the dumb animal's death cry when it suddenly understands its fate.*

We arrived in Bandar Abbas in the early afternoon. In marked contrast to arid, dusty Kerman, this old port city 300 miles southwest on the Strait of Hormuz, was lush—steamy, humid and muggy, even in late October. I sensed immediately that Bandar had an energy all its own. Tehran and the desert towns we had visited were becoming my new normal, but Bandar was another world. The oceanfront, with clusters of rickety fishing boats in the distance; stands of date palm trees; Indian-flavored music blaring from the taxi cabs and cafés; the mélange of languages—Arabic, Hindi and the local dialect, Bandari; the colorful scarves the men wound around their heads; and the mysterious beak-like masks covering the faces of the Bandari women made me feel, once more, that I was in a foreign country.

Bandar Abbas owed its multicultural, polyglot atmosphere to its strategic location on the Persian Gulf. During its 2500-year history, Bandar Abbas has had almost as many names as invaders. The Greeks named it Hormirzad. European navigators called it Bamdel Gombruc (or Customhouse Port). Under Portuguese control, it was known as Comorão, because of its plentiful shrimp. Shah Abbas settled things once and for all in 1614 when he reclaimed the town from the Portuguese and named it after himself.

We turned off the seaside road into a narrow alleyway and then another and another, and finally pulled to a stop in front of Fatemeh and Asghar's garden gate, left slightly ajar in anticipation of our arrival. At the sound of our car, Fatemeh's six children spilled into the courtyard, all wide grins and shining eyes, jostling each other to get a glimpse of their uncle and his bride.

Fatemeh and Asghar were rounder and jollier than their photo studio portraits. Fatemeh, who had appeared shy and subdued in the photo, was bubbly and animated. Asghar's children called him *Agha Joon*, dear sir, but so did Sakineh's children, because he had been like a father to them. Their own father had died before the youngest, Fakhri, was born, and for several years, Sakineh and her five children had lived with Fatemeh and Asghar.

Daee Mirzali,[27] Ali's maternal uncle, was a trim little man, about 50 years old, slightly built, with wiry salt and pepper hair swept back from his broad forehead and a black bar of a mustache tucked under his nose. He wore plaid house pants and a carefully pressed clean white shirt under a snug, black, V-necked sweater vest. His shirttails hung down halfway to his knees, in what would be, 20 years later, a bold fashion statement at Samira and Sarah's Riverside, California high school.

Daee had been married briefly, but his wife had left him long ago. For the last several years, he had been living with Fatemeh and Asghar, doing odd jobs around the house or helping Fatemeh with the cooking. To keep him busy, Asghar and Fatemeh had set him up in a small shop that sold batteries. The shop was more a social enterprise than a moneymaking venture. He would buy goods retail and more often than not re-sell them at a loss.

Daee was a kindly man with a ready smile, but fragile, and prone to melancholy bouts of drinking—usually *"eau de cologne,"* the homemade vodka available from Zan Amoo, the wife of Baba's brother. But that day, he was on his best behavior.

---

27. *Daee*, uncle, specifically, mother's brother

The courtyard was surrounded by thick bushes of honeysuckle and bougainvillea and intersected by clotheslines sagging under the weight of that day's wash. The large, raised pool in the center where the family did the dishes and laundry was shaded by a hodge-podge assortment of palm frond mats supported by a framework of roughhewn wooden poles. Plastic colanders full of tea glasses and trays of dishes lay drying on the edge of the pool.

And at the back of the courtyard, near the entrance to the house, stood the sheep, obliviously drinking the water that, according to Islamic tradition, its owner was obliged to provide before its sacrifice.

Asghar ambled over, untied the animal, and led it to the doorstep of the house. Straddling it, he took out his knife, cradled its head, and, with a soft *bismillah al rahman al rahim*,[28] quickly slit its throat. There was no tragic cry, just a soft thud as the sheep crumpled to the ground. As blood trickled onto the tiles in front of the doorstep, Ali and I quickly stepped inside.

That wasn't so bad, I thought. I had gotten through the ritual without disgracing myself or upsetting our hosts. What was unsettling was how little that ritual had bothered me.

After tea and lunch, Fatemeh distributed pillows and coverlets, and we all settled down for an afternoon nap on the floor of the hall, a sunny, whitewashed room looking out on the courtyard. Just as we were drifting off to sleep, we heard cars pull up outside the courtyard gate, then the sound of familiar voices.

Laughing, Fatemeh ran to open the gate to find sixteen Estilais who had wedged themselves into two small Peykans for the six-hour journey. There was Baba with his worry beads; Reza and

28. In the name of God, the most gracious and most merciful.

Pouran, their five children and their maid, Effat; and Sakineh and four of her five children.

"Masha'allah," shouted Ali. "We weren't expecting you for a couple of days."

"We couldn't stand it any longer without you," said Pouran.

Fatemeh's children helped the guests unload the cars while she made tea—tea for twenty-seven people, all of whom would be spending the night. That evening, she would add a little water to the stew. And perhaps the needy would get a little less lamb.

Fatemeh and Asghar's house was a feast for the senses as well as the soul: the pungent smell of charcoal and kebabs, cardamom pastries, honeysuckle, and roses. The household was in constant motion: the little boys running out to the bakery in the morning for fresh *sangak* bread, the girls bringing trays of afternoon tea laced with pussy willow. As soon as the tablecloth was rolled up after breakfast, Fatemeh began preparations for lunch, one more installment in the endless cycle of soaking rice, cleaning herbs, chopping vegetables, frying, and simmering.

Fatemeh's children coaxed Ali and me out to the shoreline a few blocks from their house. Fully dressed, we waded in the gulf's warm waters as fishing boats passed close by, their crew members grinning broadly, clearly amused at the sight of a foreign woman in a soaking wet skirt.

We arrived home in our wet clothes to find the courtyard full of music. Fatemeh and Asghar had hired two itinerant musicians who snaked around the courtyard, entertaining us with *sorna*, a bell-shaped wooden horn, and *tonbak*, a goblet-shaped hand drum carved from mulberry wood and covered with goat skin.

As much as I loved being part of this extended house party, I soon needed time to myself. With so many people in the house, it was a challenge to find privacy. If I wandered off by myself with a book, someone followed after me. "Is Ellen bored?" And, understandably, there was this persistent curiosity about me. Just a few days earlier in Kerman, while I was getting dressed, I heard the door to my room open and turned around to find Pouran and Sakineh standing in the doorway.

"May we come in?" asked Pouran.

"Of course," I said, as clutched my clothes in front of me.

Pouran and Sakineh stood in the middle of the room, side by side, smiling expectantly.

"What is it," I asked. "Is there something you need?"

"No, we're fine," said Sakineh, grinning affably. "Go ahead with what you were doing."

"Well, I was just about to get dressed," I explained.

"Please go ahead," said Pouran. "We don't mind."

Well, I minded. I wasn't used to undressing in front of an audience. At university, I had usually changed in the bathroom, out of sight of my roommates. Much to the chagrin of my high school gym teacher, I had perfected the art of showering with a towel on—while still wearing my underwear.

I minded, but I didn't want to offend my in-laws, so I took off my nightgown.

"*Masha'allah*," exclaimed Sakineh. "The left one is bigger than the right—just like Iranian women."

Satisfied, Sakineh and Pouran left me to finish dressing.

Apparently, I had just passed some kind of test.

In the old days, before a wedding, the groom's female relatives would contrive to see the bride naked, usually during a trip to the *hammam e omoumi*, the public bath with large common soaking pools, or *khazine*. There, they could make sure that the betrothed was sufficiently comely—or at least free of major physical deformities. Or maybe, as in the case of my sisters-in-law's belated mission, they could just satisfy their natural curiosity.

The custom stemmed from a simpler, more sisterly era, a time when women would spend an entire languid day each week in the public baths, soaking, drinking tea, gossiping, and being heartily exfoliated by a bath worker in the company of other women and their children. By 1971, most of Kerman's traditional public baths had all but disappeared, victims of progress in the government's war against infectious diseases. The most famous of them, Hammam e Ganjali Khan, had been transformed into an historical museum, but my sisters-in-law's due diligence about my physical attributes was as contemporary as ever.

Of course, since many Kermani homes, like Reza and Pouran's, did not yet have showers or even indoor plumbing, the city still had public bath houses, but in a different form, the *hammam e nomreh*, or numbered baths, where one takes a number and waits for a vacancy. Instead of communal soaking tubs, the more modern *hammam e nomreh* had individual shower rooms. It was not as exotic as the traditional baths, but, as I would learn, it still had workers eager to exfoliate.

Not having her own bath, Pouran used to take her five young children to the *hammam* twice a week, after school on Tuesdays and on Fridays, the Muslim Sabbath. She would pack fresh clothes, a thermos of tea, shampoo, loofahs, and crocheted bath mitts, as well as laundry detergent and a basin. She would scrub the children until they were pink, and then, while they were drying off and having tea and biscuits in the antechamber, Pouran would have her own shower. Taking advantage of the plentiful hot water, she would also wash the clothes they had worn that day.

After a few days in Kerman, I needed a bath. Badly.

I was accustomed to showering once a day, maybe more if I was going out in the evening. I was willing to forgo many amenities, but a daily bath was a hard habit to break. My new extended family was less obsessed with bathing—largely because, for many, daily baths weren't feasible. A bath was not a spur-of-the-moment affair but a lengthy, considered, deliberate enterprise. You packed for the journey; you organized your day, even your week, around it.

My expedition to the hammam would require some advance planning. I needed an escort (Ali), a guide (Ahmad), and a car (Ahmad's trusty Volvo). Once all the arrangements had been made, I bundled up my towels and a change of clothes, stuffed them in a plastic shopping basket, and drove with Ali and Ahmad to the *hammam e nomreh* a few blocks from Reza and Pouran's house. Ali took care of business at the hammam's front desk, securing a shower room for me. The male proprietor handed him the key to bath number 10 and motioned toward a long, dark corridor.

Bath number 10 was actually two immaculate rooms covered in white tile: an antechamber featuring a built-in bench and pegs to hang one's clothes and a large shower room filled with natural light streaming in from a high window.

Not wanting to keep Ali and Ahmad waiting long, I immediately got to work. My showers were usually fairly perfunctory, ten-minute affairs, not the long, concerted exfoliation projects favored by Iranians. After ten minutes, an Iranian is just getting started. But the solitude of the hot, steamy shower was so luxurious that I tarried a bit longer than usual before I reluctantly returned to the anteroom. As I was drying off, I heard a loud knock on the door. I wrapped my towel around me and opened the door a crack.

A woman, about fifty years old, was standing in the dark hallway, smiling at me expectantly. She had wrapped her chador around her Auntie Cockroach-style, the ends brought up, crossed over the chest, and tied at the back of the neck. This way of wearing the chador was a workingwoman's modesty—a pragmatic response to the pressures of convention.

"*Kaargar mikhaid?*" she shouted.

Seeing my puzzled look, she shouted even louder. "*Kaargar... kaargar mikhaid?*"

Having no idea what she wanted, I thought my safest response would be, "*Nah, merci.*"

Just before she turned and good naturedly padded off in her plastic slippers, I noticed some movement behind her, and a pair of shining eyes. It was a young boy, about 11 or 12 years old, wide-eyed, seemingly startled at his good fortune to catch what was probably his first glimpse of a foreign woman in a bath towel.

I shut the door and dressed as quickly as possible. I found Ali and Ahmad at the front desk, where Ali settled the bill, leaving a generous tip. As we drove home, with Ali at the wheel, I asked him to translate what the woman had said.

"'*Kaargar mikhaid?*' That means, 'Do you want a worker?'" explained Ali. "She wanted to know if you wanted her to scrub you."

"But what was that boy doing there," I asked him.

"What boy?"

"There was a boy standing behind her in the hallway looking at me when I opened the door."

As soon as those words were out of my mouth, Ali drove his brother's Volvo into a cement utility pole.

The three of us sat silently staring at the pole in disbelief.

"What happened?" asked Ahmad.

From the back seat, I listened as Ali gave a brief, quiet explanation in Persian. In the rear view mirror, I saw Ahmad's eyes get very wide. He and Ali exchanged a few words, and Ali started the car and headed back to the hammam.

We got out and Ahmad and Ali went to find the bathhouse manager, who summoned the boy. The young culprit listened with downcast eyes as Ali sternly reminded him of what he undoubtedly already knew—that he had been *por roo* (cheeky), that he had overstepped, that he had violated a basic trust of the hammam—namely that women, regardless of national origin, are entitled to their privacy.

In the end, there was no lasting harm done. Both the car and the boy's pride sustained only minor dents. The foreign wife's honor was intact. The brother's sense of justice was satisfied. Only the husband, thrust into the unwelcome role of the enforcer, had any lingering discomfort.

Iranian toilets loomed large for me. By the time we reached Bandar Abbas, I had visited hundreds of Iranian conveniences (some less convenient than others)—from the opulently European ceramic fantasies of upper-class Tehrani apartments, complete with bidets, to the most primitive holes carved out of the shank of a village hillside. No matter how exciting the itinerary, there were times when I viewed excursions to restaurants, historical sites, and museums as mere side trips on the way to the next toilet. Each lavatory had its own idiosyncrasies and challenges, its own special place on the spectrum of hygiene and privacy.

For example, the *mostarah*, or privy, outside Fatemeh and Asghar's house in Bandar Abbas didn't have a door. This omission didn't seem to be a problem for anyone else. The *mostarah* was located at the far end of the back garden, away from traffic. The L-shaped partition that shielded the entrance from interlopers was sufficient for others. At the sound of approaching footsteps, the *mostarah*'s occupant had only to cough discretely to avoid any invasion of privacy. I quickly developed a persistent *mostarah* cough.

Whatever the shortcomings of their privy, Fatemeh and Asghar's hammam in Bandar Abbas was a godsend—a spacious cinderblock outbuilding, about the size of a small living room, conveniently located off the back courtyard. With its plain white tiles, cement floor with a drain in the center, exposed water pipes, and plastic washbasin and laundry basket stacked in the corner, it was not luxurious in the usual sense. But it was huge, and it was secluded. To shower by myself seemed a dreadful waste of such lavish space—not to mention water—so I invited Ali to join me. After all, with twenty-five other people in the house, it was a good opportunity to have a private conversation with my husband—and get my back scrubbed in the bargain.

Emerging shiny and rejuvenated thirty minutes later, we returned to the house, only to be met by Fatemeh's icy stare. Others, suddenly transfixed by the flower pattern in the carpet, wouldn't look at us at all. Later, we would learn that the following conversation had taken place:

"Where is Ellen?" Fatemeh had asked.

"She's in the hammam," someone had answered.

"Where's Ali?"

"He's in the hammam."

"But I thought you said Ellen's in the hammam."

"She is."

"How can they both be in the hammam?"

How, indeed?

Apparently we had violated a basic trust of Fatemeh's hammam—namely that husbands and wives shower separately.

19

·············

CUTTING LOOSE

Tehran: January 1972

The winter of 1972, Tehran was encased in a sooty crust of snow. It was my first winter in Iran—my first snowy winter since early childhood—and I spent much of it cocooning when I could. My California wardrobe was no match for the bone chilling winds from the Alborz Mountains and sidewalks covered with undulating layers of gray ice. Craving calories, I stood in front of the refrigerator eating heaping spoonsful of oily sesame halva right out of the tin.

The initial euphoria of being in a new country was beginning to wear off, and I was left with the bleakness of my routine. Apart from teaching English classes and tidying up our bare apartment, I had very little to occupy my time. I tried to make art, but my feeble attempts yielded unremarkable results.

I had always thought of myself as an artist. Since childhood, when I wasn't escaping into a book I was sketching myself into another world. I was the artist in the family and among my classmates. One night, when I was six, my father came home from his accounting job to find me lying on my stomach, creating paper dolls of Geishas in flowery kimonos. He said, "You know, when you go to college, you can study art." He didn't say, if you go to college, but when—and not business or law or medicine, but art. From then on, for me there was no looking back. An artist was who I was and who I thought I would always be.

Even with their limited funds, my parents often found a way to send me to art classes. Afternoons at the University of Washington when I was six years old, summers in the park in Claremont, and, after my junior year of high school, one blissful summer at the University of Kansas's Music and Art Camp where I got a taste of what college would be like.

At UC Davis, much of my artwork was informed by family history. Working from old black and white photographs of my Italian relatives, I indulged in nostalgia for a time before my birth, translating the milky gray scale of 1930s and 40s snapshots into a funky palette of muted maroons, sage greens and teals with surprising accuracy. "How did you know the wallpaper was that color?" my mother marveled, looking at a painting of inebriated guests piled on her parents' couch at her wedding reception.

In Robert Arneson's ceramic sculpture class, I made a house raucously covered with creamy flowers. It was audacious enough to make it into a show in the student union. When I first met Ali that day in the commons, I told him that I had a piece upstairs in the gallery. Later that day, he went to investigate, as much to learn my last name as to find out what kind of work I did. He was surprised to see that works by two different Ellens were on display, but fortunately, he looked up the right one in the phone book and called to ask me out on our first date.

That ceramic house should have been on my personal historic register, protected and preserved, but I was careless with it. When we departed for Iran, I left it with the friends who took over our cottage. Foolishly, I had decided it was too awkward to pack.

I did pack my photo albums, rolled up paintings, oils, acrylics and brushes, but they had not yet arrived from the States. Thinking an infusion of equipment would spur me on, Ali bought me supplies to make canvas stretchers, but the yards of canvas remained furled and the lengths of one-by-twos lay warping in a sad heap in the corner of the otherwise empty spare bedroom, a neo-Dadaist reminder of my lack of motivation, a found-art monument to my lost talent. *If I was really an artist, I would be making art anywhere, no matter what, right?*

I was unmoored, rudderless. Just as I was no longer an Italian/Welsh-American but a *khareji*, I was no longer an artist, just a gumptionless poser, moving dusty, warped canvas stretchers from empty room to empty room. Four months before, just days after arriving in Tehran, I had left my address book in a phone booth on Toopkhane Square. If I had wanted to devise a way to distance myself from my former life, I couldn't have picked a better method. I addressed a letter to a friend in Davis using the only information I could remember—the name of his street and his landlady—but I never got an answer. I imagined my college friendships drifting away, along with my gumption.

I had chosen a life in Iran, but I didn't yet know what to do with it. I was isolated as much by my own fears, insecurities, and lack of structure as I was by an unfamiliar language and the Tehranis' unfathomable driving habits.

When Ali brought home a *Time* magazine to cheer me up, I scurried off to the bedroom to scarf it up in one sitting. Flipping through the pages greedily, I came to the arts section, and I froze. I knew that face staring back at me—it was William T. Wiley, my professor at UC Davis, looking every bit his laconic self. The article began, "California these days harbors a whole generation of stoned, amiable ironists, who work at an angle to the High Seriousness of New York."

I knew many of those amiable ironists. I took their classes, laughed at their stories over coffee, went to their gallery openings, and studied their faces for signs of approval. Wiley was perhaps the most ironic and amiable of them all. In his early thirties, he was tall and lanky with a drooping mustache and melancholy eyes that were sometimes covered by aviator goggles. When assessing student work propped up against the studio wall, he would squat down and rock back and forth on his heels, nodding his head. "That's too pretty," he'd say. He told me that truth, or versions of it, several times in my freshman year. In my sophomore year he said, "We should make a drawing together." (To my enduring regret, I was too shy to take him up on that offer.) In my senior year, he said, "You should take my graduate seminar." (I did take him up on that one.)

Like that of many of his colleagues in the West Coast Funk Art movement, Wiley's work was seriously irreverent and idiosyncratic. His, especially, was informed by a personal iconography of everyday detritus that was esoteric yet familiar. The title of the *Time* magazine article, "Quirky Angler," referred to both Wiley's penchant for salmon fishing and his ability to reel in the flotsam of everyday life to fashion wry commentary on the human condition. A perfect example was Slant Step, an icon of the Funk Art movement, a squat, ungainly, enigmatic construction of linoleum, rubber and wood with no apparent function, which Wiley bought for fifty cents in a Mill Valley, California, junk store. Soon after he deposited it in the studio of his graduate student, Bruce Nauman, Slant Step became a bi-coastal celebration of the dumb and unfathomable. Slant Step inspired many iterations by Bay Area artists, giving rise to a San Francisco group show of Slant Steps and (after being held captive in the New York studio of sculptor

Richard Serra) to The New York Society for the Preservation of Slant Step.[29,30] How could I explain this phenomenon to my new friends in Iran? And who would care?

I was 7,500 miles away from California, experiencing the High Seriousness of Iran, convinced that no one around me in my new surroundings had the arcane sensibility I had cultivated in the UC Davis Art Department. Iranian literature had a rich tradition of political satire, but I wasn't yet aware of writers or artists who were mocking high culture. There were plenty of amiable ironists in Iran, stoned and otherwise, but I hadn't met them yet, and that dismal winter, I despaired of ever finding such kindred spirits with whom to share cultural shorthand.

Seeing my former professor in the pages of *Time* was like walking along a crowded sidewalk in a strange city and suddenly seeing an old friend pass by on a bus. You wave frantically, but the friend, preoccupied with her own thoughts, doesn't see you. The bus speeds off in the opposite direction, and you know you'll never catch up with it.

I had missed that bus. Funky art was happening without me. My old American self was left standing on the curb, flatfooted, waiting for a transfer.

29. Webcast of William T. Wiley's lecture at the Smithsonian Institution's American Art Museum, September 30, 2009, http://americanart.si.edu/multimedia/ webcasts/archive/smith/wiley/webcast/index.cfm, accessed 9/11/2012.

30. Coosje van Bruggen, *Bruce Nauman* (New York: Rizzoli, 1988), p. 107 and pp. 129-131.

20

THE INSTITUTE

Tehran: 1972

While I was at sea, Ali was trying to ground himself in his new work environment. He, too, found himself in an atmosphere very different from his university experience at UC Davis, but he had returned to Iran to change things, not wallow in his disaffection. After all, why would the government give him a full scholarship to the States if it didn't expect him to come back and make a difference? After just a few months in the Faculty of Science, he was looking forward to changing the system that had nurtured him.

Like most of his colleagues at Tehran University, he had been educated in the old, time-honored Iranian way. Year after year, high school teachers or university professors would resurrect old lecture notes which students would then memorize and spit back word for word on recycled tests. You could always tell when it was time for exams. The long, high-ceilinged corridors would be full of students clutching sheaves of dog-eared, legal-sized mimeographs, mumbling to themselves as they paced back and forth.

Ali had been one of the best of them. In a country where every taxi driver could recite the poems of Hafiz or Rumi, Ali's ability to memorize was both a social skill and a useful academic tool, one that eventually saved him from himself.

Ali's path to the field of plant genetics was a circuitous one. In his third year of high school, when students were obliged to choose a major, he had chosen mathematics over biology or literature. Mathematics students were the high schools' academic elite. Upon graduation, they alone had the ability to take entrance exams for any discipline at any university. Literature students were limited to literature and the humanities, social science, psychology, geography, law, and economics. Biology students could take those exams in addition to medicine, nursing, pharmacy, general science, agriculture, and of course, biology. But mathematics students were judged capable of doing anything.

In those days, before the institution of Iran's nationwide, standardized entrance exam, the *concours*, high school graduates had to take separate exams in each of the colleges to which they were applying. The summer of 1960, Ali took six exams. At Tehran University, he applied to the colleges of engineering, science, and agriculture. He also applied to Polytechnic College, the College of Education's math program, and the Technology Institute. Except for the College of Engineering, he passed them all.

Now he had to decide which college to accept. He really wanted to enter a math program, but he knew he couldn't afford to do so without a scholarship. Only Tehran University's College of Agriculture in Karaj had offered him a full scholarship, including room and board. He asked the father of his high school friend Nader for some guidance.

"Here's what you do," his friend's father said. "Take the College of Agriculture's offer. Become first student in your major. Then with your first student scholarship, go abroad and study anything you like."

The first few months in Karaj, Ali was uncharacteristically

bored. Accustomed to solving elegant mathematical problems, he balked at having to memorize the wingspans of moths and the geometric categories of crystallized minerals. He started skipping class, taking the bus into Tehran to see movies or visit friends, or simply hanging out in the college laboratory where he could actually see the minerals instead of just hearing the professor talk about them. He had the good sense to make friends with the attendance monitor, who marked him present, but he neglected to get the notes for the classes he missed.

After a few weeks of cutting classes, his grades began to slip. Miserable and hopeless, he resigned himself to the purgatory of mediocrity. He wanted to change his major, but he didn't want to lose his scholarship. He wasn't sure he could keep his grades up if he had to work while attending school.

Ali's behavior caught the attention of Habib Mirzai, an agriculture student from Kerman who was a year ahead of him. Mirzai, an excellent student, was actually a distant relative whose family came from Badiz, the village of Ali's father. While the two had never met, Mirzai had heard about Ali's previous academic success from other family members, and watched with amazement as he squandered his opportunity. As the first semester's final exams drew near, Mirzai dropped by Ali's dorm room and introduced himself. After the usual pleasantries and exchange of family news, Mirzai got to the point.

"I've been watching you since you arrived," Mirzai said, "and I'm very disappointed. You have a great opportunity here—full tuition, room and board. Why are you blowing this chance?"

"I have no feeling for agriculture," Ali explained. "Math is what I love, but I don't have the resources to study in Tehran. I'll stick it out here for a year, and then, in the summer, I'll take the *concours* again for math or engineering. Maybe I can get another scholarship."

"You have to stay put," Mirzai replied. "You already have a scholarship, but you have to study. If you flunk out, no one will care that you wanted to study math. All they will remember is that you failed."

"But I don't have any notes," Ali told him.

"Ehhh *baba*, don't worry," Mirzai said with a laugh. "Nothing ever changes here. The notes are always the same. You can use mine from last year."

The next day, Mirzai handed him several binders full of neatly outlined course notes in his impeccable handwriting. Fortunately for Ali, his new friend was both generous and highly organized. Ali read through the notes a couple of times and aced all of his exams. His classmates were dumbfounded. *"He never studied, and he got the highest grades? What would happen if he studied?"*

What did happen was that Ali, chastened by his brush with failure and buoyed by this newfound success, began to apply himself in the competitive atmosphere of the College of Agriculture and soon got a reputation as the man to beat. After two years, when students had to choose a major, some of his classmates put off their decision until they knew where Ali would land. His main competitors, who were also keen on getting their own first student scholarships, waited for him to choose his major. Ali opted for Basic Agriculture, because it was rumored to be the easiest, all but guaranteeing him the scholarship. His rivals chose from the remaining majors, knowing they wouldn't have a chance of becoming first student if they had to go head to head with him.

He did get that first student scholarship, and he did go abroad to study whatever he liked. Armed with a master's and Ph.D. in genetics from UC Davis, Ali returned to Iran in 1971 intent on dismantling the very methods of Iranian education that had worked so well for him from elementary school through college. However much he had benefited, Ali knew that the system-wide reliance on memorization and recycled lectures did not lend itself to developing the essential analytical tools for scientific inquiry.

He knew, too, that the country needed students who could do actual research, not just read about it. The Faculty of Science's laboratories were critically lacking in state-of-the-art equipment. Many of the old guard professors, some of whom were hired when Reza Shah established the University in 1934, had become very influential in government or had other prestigious jobs. They were not involved in serious research and, therefore, not motivated to modernize the antiquated facilities.

So less than a year after he was hired to teach at Tehran University, Ali became one of seven young colleagues devising a plan to break away from the Biology Department and create a totally new learning environment—one that would promote experimentation and dialogue, questioning and debate, and the opportunity for world-class research.

They knew that they would never be able to change the mentality of the old guard, so out of both respect for their elders and disdain for outright confrontation, they decided to take the high road and create the Department of Cell and Molecular Biology, which would give rise to the Institute of Biochemistry and Biophysics.

One night, after dinner at the home of Lisa and Fereydoun Djavadi, they plotted their escape. I had heard a lot about the Djavadis, but I didn't know them well. Armed with doctorates in biochemistry from the Sorbonne, they had been hired almost two years before Ali and had already taken the measure of the situation in the Biology Department.

They were an elegant couple, at once very European and very Iranian. Tall and slim, they each had a natural grace and an effortless ability to put strangers at ease. Lisa spoke Persian with a thoughtful deliberateness, rounded by a slight Armenian accent. Her stylish sweater sets, slim skirts, and understated pearls did little to mask a tall girl's enduring athleticism and endearing awkwardness.

Slightly shorter than his wife, Fereydoun was nevertheless a commanding presence. Always dapper in well-tailored suits and silk ties, he commanded attention whenever he entered a room. He had two main expressions: a purposeful stare and a sardonic smirk. And he was a bit of a flirt—an oddity in the repressed and courtly atmosphere of the university.

They lived in Lisa's childhood home—a classic north Tehran bungalow, with thick, white walls lined with books and shiny terrazzo tile floors covered with fine Persian carpets. Their home was furnished with Iranian handicrafts and antiques passed down from her Armenian family.

I liked the Djavadis immediately—in spite of their palace connections. Lisa and Fereydoun had been high school classmates of Farah Diba, who would later become the empress. The three had kept up their friendship while they were university students in Paris, and when Lisa and Fereydoun returned to Tehran, they became caught up in the palace circle. It was this connection to the center of power that made what these professors were about to embark on even remotely possible.

That night, I watched as seven young professors sat on the floor of Lisa and Fereydoun's living room and mapped out, on sheets of three-hole binder paper, the design of the Institute of Biochemistry and Biophysics. They were giddy with excitement as they drew the locations of the laboratories, the electron microscope, the dark-room, and the greenhouse on the balcony. Feeling the effects of wine and an hour or so of watching them add to their wish list, I curled up on one of the cushiony white sofas, and Fereydoun covered me with a down comforter. When I awoke around midnight, they were ready to put their plans into action.

But first, they had to evict the Head Custodian.

HC was the chief of all custodians in the Faculty of Science. He was a tall, thin man in his mid-fifties with a grizzled beard and dark, stringy hair. His navy blue jacket was well worn but clean, his white shirt buttoned up to his chin. When speaking with faculty, he had a nervous habit of jamming his hand into his pocket and shaking it vigorously, as if aerating loose change. Respectful, without being obsequious, he communicated easily and seemed to listen intently—with only his busy, jangling pocket indicating that he might wish to be on his way to some more important, more profitable endeavor.

He had started as a lowly assistant janitor whose primary purpose was serving tea to the faculty members and their guests, and if there was any time left over after that, redistributing the dirt on the perpetually dismal terrazzo floors with his dingy gray string mop. Serving tea was a menial task, but not entirely without its benefits.

First, there was the power. No one ever really acknowledged it, but deep down everyone knew that the person who controlled the tea controlled the rhythm of the day. From sunrise to sunset, the fragrant, dark amber liquid ebbed and flowed in teapots from Orumiyeh to Zahedan, from Mashad to Abadan. Tea was the universal means of welcome, in the poorest desert hut or the alabaster estates of northern Tehran. No business deal was sealed, no marriage contract agreed upon, no friendship rekindled without tea.

"I've put the tea on," someone would say, and you would feel a calming expectancy, a sense of cosmic order.

At the Faculty of Science, the samovar was always bubbling, at the ready to wash the chalk dust from a professor's weary throat or herald the arrival of a distinguished visitor. The rattle of gold-rimmed tea glasses along the corridors marked the progress of the day.

But of course, for HC, besides the power, and the inevitable tips, there was the opportunity to eavesdrop on juicy gossip in the faculty break room and along the corridors, always a potentially lucrative enterprise. And though it was never proven, it was rumored that he was using his teatime to gather information for his other job—that of a SAVAK informer. But HC's entrepreneurial spirit and cunning ways soon opened the door to greater opportunities.

There was his wood recycling program, for one. HC appropriated discarded wooden packing crates in which the university's scientific instruments were delivered and sold them to the highest bidder without sharing any of the profits with his employer. When university administrators got wind of this activity they decided to institute their own bidding process and keep the revenues for the university.

This plan seriously cut into HC's unofficial income, so, feeling some ownership of the recycling program he had created, he devised a strategy that he felt would keep everyone happy.

"I gathered up all the crates and sorted them," he told Ali proudly. "I'd stack the worst pieces, the chipped and broken ones, in the front. I hid the clean, unbroken crates way in the back of the stack, so when people came looking to buy, all they saw was garbage."

The potential buyers, seeing only third-rate, partially usable material, offered lackluster bids, which HC, of course, could easily outbid. He would then resell the crates to a third party at a profit far exceeding what he paid the university.

When Ali was hired in 1971, the University didn't have an office ready for him. While his new friend Essie was away doing his compulsory military service, Ali used his space. However, when an office was finally available, there was no desk in it.

"Go see HC," the department chair advised. "He'll fix you up."

But when Ali approached him, HC appeared to be temporarily without his customary resourcefulness.

"Oh, I don't know, *Agha-ye Doktor*," he said, his hand shaking his pocket. "It's hard to find desks these days with all these new professors from America getting hired left and right. I could look in the basement of the Chemistry wing, but it's pretty dark down there, and besides, it's almost time for tea."

Ali had a class to teach in ten minutes, so he quickly reached in his pocket and pulled out two 100 toman bills—enough to buy 15 or 20 kilos of meat. The next day, Ali unlocked his office to find a handsome oak desk with a shiny glass top taking up one third of the room.

HC held sway over an entire wing of the Faculty of Science on a 24-hour basis. Many years before, he had taken up residence with his wife and children in the basement of the building, where they lived rent-free. That part of the basement, under what was then the Physics Department, was a considerable distance from the administrative wing and thus not frequently inspected by department staff. When the Physics Department vacated, HC and his family were left to populate the dark, labyrinthine depths of the building undisturbed. This arrangement was not exactly legal, but HC had been there so long and had made himself so indispensable that the university looked the other way.

But Ali and his colleagues, desperate for more laboratory space, couldn't look the other way. HC's laundry was hanging where the electron microscope needed to be, and his mutton stew was simmering in the future home of the centrifuge.

Exercising his squatter's rights, HC refused to leave. Ali was in charge of ordering and installing the new electron microscope on its way from Japan, and very soon he would need a place to put it. He consulted Fereydoun, the institute's director, who advised him to talk to HC and find out his intentions. Ali invited HC to his office and told him, "The older professors in the Faculty of Science might ignore your family's occupation of the basement, but the younger professors are not sympathetic. They want you to move out."

"Believe me, Agha-ye Doktor, I've been wanting to leave this basement for a long time," he whined, "but I have nowhere to take my family."

Ali wasn't buying this, because the whole Faculty of Science knew that HC owned two houses in Tehran that he rented out while he lived in the university's basement for free.

"I'm not really authorized to do this," Ali said, "but I can ask that each of our eleven faculty members chip in 100 tomans."

"Really, Agha ye Doktor," HC replied, "This 1,100 tomans won't go very far."

Ali relayed his conversation to Fereydoun, who asked him to wait a few days while he found a solution. Three days later, he told Ali to tell HC to report to a person in the Prime Ministry who would take care of him. The Prime Minister's Office had plenty of funding for, well...*special* projects. Although we will never know how much of the special projects' budget it took to seal the deal, before long, HC and his family had rolled up their carpets and packed up their samovar and were never seen again.

When HC left, he took more than his family and their bedrolls. He also took with him an old way of thinking about life in the university. Sure, the new Institute of Biochemistry and Biophysics still had a hierarchy, but everyone—janitors and students, staff, and faculty—was sitting a little higher in it. The rising tide had lifted all boats.

First, no one was assigned to serve tea.

The samovar was no longer in the janitor's closet but in the faculty break room. Students passing by in the corridor were treated to the sight of their professors making tea for each other. When the IBB cafeteria was built on the fourth floor, students, staff, and faculty took their tea breaks and lunches together.

Ali and his colleagues created an egalitarian culture of community and collegiality that fostered the team spirit necessary for scientific research. IBB was a place where anyone with talent could advance—the creative assistant professor from a working class family, the industrious female graduate student, even a young assistant janitor who started out serving tea but, with Ali's help, learned darkroom techniques and eventually opened his own photography studio. Fereydoun arranged for the cash-strapped graduate students to receive monthly stipends so they could devote themselves full-time to their studies, a perk that their peers in other departments did not have.

Ali thrived along with his students. He didn't mind the 12-hour days he and his colleagues put in to build the institute. Along with several other young professors, he volunteered to rewrite the high school biology textbook to give greater focus on scientific inquiry and experimentation rather than rote memorization, thus revolutionizing the way biological sciences were taught. He wrote the genetics and evolution sections of the senior year textbook. With the other authors, he gave seminars for high school teachers to familiarize them with this new approach.

Seeing how much time he spent preparing for his lectures, some members of his family were perplexed. "You studied for 22 years," they would say. "Why are you still studying?" Years later, my sister-in-law Pouran confessed to me that because Ali was away from home so much she was sure he was having an affair. His workload frequently was a strain on our relationship, and I often complained about being left alone, but I knew he was doing what he came to do, and I was happy for him. He was at the university of his dreams changing the system that had brought him there.

21

....

BREATHE

Tehran: July 29, 1973

The delivery room should be a *taarof*-free zone. That's how I see it. In fact, the last month of pregnancy should come with a dispensation from *taarof*. This was my first pregnancy, and I struggled with tact the way I struggled to get up from a seated position—clumsily and unsteadily.

My newfound directness was accompanied by distinctly primitive behavior. The day I went into labor, I had the overwhelming urge to strip all the beds and wash all the sheets in the apartment. The previous night, lying in bed in our apartment in Tehran, I had been kept awake by an undercurrent of masculine voices coming from the living room, an unmodulated, undulating droning that I couldn't abide. Poor Ali had to go into the living room and, gathering all his own tact, somehow explain to his father and three other male relatives that Ellen would like everyone to leave. If they were offended, they didn't let on. With characteristic grace, they granted me dispensation and moved their conversation to the house of Ali's niece.

The only male besides Ali who wasn't barred was Mansour, Naazi's eldest child, who arrived the next morning. His assignment was to look after me while Ali was at work and my sister-in-law was visiting her daughter. He was a bright and observant fifteen-year-old who had witnessed the six of his mother's pregnancies that followed his own, and there wasn't much he hadn't seen. So that afternoon, when I suddenly doubled over, blindsided by a sharp pain, Mansour very calmly said, "Perhaps you should call your doctor."

My doctor was an Iranian woman in her early forties, who had received her medical degree from the University of Pennsylvania. She was also pregnant when I first went to see her eight months before. At that visit, I explained to her that I wanted to have natural childbirth. She was surprised that I would want to forgo any painkillers, but had no great objection, as long as I knew what I was in for. It seemed that few if any of her other patients had made that request.

When I phoned her that afternoon, she was just as calm as Mansour had been, telling me to call her when the pains were closer together, so it was another eight hours before Ali and I made our way through Tehran traffic to Shahram Hospital, a well-appointed facility in the heart of the city. I was quickly ushered into one of the labor rooms where I set about putting into action all that I had learned about childbirth in the last few months. When my doctor arrived, she asked me if I wanted something for the pain, and I reminded her of our conversation.

When the obstetrical nurse came in with a tranquilizer, the doctor told her, "This mother does not wish to have any drugs."

The nurse stared at her blankly as if she didn't understand.

"No drugs," the doctor repeated. "She wants to have the baby naturally."

While Lamaze and other approaches to natural childbirth were becoming well known in the States, the movement hadn't yet caught on in Tehran. Most middle-class city women, far removed economically from their sisters in villages, expected to scream for a good, long while before they got their epidurals or other forms of anesthesia. *You want natural childbirth? Screaming is natural.*

I wanted to avoid the screaming. An American co-worker had given me a copy of *Husband-Coached Childbirth: The Bradley Method of Natural Childbirth,* so I knew there was a better way. However, I also knew that whatever better way I chose, it would not be husband-coached. Ali, who was somewhat squeamish, had no intention of being in the delivery room, and I felt it would be unfair, not to mention counterproductive, to insist that he be there against his will. Besides, I wanted him to save his strength so he could keep me company during the early morning feedings.

When I mentioned to Ali's colleague, Lisa Djavadi, that I was having trouble finding a natural childbirth class, she gave me the number of a physical therapist, a young Iranian woman trained in the States, who had taught her natural childbirth techniques. The course, which was primarily breathing and relaxation, was supposed to be eight sessions, but because I caught on fairly quickly— and perhaps because there was no need to spend time training a husband/coach—the therapist pronounced me labor room-ready after only three or four meetings. I was sorry because I had enjoyed the classes so much—the serenity of the cool, semi-dark examining room, the sound of my own rhythmic breathing and panting, the reassuring calmness of the therapist's instructions, and the sense that I was in control.

That sense of control was fleeting.

A few hours into my rhythmic breathing, I looked up to see the obstetrical nurse and my doctor standing on either side of my bed, engaged in an intense conversation. They had both been speaking English to me, but now they were speaking Persian to each other.

They were just inches away from me, but it soon became clear that they didn't think I could understand them.

"I'm just going to run home," the doctor said. "I need to give my son his medicine."

"Can't someone else do it?" asked the nurse.

"No, my husband's on call tonight," explained the doctor, "and I can't trust the maid to do it."

"Doctor, this woman could give birth any minute."

"No, she won't," said the doctor, adamantly. "I have plenty of time."

"Please don't go."

As the doctor left the room, the nurse turned to me with a cheerful smile.

"She'll be right back," she said reassuringly.

"*Dorough migid*," I shot back. *You're lying.*

The nurse looked at me as if I had slapped her.

If I had said, "I don't believe she'll be right back," that might have been acceptable. If I had said, "I know what the traffic is like in this town, and I'm afraid she won't get back in time," that would have been all right, but instead I called this conscientious, well-meaning, professional woman a liar. I was too scared and angry to think about anyone else's feelings.

An embarrassed Ali began to apologize on my behalf, but I stopped him.

"The doctor went home to give her son medicine," I said to the nurse in Persian. "You clearly didn't want her to go. Don't tell me she'll be right back."

The nurse looked at Ali. "Her Persian is very good," she said.

22

....

SAKINEH, THE BABY, AND THE BATHWATER

Tehran: August 1, 1973

"I'm not leaving," I told Ali. "I'm not going home unless Sakineh is there."

I burrowed further back into the pillows and drew the thin hospital blanket around me. My sister-in-law Sakineh was still at her daughter Batoul's house, entrenched in some project, and wouldn't be able to return to our apartment until the following day. Hearing the resolve in my voice, Ali knew better than to argue. Anyway, even if he had an argument to offer, he couldn't be convincing. He was as uncertain as I was about taking care of an infant.

Compared to my Iranian in-laws, I was a bit old to be having my first child. Most of the women in the family had married as teenagers and started having babies immediately. But at 26, I felt a bit too young to be a mother. At my first visit with my obstetrician, she asked, "You've been married almost two and a half years and this is your first child? Was there a problem?" No, there was no problem, except that for the last year or so, I had been something of an infant myself—learning to talk, learning to avoid embarrassing myself, learning to taarof…learning the business of becoming Iranian.

But when we decided to start a family and were quickly successful, we were ecstatic. In those first days of pregnancy, I also felt fragile, like a holy vessel. Now I was consumed with a sense of our daughter's fragility.

Samira was four days old, but I was in no hurry to leave. The hospital was a blissful respite from my anxieties about motherhood. I had all the comforts of home and none of the responsibilities. For the last four days, Ali had gone to work at the university but returned to the hospital for lunch and dinner, stopping at the apartment only to water the plants and pick up the mail. He slept on a cot beside my bed, and we fell asleep each night talking about how happy we were to have this beautiful child. While it wasn't exactly hospital policy to have a man sleep on a ward full of women patients, the cheerful nurses went out of their way to make him feel welcome. We feasted on meals as good as those of any restaurant— chelo kebab with saffron-laced rice, sour cherry pilaf with chicken, and eggplant stew. Breakfasts were fresh flatbread with feta cheese and plenty of quince jam.

But the best thing about being in the hospital was that I wasn't at home. Home was where I would have to start being a mother, and I was nowhere near ready. Sure, I had researched motherhood. My copy of Dr. Spock was dog-eared and underlined, but like a first-time driver who has read the manual but isn't ready to take the car out on the highway, I was filled with self-doubt and anxiety. All the talk of rashes and colic and fevers just made me feel more anxious and inadequate.

Only the day before, while leafing through *Time* magazine, I chanced upon the phrase "throwing the baby out with the bathwater" and was suddenly paralyzed with fear. *Was it really possible to do that? Of course it was.* I imagined Samira flying through the air along with the contents of her blue enameled bathtub. *What was there to stop her?* I knew that if Sakineh were waiting for me at home, there would be no flying babies or post-partum delusions. Until her aunt could be there, I preferred to have Samira safely asleep in the maternity ward nursery, tended to by people who could be trusted not to put a tired cliché into action.

When the nurse popped in to tell us that I was cleared to leave the hospital, I told her I wasn't ready to go home. "OK," she said with an affable shrug and left the room. But I knew that, even in Tehran, where government health insurance allowed women to stay in the hospital longer than in the United States, I was beginning to wear out my welcome. I sensed that among the maternity ward nurses, the novelty of the American woman who spoke Persian was beginning to fade. I was taking up valuable space, and even the generous Iranian hospitality might not withstand another day of my malingering. I would have to pull myself together soon.

In the two years since I had arrived in Iran, I had come to depend on my eldest sister-in-law, but even more so during the last weeks of my pregnancy. "Your mother's not here," she had told me. "You can't do this alone. I'll stay with you." She had come in late June, a month before my due date, and immediately started setting things in order, reorganizing cupboards, training the new cleaning lady, laying in supplies. In the first ten days alone, she dried several kilos of parsley and basil, made quince jam, and embroidered a traditional Kermani *pateh doozi* pillow for the baby. With energy to spare, she made new slipcovers for the couches.

A widow and the eldest sibling, Sakineh was the one in the family with the greatest expertise and the most flexible schedule. Over the frequent protests of her own five children, who ranged in age from 15 to 30, she frequently left home for weeks on end to assist other family members with births, sicknesses, or just plain loneliness.

Sakineh inspired confidence. As a young girl, she was bright and independent. In 1930s Kerman, she was the only girl to ride a bicycle. When she was in the fourth or fifth grade of elementary school, her uncle put her in charge of the accounting for the construction of his house. Both her father and his younger brother were illiterate, and they were often on the road, so it fell to eleven-year-old Sakineh to keep track of the hours and pay the wages of the bricklayers, metalworkers, carpenters, and painters.

With her knowledge of poultices and herbal infusions, I always thought she should have been a doctor, and in another culture, in another era, she might have become one—or a nurse, or a teacher. Instead, her parents married her off at seventeen, as parents did in those days. But marriage and five children only encouraged her talent for healing. She was the family herbalist, diagnosing and dispensing home remedies—*kalpooreh* and *khak e shir* for stomach maladies, hibiscus tea for coughs, quince seeds for a sore throat. She also doled out generous doses of common sense. "Don't eat fried foods when you have a cold," she said, "and never leave a baby in the kitchen when you're frying. Frying irritates the nasal passages." "Coffee is bad for a cold, because it's roasted. Stick to tea, or better yet, the juice of the sweet lemon."

It was Sakineh who gave me confidence in the kitchen, patiently teaching me the mysteries of Iranian cuisine. I learned to pair dried fruit with meat, to caramelize onions, to clean and finely chop kilo upon kilo of fresh herbs, to simmer stews until the flavors melded, to add just the right amount of lemon juice.

I learned to leave nothing to chance. How do you keep a meatball from falling apart when you drop it in the simmering broth? You say "*bismillah*," in the name of God.

"You must be careful with *siah daneh* (nigella or black caraway seed)," she warned me one day as we were making *torshi*, the traditional mélange of pickled vegetables. "If you're cooking with a friend and it spills, you'll have a falling out." I carefully put the cap back on the nigella bottle and stashed it in the back of the cupboard, where it couldn't ruin any friendships. I was sure that no amount of spilled nigella seeds could come between us, but I wasn't taking any chances.

From Sakineh, I learned not only Iranian cuisine but also the connection between what one eats and how one feels, a connection that I had never before bothered to make. "Never eat honey when you're eating melon," she warned me. "You'll get a stomach ache." Ridiculous, I thought. Certain that I could eat anything with impunity, I decided to experiment. At breakfast the next day, I made sure to have extra honey on my bread and a hearty serving of melon. I had about a half hour of smug victory before I doubled over with stomach pains. After that, I started paying closer attention to old wives' tales.

I had been similarly resistant to the ancient concept of *sardi* and *garmi*, the traditional classification of foods having a "cold" or "hot" nature, and the importance of keeping a balance between them. At first the concept seemed to be an incomprehensible, homespun, counter-intuitive system that defied explanation. It didn't help my attitude that doctors would roll their eyes when patients insisted that this or that malady was the result of eating too much *sardi* or *garmi*. "No, madam," I heard my physician say to a patient on the phone, "the medication I prescribed is neither *sardi* nor *garmi*."

The concept of *sardi* and *garmi* has nothing to do with food's spiciness or temperature but everything to do with the interactions between the basic properties of foods and an individual's constitution, which is either hot or cold, an idea akin to the four humors of medieval Western medicine. If you have a "cold" nature, you should balance it by eating more "hot" foods, and vice versa. All spices, except sumac, are hot, even mild ones like turmeric and nutmeg. Cucumbers and yogurt are cold—that seems easy enough. But wait, mint is *hot*! Pomegranate molasses is cold, but rosewater is hot. Is it the calorie content that determines whether a food is hot or cold? Some say that hot foods are higher in calories. But carrots are cold and green peppers and mushrooms are hot. Mulberries are hot but strawberries are cold.

I ignored *sardi* and *garmi* until one day I gorged myself on *kolompeh*, a Kermani confection made with wheat flour and filled with dates and walnuts—the quintessential *garmi* bomb. Sakineh had told me they were good for pregnant women because they would give me needed energy. What they gave me were itchy red welts. No matter. Sakineh had a topical *sardi* cure for that *garmi* as well: a liberal slathering of yogurt.

On my first day home from the hospital, Sakineh made *kebab e maitabeh*, grated onions and ground beef pressed into a frying pan, and pilaf liberally infused with cumin seeds. Cumin seeds contain an essential oil that, she assured me, would aid in post-partum recovery. But the "hot" cumin seeds also serve to mitigate the "cold" beef and rice. The "cold" yogurt and cucumbers are balanced by the liberal addition of "hot" dried mint.

Sakineh helped me find a balance in other areas, as well. Soon after we came back from the hospital, she found it necessary to tell me about *Aal*, the witch that steals babies. As a precaution, those who believe in that superstition don't name their children until they are six days old. On the sixth day, the mother sleeps with a kitchen knife on her bed to protect the baby from *Aal*. Sakineh didn't insist that I arm myself, but I'm sure if I had shown the slightest interest, I would have found a knife above my pillow that night.

Sakineh may not have been totally convinced that there was such a thing as an evil spirit like *Aal*, waiting to kidnap the baby, but she took pains to let me know it was foolhardy to engage in hubris where children were concerned. I was always forgetting to be circumspect. Whenever I waxed ecstatic about how beautiful Samira was, Sakineh gently murmured *masha'allah* to ward off the evil eye. "Parents can bring on the evil eye without knowing it," she reminded me. I was besotted with my daughter, so very soon I was saying *masha'allah* twenty times a day.

I had more to worry about than *Aal*. I was sure I was the only woman in Iran who didn't know how to breastfeed. Sakineh quickly became my lactation consultant. "Don't be afraid," she said, brushing aside my protestations of incompetence. "Just put it in her mouth. Here, I'll do it for you," she said, literally taking matters in her own hands.

"In America, what do they do with the umbilical cord when it falls off?" Sakineh asked me one day.

"I don't know.… I guess they just throw it away."

"Hmmmm.… Here, we sew it into a pillow for the baby," she said, watching carefully to see my reaction. I had an image of Samira sleeping peacefully, her head just inches away from what once had been a vital connection to me, dreaming of a time she didn't know she could remember. "A pillow…that sounds like a great idea," I said, and Sakineh went off to find the sewing box.

With the umbilical cord safely tucked away in the pillow Sakineh had embroidered, we could begin bathing the baby. I have a series of photographs Ali took of that first bath. I am sitting on the edge of the bed, watching as a laughing Sakineh holds a soapy, wriggling

Samira in the shallow water of the blue basin. With a deft nonchalance, my sister-in-law's strong hands turn the child this way and
that. The child protests at first, then thinks better of it. "See, you
like this," Sakineh tells her. Silhouetted against the golden afternoon light, she lifts the glistening baby up like the treasure she is,
as if to tell me, *See how easy that was? You can do that!* And I almost
think I can. Not right now, of course, but soon, very soon.

Sakineh's blend of fearless pragmatism and ancient superstition
brought about an equilibrium, a kind of *sardi* and *garmi* to balance
the spirit. From her, I learned that I had choices—a spoonful of
Western medicine here, a cup of hibiscus tea there.

From Sakineh, as much as from Ali, I also learned how to be
an Iranian. It was often Sakineh who was with me for hours on
end while Ali was working twelve-hour days at the university, so
I learned much of my Persian from her. Was it kitchen Persian?
Well, perhaps so, but for me the kitchen was a university. The
labor-intensive preparations of complex Iranian cuisine afforded
me ample time to practice both cooking and language, and, since
we all spent so much time there, the range of subjects discussed by
women in Iranian kitchens—religion, politics, family history, sex,
marriage, birth, death—made for a rich vocabulary.

Apart from those informal language lessons, I learned from
Sakineh how to be part of a large, boisterous family that was end-
lessly interested in one another's business. I learned to be mindful
of hierarchies—to serve tea to the eldest person first, to stand up
when elders entered the room, to be deferential when contradicting
them—all things I would have learned as a child had I grown up
in Iran. I learned the importance of keeping the nigella seeds of
my opinions in check—not carelessly tossing them about but dispensing them with tact.

But most of all, Sakineh initiated me into the sisterhood of motherhood. She gave me the basic tools I needed. Soon I, too, had a bit of deft nonchalance. I was still sometimes nervous and fretful, but now I was empowered—and all the more so because I had a network of Iranian family members to rely upon—wise older women, doting menfolk, and helpful nieces and nephews.

Before Samira and Sarah were born, I often resented having relatives visit for months at a time. As much as I loved them, my anxiety grew along with their piles of shoes in the entryway. What should I feed all these people? Where will they sleep? What will we talk about for twelve hours a day while Ali is away at work? I worried about what people would think of my cooking skills, my limited Persian, my lackadaisical approach to housekeeping. Most of all, I resented not having time to myself to read or think or just stare at a wall. But after a few weeks of motherhood, I began to re-alize that if I ever wanted to read or think or stare at a wall again, I would need to have company…lots of it. I needed helping hands and empty laps, I needed interventions, I needed busy bodies, even if they were busybodies. My Iranian relatives were only too eager to oblige. That was the seeming contradiction I learned to embrace: in order to have freedom, I had to give some of it up.

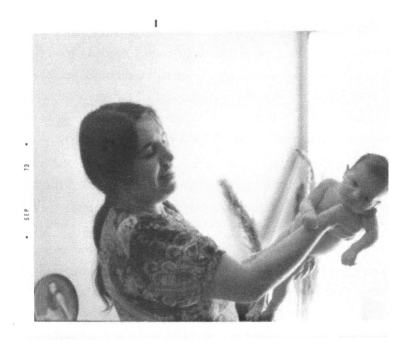

Sakineh giving Samira her first bath, August 1973.

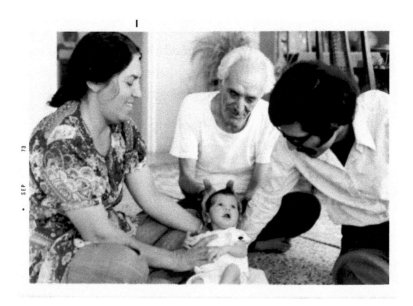

After the bath: Ali, Baba, Sakineh and Samira, August 1973.

23

....

CASPIAN SLEEPOVER

Fereydon Kenar: September 1973

It was dusk but still balmy on the Babolsar road. I rolled down the Peykan's rear side window to let in more of the sweet, soft air, a soothing mixture of salt spray and lush green vegetation. Our good friend, Mahmoud, was driving us back from a shopping expedition in Babolsar to his vacation house in Fereydoun Kenar in Mazandaran Province. With his chin tilted up as he peered over the steering wheel and his Edgar Allen Poe curls blowing in the wind, Mahmoud kept up a steady stream of cheerful banter. Suddenly, he became quiet. I could see his eyes moving back and forth from the road to the rearview mirror. In the back seat, next to me a woman was screaming, "Fuck, fuck, fuck." Her face was contorted, like a gargoyle's. Spittle was coming out of the sides of her mouth. *Spitting mad*, I thought to myself. I couldn't see the face of the man sitting in the front passenger seat, but I knew what he was doing. Nothing. He was doing nothing.

Good God, who invited these people?

I did. These people were my parents.

Come to Iran, I had said. Come meet your new granddaughter. Mom and Dad had arrived at Mehrabad Airport only the week before with a trunk full of infant clothes and hearts full of good intentions. They were planning to stay for a month. With the exception of a weekend in Ensenada, Mexico, this was their first trip outside the U. S.

Their visit got off to a rocky start. Her first unfamiliar taste of feta cheese at breakfast sent my mother to the bathroom on a wave of nausea. My father got food poisoning from a cake with cream frosting and had to go to the hospital. That was just the first day.

Very soon, I saw that while my father was open to new experiences ("Those emergency room doctors were *outstanding!*"), my mother was resistant. Having our maid serve lunch was a novelty, but one that made her uncomfortable. Her reaction was understandable. I was not yet used to servants myself. But the way she said, "How *nice* it must be to have someone *wait* on you," felt like a veiled rebuke. Although she liked the sound of Persian and was intrigued to find out that the words for "who is it?" (*ki e?*) sound the same in Italian, she quickly tired of not knowing the language, of having things explained to her, of feeling like an outsider.

"Other cultures are so interesting," she mused one day, as she emerged from the bathroom. The source of this cross-cultural enthusiasm was the European-designed plastic toilet seat lid, which was notched for easy lifting. *All right*, I thought, *people take their sense of the exotic where they find it. It's a start.*

Although we lived in a quiet neighborhood, getting to and from it in Tehran's amorphous, unfathomable traffic was nerve-wracking, especially for someone who was used to the polite, orderly ebb and flow of small-town Southern California streets. Even I, who had been living in Tehran for two years, had not yet found a way to get across town without clenching my teeth and digging my feet into the floorboards. When Mahmoud and Mahin invited all of us to join them for a weekend at their Caspian Sea retreat, Ali and I thought the trip would give my parents a welcome respite from Tehran's grit and tumult.

On our first afternoon in Fereydoun Kenar, Mother went out on the terrace for a cigarette and was soon cornered by the teenage son of one of Mahmoud and Mahin's employees, eager to practice his English. Small and wiry, with a shaved head, shiny face, and a too-tight red shirt, Yaghoub had a tenacious, nebbishy manner that quickly grew tiresome. His questions were benign at the beginning: *Where are you from? How long will you be here? Do you like Iran?* But then he asked her, "Missus, why do you smoke?"

Perhaps he was just searching for a conversational gambit, or maybe he was genuinely concerned about the deleterious effects of tobacco, but poor Yaghoub couldn't have known that he had crossed a line. No one ever dared ask Mother for an accounting of why she did anything.

"It's really none of your business," she said as she ground out her cigarette on a nearby stone and swept into the house, sure that this provincial busybody had branded her a hussy for smoking.

That night, Mahin laid out thick mattresses and comforters for us at each end of the large living room. I was looking forward to sleep after a long day on the road. Then I saw the look of horror frozen on Mother's face. "We're sleeping in the same room with you and Ali and the baby?" she asked.

"Yes," I said. "Is that a problem?"

"Of course it's a problem," she answered. "I hadn't planned on this. You should have told me."

I hadn't planned on this either. I had never been to this vacation house before, and I hadn't thought to ask our hosts if there would be a separate room for my parents. I was confident that Mahin and Mahmoud would provide comfortable accommodations, and to my mind they had. This arrangement was what I had become used to when visiting Iranian relatives. The beds were deliciously cozy and the living room was the size of four or five of the bedrooms in my parent's house. But that didn't matter to mother. She wanted privacy, not a sleepover.

The next day, Mahmoud took us sightseeing and then to Babolsar for shopping. My father, enchanted with the Caspian, announced that he was going to retire there and build a cottage by the beach. Mother, still fuming about the sleeping arrangements, maintained her morose silence. She looked at a few handicraft shops, but it was the general store that caught her eye. She felt most comfortable among the slightly foreign versions of familiar, utilitarian objects and foodstuffs: the cans of cooking oil, plastic shopping baskets, tea glasses, and sacks of rice. There were no Euro-style toilet seats, but she did find things with a foreign flair. When she decided to buy a stainless-steel rice spatula and a melamine plate with a paisley design on it, I offered to take care of the transaction.

"No," she said firmly. "I'll do it myself."

"OK," I said, "but you need to know that the clerk will write up an order form which you have to take to the cashier over there. After you've paid, you take the stamped receipt back to the clerk so he can wrap it for you."

"Shut...up...you...officious...bitch. Who do you think you are? I don't need you to tell me what to do."

Mother paid the cashier and we all left the store in silence. The silence continued on the way home until her profane outburst in the back of the car. I don't know how much English he understood, but Mahmoud said nothing. No one said anything. No one ever did. All during my childhood we never talked about Mother's episodes. I had become used to her flare-ups and the silences that followed. That was our normal. So was the guilt I felt for bringing them on by not being smart enough or quick enough. But here, in Iran, in this pristine place, in the presence of this kind and generous friend, her behavior was beyond comprehension. I saw her with new eyes. I had a new standard now. I had made another life for myself, one that didn't include crushing family members with a barrage of expletives.

Back in Tehran, Mother announced that she would like to leave two weeks early. She was surprised when I, instead of trying to change her mind, grabbed my phone book and called the travel agent to change their tickets.

This trip had given Mother a glimpse of my other life, and she didn't like what she saw: me feeling comfortable in Iran, embracing another culture—a supposed elitist with a servant. She saw me with a family, a job, a close circle of in-laws and friends—experiencing all of this in another language, sometimes sitting cross-legged, on the other side of the world.

24

NANEH FATEMEH

Tehran: 1975-77

Every Thursday afternoon, Ali brought our maid, Naneh Fatemeh,[31] her weekly supply of Iranian pipe tobacco, wrapped up in grainy pale lavender paper and stamped with a government seal. The first time, Ali did it as a favor, but Naneh began to expect it every week. The proffering of tobacco became a kind of ceremony to commemorate the beginning of the weekend. With a nod of her head, Naneh took the small packet from Ali and tied it up in the folds of her scarf, waiting for one of those quiet moments between tea and lunch or tea and a nap or tea and the dinner dishes, when she could sit alone in the corner of the kitchen and smoke.

Naneh's pipe was a simple wooden affair with an oblong bowl cocked at a right angle to its foot-long stem. Its unvarnished wood, burnished from hundreds, maybe thousands of uses, was un-adorned, save for a few turns on a lathe. Like all of Naneh's pos-sessions, her pipe might have been fetched from a forgotten trunk hidden away a hundred years before.

Naneh herself looked like an old engraving from the Qajar era.

31. *Naneh,* is an informal Persian endearment for mother or grandmother, and can also mean nursemaid. Like the English word "nanny," it is related to several similar words in various languages denoting female relatives, such as the San-skrit *nona* and Serbo-Croatian *nena,* (mother); the Greek *nanna (*aunt); and the Italian *nonna* and Welsh *nain,* (grandmother).

Her face was encircled by a large, square white headscarf, pinned under her chin, and secured tightly with a twisted length of iridescent, striped, fringed fabric, tied around the top of her head. With that headscarf and puffy face, she looked like a dried apple doll.

Summer or winter, her small frame was concealed by four or five layers of clothing, which she changed after her weekly bath: a sleeveless cotton shift, a long-sleeved calico dress with a gathered skirt, a vest, a pullover sweater, drawstring pantaloons and knee-high stockings secured by a roll of elastic cord. In the kitchen, she wore green rubber sandals, and when she went shopping, black rubber shoes.

Sometimes, bits and pieces of dialect from her native village of Badiz found their way into her speech. For instance, her word for water was not *aab* but something that sounded like *ow*, which I imagined was an Indo-European link to the French *eau*. This linguistic oddity made her seem even more like a throwback to a long-ago era.

She seemed ancient, but I wasn't certain how old she was. I imagined she had grey hair, but since she never removed her headdress, I couldn't tell for sure. It seemed strange to me that Naneh always covered her head, even when there were no men in the house, even when she was asleep. My sister-in-law Pouran explained that village women of Naneh's generation felt naked and vulnerable without head covering.

"If she didn't have that scarf," Pouran said, "her head would come apart."

With her old-fashioned villager's clothes and pipe, Naneh Fatemeh could easily have been mistaken for a nursemaid in the court of Naser-al-Din Shah, a century before, where his hundreds of wives enjoyed their own tobacco rations, just as Naneh did. The shah's wives had precious little to occupy them in the confines of the harem. Along with gossip, political intrigue, and occasional visits from the shah, smoking their water pipes was one of their main sources of pleasure.

The royal ladies in the Qajar court were so fond of tobacco that they joined the masses in protesting the king's capitulation to the British tobacco interests. In 1891, when the shah granted a concession to the British Imperial Tobacco Company giving them the right to buy all of Iran's crop in exchange for a fee of fifteen thousand pounds a year, he alienated not only the peasant farmers, tobacco merchants, and dedicated smokers, but Westernized intellectuals and mullahs alike, who were outraged at the thought of giving away their country's precious commodity to foreign opportunists. When an influential cleric issued a *fatwa*, a religious opinion or ruling, calling the use of British-controlled Iranian tobacco a war against the Twelfth Imam,[32] the entire country—including the shah's harem—gave up smoking.[33]

The ban on tobacco must surely have upset the delicate balance of the court. One can only imagine the bewildered and beleaguered shah, wandering from royal bedroom to royal bedroom, in search of solace from the slings and arrows of his enemies, only to find disgruntled wives staring him down over cold, empty water pipes. Finally, the shah cancelled the concession, and the cleric called off the *fatwa*.

Pipe smoking was Naneh's sole vice—or so we thought. Three times a day, she would sit cross-legged in a corner of the kitchen, untie her calico satchel, draw out her pipe and fill it with tobacco.

32. The Twelfth or Hidden Imam, also called the Imam e Zaman, the Imam of Time, is believed by Iranian Shias to be the Mahdi or savior who, as a young child, disappeared in the 9th century and will return at the end of time to rescue the faithful from injustice and persecution.
33. Mackey, pp. 141-142.

She'd light up, and with closed eyes, lift her chin, tilt her head back, and blow out delicate clouds of smoke.

The acrid haze soon spilled out of the kitchen and wound its way around our small apartment, a signal that another phase of the day was about to begin. It also announced Naneh's private time. At least for those few minutes, no child climbed onto her lap, no one asked her to bring tea or answer the door or stir the stew. The smoke enveloped and protected her, leaving her alone with her own thoughts.

The smoke also clung to her in a sour film. Since she changed clothes only after her weekly bath, traces of it rubbed off on the children. The smoke stayed in her voice long after her pipe was put away, adding a raspy dimension to her melodic Badizi drawl.

I didn't mind any of this. In fact, something about Naneh's thrice-daily habit gave me a peaceful feeling, a sense of order. Tea breaks or the *muezzin*'s call to prayer may have given our days their rhythm, but it was the smoke from Naneh's pipe that provided a gentle counterpoint.

Naneh Fatemeh was, for all her villager's simplicity, the best naneh we had ever had—and we had hired a memorable few in the preceding four years. Naneh was quiet, reliable, and cheerful. She loved the children and they loved her. With Naneh, there was none of the drama of her predecessors.

Perhaps it was I who imbued these relationships with drama, for I had no experience with servants. I was completely at sea. Unlike most of my Tehrani friends, I hadn't known the constant presence of household servants. When I was growing up in California in the 1950s and '60s, no one I knew employed even a weekly cleaning lady. My mother would never have let a stranger work in her house—even when she was finally able to afford help. She was a perfectionist with a Platonic ideal of housekeeping but no enthusiasm for it. Her standards were so high that even she could not achieve them without a Herculean effort. Work remained undone because she didn't want to have to explain to anyone how she wanted it done. In fact, she was certain that no one else would be intelligent enough to understand.

Ali's childhood experience with servants was not much more extensive than mine. When they were able, his family employed a baker and a laundress who came once a week, and a gardener who did odd jobs around the property. For Ali, having a live-in maid was an imposition. He didn't want someone in the next room listening to his conversations. He didn't want to deal with a maid's problems or those of her children or her children's spouses and their children—an extended family of problems. He valued his privacy far more than he valued an immaculate house.

For both of us, the idea of servants ran counter to our idealistic notions of egalitarianism. We were skeptical when people said that their servants were like family. What did they mean? Did they eat together? Did they socialize with them and their families? Did they provide for them when they could no longer work?

If I was so uncomfortable with the idea of having a servant, why did I want one?

First of all, I still had that uneasy relationship with the broom. I could not summon up the requisite nonchalance, the necessary sense of ordinariness about housework to get it done quickly and without operatic commentary. But more than that, I struggled with the pressures of life in Tehran. From those first days at Mahin's house, I was aware that Iranian women had high standards of housekeeping, admirable standards but ones I felt I could never attain by myself. The constant flow of dinner guests and house guests who stayed for weeks on end, both invited and uninvited, required that the house always be immaculate, the pantry stocked, the samovar at the ready.

Convenience foods were hard to come by. It was several months before we had a washing machine, and a year or so before we had a vacuum cleaner. My time was limited, and everything took so much longer in Tehran. Almost as soon as I arrived, I was teaching English and bringing home papers to grade. After a few months of shopping, cooking, and preparing lessons until two in the morning, my bleeding-heart liberal's disdain for employing servants disappeared.

Desperate for help, we put out the word to family and friends. For a while, we had a succession of barely competent village women who would come in once a week to clean. They would be prompt and dependable for a few weeks, and then, without warning, decide to go home to their villages, not seeming to care that an abrupt, two-month vacation might wreak havoc with our work schedules.

When I was expecting Samira, I knew that I would need to have live-in help if I wanted to continue working. Even if Ali and I just wanted to go out at night, we would need to have a *naneh*. I wouldn't be able to call on a neighbor's daughter to stay with the baby. While middle-class American teenage girls saw their first babysitting jobs as rites of passage, their Tehrani counterparts wouldn't stoop to such work, believing it to be below their station.

Many middle-class Tehranis at least had someone come in occasionally to clean the stairs or wash the windows. Some had old family retainers, men or women servants who had been with the family for decades.

Some wealthy Tehranis were able to hire young ladies from the Philippines. An older Filipina woman, a kind of *grande dame* who acted as a combination employment agent/confidant/chaperone and den mother, supervised these young women. In negotiating with prospective employers, she would make sure that her charges would have their own rooms and Sundays off. Each Sunday, the ladies would dress up and visit her for lunch at her well- appointed home in northern Tehran, where she held court.

Even if we could have afforded their higher salaries, these elegant young women were not for us. Not only did their day off fall in the middle of the Iranian workweek, our household never would have passed muster. We didn't have a maid's room, and anyone who worked for us would need to sleep in the children's room. So we were mostly limited to widowed villagers who were perfectly happy to sleep on a futon on the bedroom floor.

The arrival of a new maid was a new beginning. Each brought with her the promise of a calm, orderly, pristine existence, a partnership of mutual benefit. This optimism usually lasted about two weeks.

Our first live-in maid was Kobra. She was a tiny, wiry, angular woman in her forties with a long, slightly lupine face. Even the sheer white headscarf that covered her dark hair was pointed and severe. She would gather up the ends of it and pin them under her chin, so that the fabric stuck out at angles, somewhat like an ancient Egyptian headdress. She was gentle with the children and seemed intelligent, but she had a sly, calculating manner and a way of taking directions that made me think she was only grudgingly acquiescing to my wishes.

I also soon found out that the person who runs the kitchen runs the house, or thinks she should. As soon as Kobra started the midday meal, the dynamics of the household changed. She didn't exactly order me around, but her manner became brusque. When she was cooking, she was not to be interrupted. Citing hygiene concerns, she would not stop to change a diaper if she was in the middle of food preparation. She let me know that I was her backup, whether or not I was in the middle of my own work.

Now that we had a stranger living under our roof, my sister-in-law Sakineh set about cautioning me to be more careful about keeping track of the household inventory. Sakineh was particularly knowledgeable about inventories—hers and those of everyone else in the family. Her extended visits at the homes of family members gave her an intimate knowledge of the workings of every household. She knew how many sets of mattresses and comforters were stacked in Pouran's *anbari*, how many jugs of vinegar or pickles Fatemeh had in hers, how many embroidered Kermani tablecloths Naazi owned and who gave them to her, how many gold bracelets Mina received from Ghasem on the birth of their first son. In her mind's eye, she could picture every closet, every chest of drawers, every dark and dusty storeroom that she had helped some overworked relative to organize, and she could recite the contents of each one with mind-numbing accuracy.

Sensing that I didn't share her appreciation of the finer points of employer-employee relations, Sakineh feared where my naiveté might lead. One day, when Kobra was busy in the children's room, Sakineh cornered me in the kitchen.

"Do you know how many eggs you have in the refrigerator?" she whispered.

"No, how many do you need?" I answered, wondering why I was whispering as well.

"I don't want any eggs," she said. "I want to know if *you* know how many eggs you have."

"Well, not really."

"You need to know these things," she said, taking the eggs out and counting them. "There—twenty-three eggs," she announced, fixing me with a steady gaze. Nodding toward the children's room, she whispered, "You can't assume everyone's like you."

But it was difficult for me to assume otherwise, to live with someone whom I suspected might steal from me. I preferred to think that if I treated a person fairly, they would treat me fairly in return. I was prepared to pay an equitable wage, give time off, provide a comfortable living environment and good food, and be sensitive to the needs and feelings of others. In return, all I asked was respect for my wishes and my private property.

Of course, I practiced reasonable caution. I didn't leave money or valuables lying around.

"Let's not make thieves of people," Ali would say, preferring not to tempt fate—or a servant.

I agreed, but I had little interest in keeping a running egg tally.

What I was more interested in was the children's safety. Our second-floor apartment abounded with opportunities for disaster—open windows, balconies, stairs, electric wall sockets, fruit knives left on the coffee table. The only outside play area available to us was the second-floor porch outside our front door, with un-gated steps leading to the building's courtyard entry below.

The neighborhood itself was not child-friendly. There was no park nearby, and the busy main street, Geesha Avenue, had high curbs and uneven, broken sidewalks that made pushing a stroller nearly impossible. Even so, Kobra was eager to take two-year-old Samira out for walks. Of course, Samira needed fresh air and the stimulation of new surroundings, but her *naneh* needed them just as much. As anyone would be, Kobra was restless after being cooped up in the house with two small children for days on end, so she frequently devised excuses to go shopping—usually for things she insisted were best bought at the old bazaar, a long, crowded bus ride away in congested south Tehran.

"It's so much cheaper there, Khanum," she said one day, as she was getting ready for a trip to the bazaar.

"Fine," I said, "but I don't want you taking Samira. It's too crowded and full of exhaust fumes. It's not healthy. Besides, when you're loaded down with packages, you can't hold her hand. It's just not safe."

"*Chashm, Khanum*," she said. *Yes, madam, upon my eye.*

"I'm serious, Kobra."

"*Chashm, chashm.*"

A few weeks later, Kobra asked permission to take Samira with her to do some shopping in our neighborhood. When forty-five minutes had passed and they were not yet back, I began to worry. Kobra came back two hours later, laden with packages and carrying Samira, who immediately said, "*Maasheen bood!*" In Samira-speak, that could either mean "there was a car" or "there was a bus." I knew immediately there was a bus. Kobra's guilty look confirmed my suspicions.

I could well imagine that excursion, one I had taken myself. I saw Kobra and Samira wedged into a swaying, sweaty, overcrowded bus that jerked and thrust itself through south Tehran's ever-shifting muddle of taxis, trucks and the occasional horse-drawn carriage; the blue haze of exhaust filling their lungs; the din of the artisans' hammers drowning out the child's cry; the jostling; the broken sidewalks and uneven cobblestones waiting to trip someone burdened with packages and a baby, hurrying to get home before her employer realizes where she has been.

A visit to the bazaar is an edifying outing for a young American wife smitten with romantic ideas about traditional Tehrani life. It's a stimulating, multisensory experience, an antidote to the confinement of apartment living, but it was hardly the way I wanted my two-year-old to spend an afternoon away from me. I could overlook a lot of things, but not the flagrant disregard for my explicit wishes concerning my children's wellbeing. The trip to the bazaar may not have been as harrowing as I had imagined, but what was important was that Kobra had ignored my instructions. That night, Ali and I let her know that she must leave in the morning. She accepted our decision with equanimity. But the next day, after she had gone to her daughter's house, I noticed that a large aventurine pendant I had thoughtlessly left on the kitchen counter was missing. All the eggs, however, were still in the refrigerator.

Ali and I were prepared to spend the rest of the summer without any household help, but with classes starting at the university, we would need someone soon. We were losing all hope, until one day Ali's niece Batoul told us her husband had a friend in an employment agency who had found just the person for us.

The next day, Ali and I sat in the agency's office, sipping bitter tea that, like most office tea, tasted as if it had been brewed from old ledgers. The office was full of employees and cronies lounging around, each with their own tea glass, pretending not to listen to our conversation.

"This girl I found for you is no ordinary servant," our contact assured us. "Her name is Parvaneh. She speaks four languages—Persian, English, Arabic and French. She's even lived in Beirut. She's probably more fastidious than most employers."

"Probably not this employer," Ali said, nodding at me, "but all right, please send her over."

"She'll be there by five tomorrow evening."

The following day, to avoid scaring away the new help, we frantically cleaned house. Five o'clock rolled around but no Parvaneh. There was still no sign of her at seven o'clock, when Batoul and her husband came for dinner to check out the new employee. Finally, Parvaneh arrived just after eight, chipper and unapologetic.

"Would you like some supper," I asked her.

"No thanks, I've already eaten," she replied.

"Well, I should think so," Batoul muttered under her breath. "Someone who is three hours late definitely should have eaten already." So grateful was I to have a *naneh* again that I was ready to overlook this inauspicious beginning, chalking it up to miscommunication or bad traffic.

Parvaneh was a friendly, bouncy nineteen-year-old from Rasht, in Gilan Province, near the Caspian Sea. With her brown hair in a fashionable bob, contemporary clothes, perky manner, and lack of *hijab*, she looked like any carefree, modern, middle-class Tehrani schoolgirl.

She told us she had finished high school in Rasht and had come to Tehran to further her education because the capital had many more educational opportunities than her provincial hometown. She planned to take English classes in the afternoons to prepare for the university.

Good, we thought. This will be a win-win situation. I can work while the children are in the care of a lively, intelligent young woman, and she will have the opportunity to continue her education. Perhaps I can even tutor her in English. Ali can help her prepare for the university entrance exam. This will be a chance to make a real difference in a young person's life.

Parvaneh quickly caught on to our routine, and she seemed genuinely interested in the children. She was a far more energetic playmate for two toddlers than Kobra had been. However, after a few weeks, I noticed that she never seemed to study.

"Don't you have homework?" I asked her.

"I did it after class, at a coffee shop," she assured me.

She also never asked to practice her English with me. It seemed odd that she didn't want to take advantage of having a resident native speaker available to tutor her, even informally, but then we were all busy—Ali with teaching, I with graduate school, she with the children and housekeeping—so it was reasonable that she might not want to ask for private lessons. But her lack of interest worried me.

"Don't you want to practice your English?" I asked her.

"Well, I don't need to," she replied. "I'm taking a math class instead."

Gradually, her afternoon outings became longer—a half hour more here, another hour there. She always had a plausible excuse: she had to stay after school to talk with the instructor, she had missed the bus, or she needed to do some errands. We cautioned her about the importance of punctuality, and for a while she would be diligent about returning on time, but eventually she began to slack off again.

One Friday, after Parvaneh had been with us for a couple of months, we received a call from a man with a Rashti accent who said he was Rashid, Parvaneh's brother.

"I've just come from Rasht and I'd like to speak with you," Rashid said.

"By all means," Ali said. "When would you like to come?"

"I can be there in ten minutes," he said.

Parvaneh tried to disguise her apprehension at the imminent arrival of her brother, but it was obvious that she was nervous. As soon as he arrived, I could see why she was so anxious.

Rashid was a tall, imposing, muscular man in his early thirties with the ruddy complexion of someone who spent most of his time outdoors. He seemed uncomfortable in his dark suit with his white shirt collar and tie straining at his thick neck. The Persian word for ruffian or bully is *gardan koloft*, literally "thick neck," and his cold demeanor did nothing to dispel that stereotype. He sat stiffly in his chair and glowered, first at us, then at his sister. He accepted a cup of tea, but he dispensed with the usual pleasantries and got straight to the point.

"What are you doing here?" he asked, glaring at Parvaneh.

"I'm taking care of the children and going to school," she replied, in a smaller voice than usual, but clearly and evenly, just the same.

"You can do that in Rasht. There's no reason to be in Tehran," he said. "Get your things. You're coming with me."

"I want to stay here," Parvaneh said, her voice gaining strength.

"We don't even know these people," said Rashid.

Ali explained that he and I were both at the university, and that the employment agency had arranged Parvaneh's placement with us, assuming that our home would be a safe and beneficial situation for her.

"Look," Ali said, "Parvaneh is free to go, if that's what she wants. But I know you want the best for her. If she wants to study, Tehran's the best place. We promise we'll look after her."

Rashid thought for a moment and then relented. He probably thought that a university professor and his American wife might treat his sister less like a servant and more like the daughter of the house, and he was right. Rashid put aside his concerns and left his sister in our care.

A grateful and relieved Parvaneh resumed her duties with renewed enthusiasm, well aware how close she had come to suffering the indignity of being dragged back to Rasht. Ali, however, was worried. The responsibility of a spirited young girl in the house—especially one with a disgruntled older brother—was more than he had bargained for. If she were to get into trouble, Rashid would hold him accountable.

But with her victory over her brother behind her, it was becoming increasingly clear that Parvaneh had a lot more than studying on her mind. One day, I came home from the university to find the stereo turned up full blast. Through the stained-glass sliding doors, I could see the blurry image of Parvaneh bobbing up and down, dancing intently to Fleetwood Mac. Not hearing me when I entered the room, she continued dancing, oblivious to Samira and Sarah, who were watching her, crying at the top of their lungs, competing with Stevie Nicks for her attention.

When Ali's handsome younger brother Ahmad came from Kerman for a visit, Parvaneh went into high gear. Instead of busying herself in the kitchen or the children's room, she planted herself at the dining room table and proceeded to flirt shamelessly with Ahmad while painting her nails. Ahmad had brought photos of his recent wedding in Kerman, which he shared with all of us. Nevertheless, Parvaneh was undaunted. She was so preoccupied with making an impression on him that she spilled nail polish on the carpet.

"You realize he's married," I said to Parvaneh as she kneeled under the dining room table, scrubbing away at the carpet with acetone. "He's the groom in those photos." She said nothing, but gave me a look as if to say, *He might be married, but that doesn't mean I don't have a shot.*

Ahmad's reaction was not the one Parvaneh had intended. He pointedly ignored her. Privately, he let us know that we needed to curb this girl's behavior, that we had let her become *por roo*—cheeky.

Clearly, Parvaneh was as confused as we were about her status in the family. What was her place? Should she be allowed to visit with guests or should she make herself scarce? How much freedom should she have?

One day, Ali came home early from work and announced that he had just seen Parvaneh on the street near the university talking to a group of boys when she was supposed to be in class. That certainly explained her chronic lateness and her lack of homework. For Ali, the issue wasn't just that she was ditching class and lying to us about it. It was that she was hanging out with boys. Spending time with male classmates might have been perfectly acceptable for an American girl in the States, but he was having none of it here, where most families forbade dating and controlled their daughters' social lives until they could arrange their marriages. Context was everything. What was possible in the States was, to say the least, problematic in Iran. Ali's concerns were fueled by the prevailing social mores and his sense of responsibility for Parvaneh's welfare, a responsibility underscored by our encounter with her brother.

When we confronted her about not being in class, Parvaneh told us she hadn't been enrolled for a few weeks, but would start again soon. By this time, Ali and I had had it. We couldn't trust her to be attentive to the children, and we couldn't depend on her to tell the truth about her activities outside our home. I shared my concerns with my friend Nyusha, a university student with an infant of her own. Nyusha was a young, idealistic liberal with an independent mind and little patience for Islamic strictures against young women's freedom. A graduate of a Catholic high school for girls run by French nuns, she came from a family that was only nominally Muslim. Unlike most young women her age, she didn't wait for her family to arrange a marriage for her. She and her university professor husband had married soon after she became pregnant.

"This just isn't working," I said to Nyusha. "I can't be sure what she's doing when she's out and about. What if she gets pregnant while she's in our house?"

"Well, if she's not working out for you, perhaps she could work for me," said Nyusha, who was certain I was making too big a deal about Parvaneh's comings and goings.

Parvaneh packed her bags and went to Nyusha's house, a few blocks away. We were once again without household help, alone but relieved.

Two months later, I saw Nyusha at a party and asked her how Parvaneh was doing.

"I had to let her go," Nyusha said.

"What happened?"

"It was a disaster. When you first told me about her, I was sure you were being too critical," she said. "I thought, 'Ellen's an American. She doesn't understand how to get along with Iranian servants.' I was sure I could do better."

"For a while, everything was fine," Nyusha said. "But after a few weeks, she started coming home late every day. The minute she got home, she would head straight for the shower. It was obvious what she was doing. I don't think she was going to classes at all."

Both Nyusha and I had been sympathetic to Parvaneh's desire to be a liberated, educated young woman, to better her lot in life. We had hoped we could give her the support she needed to attain her goals. Parvaneh wanted the same kind of freedom enjoyed by many American girls her age, but she was not willing to do the hard work necessary to win that freedom in her native environment.

She wanted the student life she saw in Western movies, minus the sleepless nights cramming for exams or writing term papers. She aspired to the trappings of Western-style liberation, but not to the essential experiences needed to sustain them in Iran.

With Naneh Fatemeh, there were none of the complexities and ambiguities surrounding our relationship with Parvaneh. But even with Naneh's outward simplicity, it was easy to underestimate her, to fail to see the person she was under all those protective layers of cloth, to see her only in relationship to myself. However, sometimes a gesture, a catch in the voice, a chance remark would hint at the existence of another Naneh, a secret Naneh.

If she hadn't been there when the census taker came, I might never have bothered to know Naneh's last name. When the bell rang, she waddled over to open the door, letting in flies, the smell of tar from the neighbor's new roof, and a crisp young man holding a clipboard.

"Fatemeh Mullahzadeh," she told him when he asked her name.

"How old are you?"

"As old as the shah."

Now I knew her age, fifty-six, and her family name, Mullahzadeh, child of a mullah. One of Naneh's ancestors must have been a respected member of the village. One of her forebears must have been literate, or at least able to memorize the Qur'an and interpret it. Perhaps he had taught the Qur'an to the small children the harried village women sent to him so they could have a few hours of relative peace.

We hadn't asked for her identity card as security, although that was a common practice. One of my friends had stashed her servants' identity cards in her cashbox, thinking they wouldn't be able to leave without them. However, they did leave, stealing back their identity cards and the contents of the cashbox, as well.

Sadly, up to that time, Naneh's family name had been irrelevant. It was still irrelevant. That was the thing about Naneh. All the personal details of her life were interesting separately, but they never added up. They never adhered to her. They went unexamined. They hung in the air for a moment like plumes of pipe smoke, then disappeared.

For instance, one day, while we were taking a tea break, she told me that only two of her eight children had survived.

"What happened to the others?" I asked.

"They got sick and died," she said, tamping down her pipe tobacco.

"How? All at once?"

"No, at different times. They all had measles, but the spots didn't come out. They stayed inside, in the liver."

She had lost six children in this way and was able to talk about them as if they were lost balloons or dandelion puffs born away by the wind. I wondered if she often thought about them, if she tried to imagine what they would have been like if they had lived, if she blamed herself, or simply thought their deaths were *ghesmat*, fate.

She didn't embellish the story, nor did she ask for sympathy. What would have been the point? Ever the pragmatist, she wanted my sympathy only when she had an upset stomach. At those times, she didn't get much from me except Kaopectate and strong tea. Instead, I offered sympathy for the loss of her children. I should have been smarter.

One bright autumn day, we went on a family picnic in the garden of a friend in Karaj, 25 miles from Tehran. We spread our tablecloth under a tall apple tree and started unpacking our lunch. Before I knew what was happening, Naneh had tied the ends of her chador behind her neck, kicked off her black rubber shoes and scurried up the tree.

"Naneh, come down from there," I shouted. "You'll fall."

But, of course she didn't fall. At fifty-six, she still had her villager's agility. Never taking her eyes off the fruit, Naneh just smiled to herself and kept on climbing. The children and I watched as Naneh tossed down apples from her perch ten feet above us. This woman, as old as the shah, was twenty-six years older than I and far more fearless. In that moment, I saw Naneh as she must have been in her youth.

I had never seen Naneh without layers upon layers of clothing until the day I had to call her out of the bath to answer an urgent phone call from her daughter.

"What? Come out like this?" she had cried from behind the bathroom door. "Like this" meant wearing a sleeveless shift which exposed delicate, thin, white shoulders. Her head was bare, and I saw for the first time the little tendrils of dark salt and pepper hair. It was like seeing the real Naneh, not the Qajar-era throwback but a timeless, private Naneh hidden beneath the Naneh I thought I knew. I was seeing her not only as she might have been in her youth but as a mature woman, not the crone who crouched in the corner with her pipe.

Every Friday, on her day off, Naneh went to her daughter's house in south Tehran. We would often send along fruit or pastries or used clothing for her daughter and her family. Naneh would pack up everything the night before and leave early for the bus stop in the morning, often just as we were waking up.

One Friday morning, after Naneh had gone, a neighbor rang the doorbell.

"*Salaam, Agha-ye Doktor,*" she said to Ali. "Forgive me for bothering you, but I really feel I need to speak with you."

"Of course," said Ali.

"It's your maid," she said. "I think you need to watch her more carefully."

"What do you mean?"

"Well, every Friday morning, she leaves your house with a big black garbage sack slung over her shoulder."

"Oh, I'm sure those are her things she's carrying—or things we've given her," Ali replied.

"Are you certain?" the neighbor asked. "I've been watching her. She puts the garbage sack outside by the door first thing in the morning, goes back upstairs, collects the rest of her things, and then she leaves."

"Thank you for your concern," Ali said, "but we trust Naneh. I'm sure she's not stealing."

The neighbor smiled and shook her head. "All the same," she said, "it wouldn't hurt to keep an eye on her."

Ali related the conversation to me, and we laughed at the neighbor's cynicism. "Why do people always assume that maids steal?" I said. "It's so unfair."

But the suspicion the neighbor had planted began to nag at me. Was I imagining it, or had Naneh's behavior toward us changed in the last few months? I remembered that lately she had become increasingly short with Samira, who was no longer a malleable toddler, but a four-year-old with a mind of her own who needed more intellectual stimulation than Naneh was capable of giving her.

Naneh had also started grumbling about my new work schedule. While I was teaching or going to graduate school, I was rarely gone the entire day, and some days I worked from home. But after graduate school, I was hired at the Tehran Museum of Contemporary Art, where I worked from 9 a.m. to 5 p.m., five days a week.

"You never told me you were going to work full-time," Naneh said, after several weeks home alone with the children. "This wasn't part of the bargain."

She was right. It hadn't been part of the bargain, so we gave Naneh a raise, which she happily accepted. We also agreed to find a pre-school, which would take some of the pressure off her and give the children new experiences. But I had always assumed Naneh and I had another bargain—however tacit—namely that if I treated her fairly, she would treat me fairly in return. I decided to see if that bargain was still in effect.

The following Friday morning, I got up early to find Naneh in the kitchen smoking her pipe. Ali's brother Ahmad, who was visiting from Kerman, was still asleep in the living room. While Naneh was getting ready to leave, I slipped downstairs and opened the front door.

As soon as I saw the black garbage sack, my heart sank.

Inside was a collection of household items—steel wool and laundry detergent and lentils and rice and tea biscuits—inexpensive things I would gladly have given her, but things she had taken without asking, things she thought I wouldn't miss—things she must have felt entitled to precisely because I had so much. She was right. I wouldn't have missed them.

I brought the sack upstairs and put it on the kitchen table in front of her.

Naneh put down her pipe and looked away.

"If you had asked me, Naneh, I would have given these to you," I said.

"*Eh, Khanum....*"

"Why did you do this, Naneh?"

"*Eh, Khanum...,*" she said, her eyes filling with tears.

By this time, Ali and Ahmad had joined us. Ali surveyed the scene and made his decision.

"Naneh, I'm sorry, but you'll have to go," he said. Handing her a sheaf of bills, he said, "Here is your salary for the rest of the month."

Ahmad winced. He didn't say anything, but it was clear that he was disappointed in us. Maybe he was embarrassed that he had to witness that scene, or maybe he couldn't believe we were letting Naneh go over some soap and a few handfuls of lentils. After all, servants steal things all the time. Hadn't Sakineh warned me to be more vigilant? People who insist on leaving their eggs uncounted should expect to be disappointed.

We could have made allowances for human weakness. We could have made minor adjustments in our lifestyle, locked things up, inventoried. We could have policed our own house, made spies of our children, or rifled through Naneh's bags every Friday morning to make sure that she was not spiriting away packets of Tide.

Instead, we lowered our standards and did our own housework until we could find someone to come in one day a week. We had our privacy back.

To be sure, we were among the fortunate. However fractious our interactions with the nanehs sometimes were, I benefited greatly from them. They enabled me to further my career; they enlarged my understanding of Iran's diverse society; they kept me from going crazy juggling a household and work or graduate school. I have no regrets...except one.

That Friday morning, as I watched Naneh disappear down the *koocheh* that last time, I was filled with sadness. I knew I had failed in this relationship. In spite of my initial cynicism about servants being part of the family, I had come to feel that Naneh was indeed part of ours. What I had not understood was how to make allowances for family, to find a way to coexist with people's weaknesses, to forgive.

Naneh Fatemeh and Sarah, circa 1976.

PART IV: Revolution

25

·················

RAY'S PIZZA

Tehran: March 1978

We had spent the morning packing for our road trip to Khuzestan, the southwestern province bordering Iraq. With Sakineh's help, we loaded the car with a flask of tea, biscuits, children's books, and that week's favorite dolls to keep Samira and Sarah entertained on the two-day journey. The five of us were going to spend the week before the Persian New Year in Ahvaz. Ali would be attending the Iranian Genetics Society meeting at Jundi Shapur University, but we would have ample time to see the sights: the Dezful bazaar, Haft Tapeh archeological museum, King Darius's winter palace, and the tomb of Daniel in Susa.

We decided to treat ourselves to lunch before getting on the road and settled on a place we knew the children would enjoy, Ray's Pizza Pantry, a fashionable yet family-friendly restaurant on Vila Street, across from the Ministry of Science and Higher Education. Ray's had several popular locations in town, usually packed with middle-class Iranians and foreign expatriates. Each of the locations had a cozy ambience, a mixture of Persian handicrafts and Italianate kitsch, and a variety of pizzas and Mexican food.

Ray's Pizza Pantry had been cultivating foreign clientele for several years. It had been one of eight Tehran restaurants to have a presence at the 2nd Asian Trade Fair in 1969.[34] The owners' familiarity with Italian and Mexican cuisine provided a welcome antidote to my frequent bouts of homesickness.

As we approached the entrance to the basement restaurant, Ali and I stepped aside to let Sakineh descend the stairs first. With her dark, flowered chador flowing behind her, she took the lead. Suddenly, out of the shadows, the manager appeared at the foot of the stairs, blocking Sakineh's progress.

"Excuse me, Khanum," he said, "you'll have to remove your chador."

We all froze in disbelief. Samira and Sarah stared wide-eyed at this man. They were old enough to know that some women preferred to wear a chador, that on some occasions—when they prayed, when they went to a mosque—women had to wear a chador, but they'd never before seen a woman prevented from wearing one.

Sakineh, her sturdy frame straight, silently took the man's measure.

Suddenly, I felt Ali push past me on the stairs. "What do you mean?" he demanded. "Why should she take off her chador?"

"Agha, we have many foreign customers here, and…."

"Oh, come on," Ali said, pointing to me. "This lady is a foreigner and she's not bothered by a chador."

"*Basheh*," said Sakineh. It's OK.

Before Ali could say anything else, Sakineh pulled the chador from her head, draped it across her arm, and breezed down the stairs past the manager and into the restaurant.

---

34. Petrossian, Vahe. *19 Days in Iran*. Tehran: Iran Chap, no date, pp. 298-299.

"Sakineh," I said, rushing to catch her before she slid into a booth. "You didn't have to do that. We can go somewhere else."

She thrust her chin up as if to say, Vellesh kon—*Let it go. It's of no importance.*

"But it's not right," I protested.

"Hijab too del e aadam e," she explained. Modesty is in a person's heart.

"Years ago," she went on, "Reza Shah made us take off our chadors. A few years later his son said we could put them back on. Today, they want me to take mine off again." Her shrug said: *These people are of no consequence. I know who I am. I know what I believe.*

Unlike her daughters' generation, Sakineh was firmly in the chadori camp of the family. She had worn a chador since her marriage over thirty years before. But she had a history of independence. The eldest of the seven children, she was the only one to attend a co-ed elementary school, in the days before boys and girls were separated, and her brothers and sisters credit that early experience with instilling in her a kind of unconventional spirit and sartorial sophistication. As a teenager in the 1940s, she was the only girl in Kerman to ride a bike. A chador would have got in the way of that activity.

But from the time of her marriage at seventeen, she wore the chador, as was expected of a devout Muslim wife and mother living in a small provincial town. She prayed every day. She fasted during Ramadan. She gave food to the poor. She believed.

But Sakineh was also fundamentally non-confrontational. That is not to say that she was weak or ineffectual. To the contrary, she was an energetic defender of the family's well-being, protecting it from debilitating discord. However, she was always the placater, the mediator, the settler of ruffled feathers. Just as she had an herbal cure for every ailment, she had a poultice of soothing words for every nose out of joint. She would spread flagrant rumors of good will. True or not, whenever you voiced some doubt about someone's fidelity or motives she would say, "Oh, but So-and-So Khanum really likes you." For good measure, she treated So-and-So Khanum to a reciprocal account of your own fond feelings.

Sakineh very likely didn't want us to start our vacation with a bitter argument over a length of cloth. She didn't want any of us to be upset. But she also didn't want that restaurant manager to think that what he said mattered to her.

What mattered to the manager was to keep his job. Barely a year before the revolution that would depose the Western-influenced shah and eventually mandate *hijab* for all women, he was forced to ask a faithful Muslim to take off her chador in deference to foreigners. Charged with the responsibility of protecting the imagined standards of Western customers, he very likely went against his own standards. It was highly probable that he came from a traditional family in which most of his female relatives wore chadors. How would he have felt about turning a member of his own family away? More importantly, how did he feel months later when women were harassed and arrested for not having proper hijab? In no small measure, the flames of the revolution were fueled by the burning consciences of the faithful who, during the shah's era, were often forced to compromise their own values in the name of progress.

We made the best of our lunch and headed for Khuzestan. As we left the restaurant, Sakineh's chador was once again draped over her arm. She didn't put it on again for the rest of the trip—not for the conference's social gatherings, not for the Dezful bazaar, not for the sightseeing trip to Susa—not until she got back home to Kerman.

A few months later, my friend Julie and I were having a leisurely late lunch at that same restaurant. The lunch crowd had left, and ours was one of the few tables occupied. When we got the check, which was, of course, written in Persian, Julie noticed it included a charge for a bottle of Johnnie Walker Red Label. She called the waiter over and showed him the bill.

"We didn't order this," she said calmly, pointing to the *veesky* on the tab.

Only the waiter's darting eyes betrayed his surprise that two foreign women could read Persian and knew that they were being overcharged. With a mumbled apology, he turned on his heels and went back to the waiters' station to correct the bill.

Apparently, the reverence of Ray's Pizza Pantry for the sensibilities of foreigners did not preclude cheating them.

26

·················

THE LONG, HOT SUMMER

Tehran: August 1978

Salman, the corner grocer, was out of eggs. I mean, truly out of eggs. This time, there was no barely perceptible lifting of an eyebrow signaling me to come back when the store was empty of less favored customers. A pyramid of tea biscuits now occupied the place on his countertop where he usually kept the stack of egg flats.

I left his store with my empty plastic shopping basket and stood on the corner in the August heat, wondering what to do next. I couldn't go home without eggs again. How long had it been since the children had eaten eggs? Three weeks? A month?

I decided to strike off in search of new territory. If Salman didn't have eggs, someone else might have them. But would that someone sell them to me if I weren't a regular customer? I began to see the all-my-eggs-in-one-basket folly of cultivating only one neighborhood grocer.

Desperate for a chance at another grocery store, I turned into a side street in an unfamiliar part of the neighborhood. I went into the first shop I found, but again came out empty-handed. After wandering for a while, I saw an old man ahead of me on the sidewalk holding the hand of a little boy, probably his grandson. The man had an empty shopping bag, too, so I decided to follow him. With any luck, I reasoned, he'll lead me to eggs. I caught up with the pair and followed them at a reasonable distance. I hung back when they stopped in front of a piece of flatbread that someone had dropped on the sidewalk. The old man slowly bent down, picked up the bread and, as a sign of respect for the staff of life, carefully propped it against a nearby tree so that it wouldn't be trampled.

Soon, my quarry turned down another street and into a corner grocery store—one I had never seen before. I followed them and got in line behind them—the only other customers.

"Do you have any eggs, Hassan Agha?" the old man asked.

The proprietor glanced past him at me, as if wondering how he should reply.

"Sorry, I can give you only six," answered Hassan Agha, who apparently did not use eyebrow signals.

He reached under the counter and brought out six eggs, which he put in a paper sack and handed over. The old man paid and, with his hand on his heart, bowed in thanks and left with the little boy.

I stepped up to the counter. "I'd like some eggs, please," I said.

Hassan Agha glared at me, unhappy at being caught in the possession of eggs he must have been saving for his regulars. I was clearly an interloper, but just as clearly, Hassan Agha was a decent man. He could have said he had just given away his last eggs. Instead, he reached down and took six more eggs from their hiding place and put them in a bag for me.

August in Tehran was always irritating, tiring, and oppressive, but August 1978 was particularly unsettling. Something was in the air. Mixed with the dust and exhaust fumes was an electricity and tension that had less to do with the summer's brutal heat than with the smoldering political discontent.

In spite of the new, French-built hydroelectric plant in

Khuzestan Province, Tehran experienced frequent power outages, leaving us without air conditioning for hours at a time several days a week. There were continual shortages. Lately, the only chickens in the stores were the pitiful, frozen, hormone-laced ones imported from Holland. And for the first time I could remember, vodka was in short supply. But these petty annoyances paled beside Iranians' increasing dissatisfaction with their government.

Discontent could be found across a broad political spectrum. The reasons people gave for the widespread unhappiness differed greatly. Some said there was too much repression, others too little repression. However, one thing was clear to Ali and me: the country had traded its moral compass for oil and thereby lost its opportunity to create a truly modern state.

This malaise was several years in the making. The seeds of this most recent discontent were sown in 1953 when the CIA engineered a coup to overthrow the popularly elected prime minister, Mohammad Mossadegh, and in 1964 when the shah exiled Khomeini. The shah's celebration of 2500 years of monarchy was, for some, a brief diversion from the trouble that was brewing. For others, it added more fuel to the fire.

When I first arrived in Tehran in September 1971, the country was gearing up for the celebration. What should have, in some way, included the entire nation was instead a lavish blow-out attended by Iran's elite and foreign royalty, showcasing not the richness of Iranian culture but rather Iranian royalty's ability to emulate European culture. At the time, the cost of the affair was a state secret, which only served to fan wild speculation. An acquaintance of ours, who was one of several accountants assigned to the event, knew some of the costs but was sworn to secrecy. Since the fall of the shah, the price tag has been estimated at between $50 million and $300 million.[35] However, according to the Minister of the Royal court during that period, Amir Assadollah Alam, the actual cost was $120 million.[36]

While the higher estimates might include infrastructure costs, such as roads and airports, much of the money was spent in the construction of a 160-acre tent city near Shiraz. There, among the ruins of Persepolis, the wellspring of Iranian history and culture, foreign dignitaries were treated to the best that Paris had to offer. Iran, so rich in literature, fine arts, and cuisine, was represented chiefly by its caviar and carpets. France was present nearly everywhere else. The organizers flew in a French hotelier and a staff of 159 chefs, bakers and waiters who plied the guests with French cuisine and French Champagne. They imported forty-three thousand yards of flameproof European cloth for the tents, as well as Baccarat crystal, bed linens, Guerlain-perfumed oils, chandeliers, and furniture from Europe for the Louis XIV décor.[37] Even the uniforms worn by the Iranian Army depicting Persian soldiers throughout history were created by French artists.[38] Bathroom fixtures, however, were imported from the United States.

It's one thing to dismiss the richness of Iran's complex and sophisticated culture as insufficient for guests, but it's quite another thing to ignore the economic impact that such a festival might have had on the local economy if more of those millions had stayed in the hands of Iranian designers, chefs, bakers, waiters, farmers, weavers and furniture makers. Instead, much of the money spent

35. Mackey, p. 236.

36. Alam, Amir Assadollah, *The Alam Diaries (1967-1977)*, Alinaghi Alikhani, ed. Ketabsara Publishing Co., seven vols. (in Persian).

37. Mackey, pp. 236-237.

38. Shawcross, William. *The Shah's Last Ride: The Fate of an Ally*. New York: Simon and Shuster, 1989, p. 42.

on the tent city generously lined foreign pockets.

Watching the pageantry on Mahmoud and Mahin's black and white TV, I was transfixed, like millions of my new countrymen, by the images of the shah and the empress standing regally still, as the friezes of Persepolis came to life before them. However, my teenage fascination with the royal family was now tempered by my growing understanding of the government's repression—the censorship and the torture and executions of political prisoners.

During the ceremonies, the shah stood at the tomb of the great king of the Persian Empire and intoned,

> *Cyrus, we stand before your eternal dwelling place to speak these solemn words: Sleep in peace forever, for we are awake and we remain to watch over your glorious heritage.*

These solemn words were meant to solidify the shah's image at home and abroad as the rightful, ever vigilant heir to the twenty-five hundred years of dynasties before his. However, they became a source of amusement for many of his people who were unconvinced that their king was looking out for their best interests. The ubiquitous phrase, *"Kourosh, asoodeh bekhab; maa bidaarim"* (Cyrus, sleep in peace; we are awake), became one of the first Persian sayings I learned. Privately, friends and family members invoked it to raucous laughter whenever the electricity went out or there was a shortage of onions.

Instead of solidifying domestic support for the shah, the celebration only magnified his many shortcomings. Its extravagance was seen as a slap in the face by both the struggling middle class and the poor villagers suffering from that year's drought and meager harvests. Remembering the relatively humble beginnings of the shah's father and the pervasive influences of foreign powers during his son's reign, many intellectuals scoffed when the shah equated the forty-six-year-old Pahlavi dynasty with that of the great Achaemenians. But for those who had no use for the monarchy at all, the festivities were the ultimate blasphemy.

In the seventh year of his exile in Najaf, Iraq, Ayatollah Khomeini declared, "Anyone who organizes or participates in these festivities is a traitor to Islam and the Iranian nation." He called the title *Shahanshah*, the King of Kings, "the most hated of all titles in the sight of God....Islam is fundamentally opposed to the whole notion of monarchy....Monarchy is one of the most shameful and disgraceful reactionary manifestations."[39]

In 1973, the shah negotiated a major increase in the price of oil. The country's increased wealth from oil production, which should have enhanced everyone's standard of living, was the cause of much dissent. While this new infusion of cash benefited many social programs and cultural institutions, enough of those revenues were funneled away from the people to the shah's family and his entourage, to foment widespread anger.

Lest the world forget that the current King of Kings was the protector of thousands of years of Persian civilization, in 1976, the shah decided to abolish the *hejri* (Islamic solar) calendar dating from the Prophet Mohammad's migration from Mecca to Medina. He replaced it with the Imperial calendar, dating from the year that Cyrus the Great ascended the throne. This symbolic act, which effectively subordinated Islam to the monarchy, was just one more insult to the Muslim clergy and their devout followers. Many secular and religious Iranians alike saw it as yet another manifestation of the shah's arrogance. The nation went to bed in 1355 and

39. Shawcross, p. 116.

woke up in 2535. But like many other Iranians, Ali and I largely ignored the new calendar. When we weren't dealing with official correspondence, we used the old calendar.

In spite of the shah's modernization efforts, by 1978, there was still a great disparity in personal wealth among the social classes. The government prevented economists in the Plan and Budget Organization from publishing a report showing that in the cities, the rich were getting richer while the middle class lost ground, and the consumption of both groups was three times that of their rural countrymen.[40] Of course, we didn't have these figures at the time. All we knew was that our buying power was dwindling rapidly.

The Islamic fundamentalists were angry about the pervasiveness of Western secular influences at the expense of traditional Islamic culture and the loosening of social mores that came with the influx of oil revenue. They decried the rise in sex without marriage, birth control, abortion, and drinking, the proliferation of mini-skirts, salacious movies, and co-ed university classrooms. The clergy viewed the shah's land reform, the centerpiece of his 1963 White Revolution, as pandering to Western democracies while eroding the wealth and influence of the mullahs and the feudal landowning families that supported them.

Historically, the British had little respect for Iranian sovereignty and had repeatedly tried to influence the Iranian government through the mullahs. At the same time, in the interests of political stability, both Great Britain and the United States had supported a powerful king to prevent the spread of communism and block the Soviet Union's access to the Persian Gulf.

The SAVAK was instrumental in maintaining this equilibrium.

---

40. Joseph Kraft, "Letter from Iran," *The New Yorker*, December 18, 1978.

Far more oppressive than the economic situation was the constant fear of political repression. Many who were against the shah—secular nationalists, leftists, and Islamic fundamentalists alike—had friends, relatives, or relatives of friends in the shah's prisons.

Ali and I were not politically active and certainly not members of any political group, but by 1978, we had one or two degrees of separation with no less than eighteen people who had been or were still in the shah's prisons. There were thousands more, and the silence of their cautionary tales was deafening. They were all around us, every day, the broken ones, the famous ones, the forgotten ones. You could be oblivious for just so long before hearing their muffled voices just outside your consciousness. Maybe it was the SAVAK agent posing as a student in your classroom that made you remember them, or a friend's mother, gray with worry about the child who was taken away in the middle of the night, or maybe it's a woman who says she's the English department secretary who calls you at home one night to ask if a certain student closed down your class so he and his classmates could go on strike. You tell the secretary that he didn't (even though he actually did), then you wait to see if that student shows up the next day. (He does, thank goodness.)

One of those imprisoned was Mohammad Hanif Nejad, a student one year ahead of Ali in the College of Agriculture. A cofounder of the People's Mojahedin of Iran, he advocated armed struggle against the regime. He was imprisoned and tortured before being executed in 1972. And there was one of Ali's boyhood friends, a rather nondescript kid who had metamorphosed into a handsome, erudite young man on his way to becoming a physician until he discovered politics. Ali loved talking to him. Then one day he didn't exist anymore.

Reza Baraheni, a professor in the English department at Tehran University and a co-founder of the Writers Association of Iran, was imprisoned and tortured in 1973 for his writings about political oppression and the marginalization of ethnic minorities in Iran. He was freed after 102 days, as a result of the efforts of the American chapter of PEN and the Committee for Artistic and Intellectual Freedom in Iran. His book, *The Crowned Cannibals: Writings on Repression in Iran*, which he published in 1977 while in exile, is a scathing, first-hand account of the brutality of the shah and his henchmen, the SAVAK.

Nearly fifty years after *The Crowned Cannibals* was published, it's easy to forget the excesses of the shah's regime. The popular Western media focuses on the forces of repression now firmly entrenched in the Islamic Republic. Before the revolution, one might have said, "No one could be as bad as the shah." Now, it's tempting to say, "It wasn't that bad under the shah." The brutality and backwardness of the Islamic Republic overshadows what was inarguably a repressive regime.

Most of the political prisoners we knew or knew of during the shah's time were arrested for ideas—having them, writing them, reading them, sharing them. Many simply wanted the shah to adhere to the Iranian Constitution of 1906, which requires him to leave the business of government to the parliament. They were arrested for minor offenses like reading the banned works of Karl Marx, Mao Tse-Tung, or censored Iranian writers, or just attending a protest, like Ali's friend Farzin.

Years before, while a university student, Ali, himself, narrowly missed being arrested. When Queen Elizabeth visited Iran in March 1961, many Iranians still had decades' worth of grievances against the British: the jockeying with Russia for key trade and military routes through Iran; the British Imperial Tobacco Company and its nearly successful plan in 1891 to control Iran's tobacco crop; the oil concession first granted to the Australian William D'Arcy in 1901 which led to the entrenchment of Britain in southern Iran; the unfair share of the profits taken by the Anglo-Iranian Oil Company and its mistreatment of Iranian employees at the company's oil fields in Ahvaz and the Abadan refinery; and the role of the British government in the 1953 plot to overthrow Prime Minister Mossadegh, who had nationalized that oil company.

Along with hundreds of other students, Ali and his friend Farzin cut classes to join in the non-violent protests. Both boys were fearful because, only a year before, Farzin had been arrested during a demonstration and had spent several months in prison. They followed the orderly crowd for a few minutes until the police appeared and started arresting protesters. Immediately, Ali and Farzin turned around and started zigzagging through the crowd, darting into side streets until they came to a dead end. Farzin escaped down a basement stairwell. Ali ran into the first open shop he saw—a fabric store that sold men's suiting. The startled shopkeeper behind the counter had only to look at Ali's wide eyes and sweaty red face to know the whole story. He flipped open the counter's gate, motioned for Ali to join him on the other side and unfurled a bolt of cloth in front of him. When the police burst in, they saw only a shopkeeper and his assistant engaged in serious conversation about the merits of worsted versus twill.

By the summer of 1978, things had gotten ugly again. Many of the shah's own supporters were angry with him for not taking a hard enough line against the protesters. At the behest of U. S. President Jimmy Carter, the shah had made some concessions to human rights. He relaxed some security controls, allowed student demonstrations with comparatively little police intervention, tolerated public criticism from the main opposition party, the National Front, released a few political prisoners, and declared that the SAVAK would end its practice of torture. In response to widespread corruption within his court, he also established a code of conduct for the royal family. However, when anti-government factions seized the opportunity to use these concessions to bolster their positions, the shah cracked down again.

It wasn't just Iranians who were unhappy. The British and the Americans were also worried. Both had always wanted a stable Iran and a compliant king. Historically, the British had little respect for the shahs and their sovereignty and had repeatedly tried to influence Iranian politics through the clergy.

We would soon see just how powerful that clergy was becoming.

27

······

WIND CATCHERS, FLAK CATCHERS

Tehran: 1977-78

In late 1977, almost two years before the Iranian Revolution, I completed my master's degree in English literature at Tehran University. A few months later, I was hired at the Tehran Museum of Contemporary Art as Manager of Education Services. The museum, a project of Empress Farah, had opened a month or so earlier to great fanfare, both for its exquisite architecture and for its spectacular collection of European, American, and Iranian modern art. It soon became a new center for contemporary Iranian artists, but what some welcomed as progress others saw as a threat.

The empress had hired her cousin, architect Kamran Diba, to design the building, which abounded with references to traditional Persian architectural forms—especially the *baadgir*, or wind catcher. Traditional *baadgirs*, which I had seen in the desert town of Yazd, channeled breezes down into the house where they were cooled by an indoor pool, but here they were transformed into light catchers that helped illuminate the galleries. A central ramp of gleaming polished concrete wound down through the center of the museum and ended in a lower-level atrium with a *hoze*, a rectangular reflecting pool—not of water but of oil. Diba had commissioned this black pool, "Matter & Mind" by Japanese artist Noriyuki Haraguchi, for the new museum in an obvious reference not only to the *hoze* of traditional Iranian architecture but also to the oil that fueled Iran's economy and ultimately funded the museum.

David Galloway, the museum's first curator, was an American art critic based in Germany who had been tapped by the empress to help build the museum's collection and organize major shows of European and American art. The empress charged Americans Galloway and Donna Stein and Diba, who was also the museum's first director, with putting the collection together. In a few months, they amassed what would become the largest collection of late-19th and 20th century western art outside the West, with impressive works representative of the major art movements. The museum's 5000 square meters also afforded generous space to Iranian artists, such as Nasser Ovissi, Parviz Tanavoli, and Parviz Kalantari. But while the architecture was informed by traditional Iran, the collection was predominantly western.

I loved working in that building with its spiraling rhythm, its light, its energy. Each day, I sailed up and down the winding ramp, making friends with the Van Goghs, Giacomettis, Picassos and Warhols. I took restorative breaks in the galleries, or wandered in the sculpture garden outside my office window. I felt lucky to work in a museum where two cultures co-existed so amicably...or so I thought.

I answered a phone call one day from an Iranian woman who wanted some information about current exhibits. Before hanging up, she asked, "Is this a museum for foreigners?"

"Not at all," I assured her. "It's for Iranians. *"Manzel-e khodetoon hast."* This is your house. The museum did belong to the people, but in reality it housed two cultures existing side by side. It was not just a matter of Iranian artists sharing space on the walls with their European and American counterparts; it was also the museum's western-educated administrative and curatorial staff working among the more traditional and religious support staff. Soon I would see that, for those in the latter group, the museum, in its current form, would never be their house.

In the early summer of 1978, I was helping organize a reception at the museum that would feature the Danish ambassador. As did all our receptions, this one would include alcohol. In fact, beer and wine had always been available in the museum's cafeteria. Weeks before the event, I made sure that two of the women who worked in the cafeteria would be on hand to help serve at the reception. But just a few hours before the guests were to arrive, one of these ladies asked to speak to me.

"Khanum Estilai," she whispered, nervously adjusting her headscarf. "I'm willing to work tonight, but I can't serve alcohol."

"Why not?" I asked.

"My son has forbidden it," she explained.

"I don't understand," I said. "You've been serving beer and wine in the cafeteria all these months."

"Yes, I know, but my son won't let me do that anymore," she answered. "Oh, and my friend won't be serving alcohol, either."

I looked over at her friend, also wearing a headscarf, standing off to the side watching this exchange. Both women were polite and respectful as always, but now they were displaying a newfound power and resolve. Clearly, in their minds, they had just scored a small victory for Islam over the infidels at the museum.

I knew that it was pointless to argue with them. No reasoning about the lateness of the hour would dissuade them from upholding their Islamic principles. I thanked them for letting me know their position, and quickly set about finding others to take their places.

This defection had caught me off guard. I could no longer assume a benign disinterest on the part of the janitors, guards, and support staff. They were watching and judging and making choices. Suddenly I saw the museum from their perspective—the provocative images, the *bihijab* female employees, the nodding to architectural traditions while dismissing others, a place seemingly at odds with their values and culture. My temporary staffing problem would soon prove to be a harbinger of more dissatisfaction to come. A few weeks later, another event occurred that made me see just how myopic we all had been.

Sometime in 1978, before he returned to Germany, David Galloway had produced a rich and innovative catalogue to accompany a large show of cutting edge, contemporary art, *The Book of the Art of Artists' Books*. Hundreds of copies of the thick catalogue were produced in Germany at considerable expense. Shortly after the catalogues arrived, my boss, an American in his mid-fifties, burst into my office, red-faced, frenetic, and brandishing a mat knife.

"Where is your copy of that new catalogue?" he demanded.

"It's not here," I said. "I took it home to read."

"Well, I need it back," he shouted. "Now!"

"Okay…but why?"

"Just look," he said, as he opened his copy and thrust it in my face. I stared at it for a second, horrified, and then burst out laughing.

There in the middle of the book, low on the page near the inner margin, was a small black and white photograph of two men engaging in oral sex.

"Whose idea was this?" I asked. "What were they thinking?"

"I don't know," he replied, "but I need to cut out all these pages. Hundreds of them." He snatched back his copy and, clutching his mat knife, disappeared in search of the rest of the offending pages.

I don't know if the photo was the choice of Galloway or his graphic designer, whether the curator had seen it or if it was simply someone else's last-minute addition to the layout, but clearly its inclusion indicated someone's ignorance of the prevailing mores of the country, or at least an inability to understand that these mores were relevant to this museum. Outside of a small group of *avant garde* intellectuals and aesthetes in major international centers of art, where would this catalogue photograph have been acceptable? Most likely not in many government-sponsored museums around the world, and certainly not in Iran. The public never saw the offending page, but as it turned out, there still was much in the museum that wasn't acceptable to a growing number of dissatisfied and disaffected Iranians.

Later that fall, one of the museum staff found a note stuck in the frame of Tom Wesslemann's *Great American Nude,* a painting of a big, blowsy blonde whose most predominate feature was bright pink nipples. The note said, "Next time, this will be a bomb."

28

. . . .

THE RED AND THE BLACK

Tehran: Summer 1978

On January 7, 1978, an anonymous article entitled "Iran and the Red and Black Imperialism," appeared in the Tehran newspaper *Ettela'at*. Sent to the paper by the Imperial Court and claimed by his enemies to have been written by the shah himself, the article described an unholy alliance between the Soviets and the clergy, the red and the black.[41] It also accused Khomeini of spying for the British. When theology students gathered in the holy city of Qom to protest the letter, police fired on the crowd, killing at least twenty people. The following month, during the ritual observation of the fortieth day after these deaths, the shah's army turned their guns on the mourning procession, killing one person. After the ensuing day and a half of riots, the casualties totaled either 19 dead and 100 injured (the government's figure) or 432 dead and 1,500 injured (the opposition's figure).[42] Across the country, more protests and bloodshed followed. But it was the events of August 1978 that galvanized the country and paved the way for the revolution.

That August, we were preparing for Ali's sabbatical at UC Davis in the fall. I hadn't been back to the States for two years, and I was

41. Kraft, p. 20.
42. Mackey, p. 278.

looking forward to a respite from the turmoil. I longed for a languid American summer. I wanted the children to run barefoot on the grass. I wanted to choose between Roquefort, Thousand Island or French. I wanted not to have to watch what I said.

But before we could go to the States, Ali had to go to Moscow for the XIV International Genetics Conference, from August 20 to August 31. His sister Naazi and her son Farzad would keep us company while he was away. It was a particularly sweaty, uncomfortable summer, with frequent power outages and food shortages. I dreaded Ali's absence, but there was no chance the girls or I would accompany Ali, even if we could have afforded the trip. The shah, that stalwart foe of Communism, that darling of Washington who vowed never to let Iran become Iranistan, would not allow husbands and wives to travel together to the USSR for fear they would defect. Even without the ban on visas, there was little chance of a mass exodus. Most Iranians knew that Russians were no better off than they were. In fact, while both countries were lacking in basic human rights, middle-class Iranians probably had a far better standard of living than their Soviet counterparts. Even if the average, middle-class Iranian were to defect, he would have been more likely to choose Paris. The shopping was so much better there.

Ali left Tehran on August 17, 1978, for Moscow. He spent a few days in Leningrad visiting the Hermitage and other cultural sites before returning to Moscow for the conference. This international gathering was a great coup for the Soviets, who, as late as 1964, had been touting the bogus findings of Trofim Lysenko on the inheritance of acquired characteristics as proof that environment trumps genetics. Although they had once declared genetics to be a bourgeois pseudoscience and imprisoned and executed geneticists, the Soviets were now hoping that the international scientific community might forget that not-so-long-ago interlude with dogs that had supposedly inherited missing limbs from their amputee parents.

When he reached Moscow, Ali met up with our American friends, Marvin, a Fulbright professor in the English Department of Tehran University, and his wife Joan, a geneticist who, like Ali, was there to deliver a paper at the conference. One evening, while Joan was busy preparing for her talk, Marvin and Ali wandered around Red Square looking for a place to eat. Suddenly, a young Russian approached our friend and struck up a conversation. With Marvin's wavy gray hair and full beard, he was a dead-ringer for Hemingway, and the young man, eager to meet Westerners, was immediately drawn to him. An aspiring writer, he was even more attracted when he learned that his quarry was a professor of English literature.

"I can't seem to shake him," Marvin whispered to Ali. "What should I do?"

"See if he knows any good restaurants," Ali replied. "We'll take him to dinner."

The young man took them to a nearby restaurant in what had once been an old church. Apparently well connected, he was able to bypass the serpentine line of hopeful diners and usher them through a separate entrance.

Whoever their dinner companion was—government agent or just a hungry, networking writer—he probably didn't get much in the way of intelligence from his new acquaintances, but he certainly gave Ali some information he hadn't expected.

After an excellent dinner, during which he had extracted a promise from Marvin to read some samples of his work, the young man suddenly turned to Ali and said, "It seems you have a new government."

"What do you mean?"

"Ah, you haven't seen the papers. You have a new prime minister. Jamshid Amuzegar is out and Jafar Sharif-Emami is in."

Ali returned from the Soviet Union to a very different Iran.

"So, I go away for two weeks and the government changes," he said when he walked in the door. In his absence, the shah's carefully constructed house of cards had begun to collapse.

I handed Ali a stack of newspapers I had saved, and he set about catching up on the events of the last two weeks. He had been away just a few days when, on August 20, I came home from grocery shopping to find grizzly television reports of a fire that destroyed Cinema Rex, a movie theater hundreds of miles away in Abadan, an oil refining center in the southern, oil-producing province of Khuzestan. Some 430 people, mostly women and children, were watching the popular actor Behrooz Vosoughi in the film *Gavaznha* (The Deer) when the theater suddenly caught fire. The extreme heat of the inferno and the exit doors, locked from the outside, made escape or rescue impossible. There were no survivors. Most victims were burned beyond recognition and their bodies buried in a mass grave.

Both the shah's government and Islamic militants accused each other of starting the fire and locking the doors. Was the fire started by Islamic militants, who had a history of torching cinemas because they were deemed profane, or was it started by the shah's forces, to make the opposition look bad? Did the SAVAK chase insurgents into the theater? Was it some inept police officer who locked the building to prevent their escape? At the time, no one really knew, and that uncertainty fueled rage on both sides. What was clear to everyone was that it was arson, it was political, and it was barbaric.[43]

Jamshid Amuzegar, the prime minister at the time, was trying to make reforms to quell the opposition, but after the Cinema Rex fire and the protests that followed, he resigned. Jafar Sharif-Emami was appointed, presumably because he came from a religious family with ties to the clergy.[44]

On Friday morning, September 8, we were still in bed when we heard our doorbell ring several times. Ali, still half asleep, ran to the window to find his boyhood friend, Farzin, standing in the *koocheh* below. A neurosurgeon at nearby Pahlavi Hospital, Farzin lived just two blocks away from us. However, we hardly ever saw him or his family because we all were so busy. It was highly un-usual for Farzin to drop by unannounced, especially early on a Friday morning.

"Hey, what's up," Ali said, laughing as he leaned out the window.

"Sorry to wake you," Farzin said. "I need to borrow your car."

"Of course," said Ali, not stopping to ask why. He ran and found his keys, threw them down to his friend, and buzzed open the door to the garage. Moments later, Farzin sped down the *koocheh*. A few hours later, we found out why he was in such a hurry to borrow our car.

---

43. In 1979, Monir Taheri, a police captain in pre-revolutionary Iran, was wrongly accused of the crime and executed. In 1980, after months of protests by the vic-tims' families, a Revolutionary Tribunal reopened the case and found six people guilty. "The principal defendant admitted to starting the fire with three other religious activists." *Human Rights and Democracy for Iran: Monir Taheri: One Person's Story.* http://www.iranrights.org/memorial/story/-3246/monir-taheri. (Accessed March 13, 2014.)

44. Kraft, op.cit.

When we turned on the radio, we learned that late the previous night, at the behest of the military and with the consent of the prime minister and cabinet, General Ovissi had declared martial law in Tehran and eleven other cities. No groups of more than three people could congregate, and no public demonstrations were allowed. However, most people did not hear the announcement of the decree until the following morning.

Later, we began to hear the radio reports of a disturbance in Jaleh Square, located in a working-class Tehran neighborhood seven or eight kilometers southeast of our apartment. Soon friends and relatives began to call as people shared what they knew. We learned that in the early morning hours, a crowd had begun gathering in the square. As soon as martial law was announced over the radio, the demonstrators began chanting. They were met by the troops, who ordered them to disperse. When they did not, the soldiers fired into the crowd. It was then we realized that Farzin must have been called to the hospital to help care for the wounded.

About 11 o'clock that evening, when a clearly exhausted Farzin returned to drop off the car, we convinced him to come upstairs for a quick cup of tea. He had indeed spent the last fifteen hours at Pahlavi Hospital, tending to the casualties.

"The hospital floor was so thick with blood," he said, "that we couldn't walk. Our feet stuck to the floor." With that, he put down his tea glass and made his way home.

We later learned that in the morning the soldiers had opened fire on a crowd of unarmed civilians, killing and wounding hundreds.

Amid this turmoil, we prepared to leave for Ali's sabbatical. We needed to rent our apartment—charging just enough to cover the mortgage payments—and were hoping to find foreign tenants who were planning to stay for only one year. Even with the violent protests, foreigners were still coming to Tehran—Fulbright professors and medical personnel, engineers, and construction crews. A Polish orthopedic surgeon answered our ad but decided that our tiny apartment was too large for him and his wife. We had almost given up hope of finding a tenant when we got a visit from two Indian engineers, in Tehran for a year's assignment with a construction company. Their wives were living in India.

"It will be just the two of us," they assured us, "and we will hardly ever be here."

Anxious to begin our sabbatical, we sealed the deal, which included the use of our telephone line. The tenants wouldn't rent without a phone, and the Ministry of Post, Telegraph and Telephone wouldn't allow us to temporarily put our account in the tenants' names. Putting in a new phone line for them would have taken another five or ten years. With Tehran in a state of turmoil, we felt fortunate to have foreign tenants at all. How many more protests would there be? How many more demonstrators would be jailed or killed? How many more foreigners would be willing to work in Iran? We decided to trust our Indian engineers.

29

THE REVOLUTION WILL BE TELEVISED

Davis: Fall 1978

I filled my lungs with it—the City of Davis' signature autumnal smell: ketchup on fried eggs. The aroma of the tomato canneries just outside of town, the rotten apple scent of fallen leaves, and the tentative chilliness of September mornings imparted a familiar electric expectancy.

Fall was always my favorite season in Davis. For me, fall—not spring—had always been the season of new beginnings. The term "clean slate" conjured up the new classroom and all its implied opportunities. Fall meant pristine notebooks with purposeful handwriting still neat and upright, not yet splayed and skewed by the excesses of too many late nights and badly ordered priorities. It meant new classes that promised to transform. It meant reinventing myself. In the fall, anything was possible.

We arrived in Davis in mid-September 1978, settling into a three-bedroom tract house in east Davis, a block away from the elementary school where Samira would start kindergarten. Ali set to work researching the cytogenetics of safflower, and I settled down to write a paper, based on my master's thesis, which I was planning to deliver the following summer at the International Modern Language Association conference in Innsbruck, Austria.

But mostly, we just reveled in the normalcy of our temporary existence.

Surrounded by farmland and rice fields and orchards, Davis was the perfect antidote to the turmoil of Tehran. The university still had some of the brown-shingled buildings and cow barns left over from its beginnings as the University Farm serving UC Berkeley, some 65 miles away. After seven years in Iran, we found the small town had grown without sacrificing its charm. The locals still proudly proclaimed there were more bicycles than people. When Ali and I were students in the late sixties, we had to content ourselves with one small off-campus bookstore, a handful of forgettable restaurants, and, for nightlife, Deebo's, the funky, seedy, sawdusty dive where my art professor, William T. Wiley, occasionally jammed with a small blues group from the Bay Area. Seven years later, the downtown, just a short walk or a double-decker London bus ride from the center of campus, had far more amenities—two theater screens instead of one, and a proliferation of bookstores, coffee houses, gift shops, restaurants and galleries—all accessible without spending hours in smog-choked traffic or trying to cross the street without getting run over or having to jump over the gaping maws of gutters.

We played house. We filled our east Davis rental with beds and dressers borrowed from Ali's major professor and his wife, as well as living room furniture that we bought to take back to Iran. To alleviate Ali's chronic back pain, we even bought a La-Z-Boy recliner, that icon of American middle-class leisure and contentment. Samira and Sarah, all bumblebee bodies and spindly legs in their leotards and tights, took gymnastics and ballet at the Davis Art Center. Even I tried ballet, although I was much less ungainly in my art class. We watched *Little House on the Prairie* and, come

December, festooned the house with homemade blue and red gingham Christmas ornaments.

This is what life would be like if we lived here, I imagined: taking the children to parks with grass they were allowed to play on, watching too many made-for-television movies, roaming the stacks in the university library at will, saying whatever I thought.

As I pulled up in front of the small tract house in east Davis, just a few blocks away from our own, I felt that familiar frisson of anxiety I always experienced in new social situations. This was my first visit to my new friend Sharon's house. Sharon was the instructional aide in Samira's kindergarten class, and her daughter Anna was Samira's classmate. Sharon had a sunny, confident demeanor and a round, open face always ready with a smile. In the few weeks since I had met her, I could see that she was a multi-tasker, a practical can-do person who quickly found solutions to problems—qualities she would put to good use a few years later when she finished her teaching credential and took over her own K-3 classroom. Now, she glided among the kindergarteners, dispensing stickers, and hugs, letting them know that they were capable of any feat they set their minds to.

Sharon had noticed that Samira, not yet used to American ways, seemed shy and overwhelmed by her new surroundings, so she enlisted Anna's help in making her feel welcome. It worked. Samira quickly began to thrive, and the girls became fast friends.

The moment I entered Sharon's house, my usual stiffness and anxiety fell away. I was immediately enveloped in the earthy, dark coolness of the living room. As Sharon made tea, I sat on the wine-colored sofa and took in my surroundings. *So different from Tehran living rooms*, I thought, as I sank deeper into the cushions. In Tehran, I would be sitting primly on someone's idea of a Louis XIV sofa or straight-backed chair, not slouching languidly in a sea of velvet cushions and ottomans.

The only straight-backed chair was occupied by a Charley Mc-Carthy dummy, his posture even worse than mine, head at a rakish angle, mouth slightly open, as if he were just about to say something snarky. Thick coils of colorful wool yarn and a half-finished scarf filled a basket in the corner by the rocking chair, one that, I soon learned, had served for generations on the wrap-around porch of Sharon's family home in Marshall, Texas. Floor-to-ceiling bookcases lined the walls, the contents—psychology textbooks, novels, fairy tales, cookbooks—were crammed every which-way. A tabby cat, Peach Lemon, sauntered in and out, oblivious to the half-dozen zebra finches hectoring each other in a five-foot cage by the window.

It was a room full of personality and idiosyncrasies. It encouraged beginning in the middle of the conversation and dispensing with pleasantries. Like its owner, the room had an American openness, that willingness to expose one's self, to say, "*This is who I am. Relax. Curl up on that couch. Put your feet up. Tell me what you're thinking.*"

The average Iranian living room, or *mehman khaneh*, is not a cozy, idiosyncratic refuge but a public space. Just as in many Western homes, it's not the room people actually live in. That's the hall, a kind of family room. The perimeter of the *mehman khaneh* is often lined with chairs to accommodate large numbers of visitors and facilitate the circulation of endless glasses of tea and trays of pastries and fruits.

Sometimes, the information people leave out is more telling than what they put in. Whether elegant or sparse, tasteful, and gracious or starkly primitive, the Iranian living room reveals little about the interior life of its hosts. Of course, each traditional middle-class

mehman khaneh has its own special charm. There are endless varia-
tions of intricate carpet designs, filigreed silver, Isfahani enamel-
ware, inlaid boxes and picture frames, embroidery, and brocade.
But no matter how beautifully or expensively decorated these
rooms might be, the owners' idiosyncrasies are hidden from view.
Charley McCarthy would not be invited to the party.

That division between the personal and public was reminiscent of
traditional Iranian houses of generations ago, with their *biruni* (the
outer rooms for guests) and the *andaruni* (the inner rooms which
served as women's quarters), an architectural necessity that existed
until the end of the Qajar era. While modern Iranian society in
the 1970s had progressed from the strict separation of the sexes,
Iranians still kept a certain part of their lives separate from out-
siders—at least until they knew them well. Levels of wealth and
taste might be on display, but not what the host was reading. Those
rooms themselves revealed nothing of the host's interests or preoc-
cupations other than her earnest desire to please her guests.

While I appreciated the elegant, gracious hospitality of Iranian
hosts, there, in Sharon's living room, I realized how much I had
missed the informality of Americans. I had become better at *taarof,*
but I was relieved to have a break from it.

While we were living our make-believe life in Davis, we were
keeping close tabs on the situation at home and having long, loud
political discussions with friends about the future of Iran. Ali got
hold of a copy of Ayatollah Khomeini's *Velayat-e Faqih* (Guardianship of the Jurist), a series of thirteen lectures he delivered to
Muslim clerics in 1970 while in exile in Najaf, Iraq. The collected
lectures, which had been banned in Iran by the shah, laid out the
justification for an Islamic government.

Khomeini spoke of an Islam threatened by enemies from all sides: from without, by the Jews, imperialists, and orientalists (Western interpreters of Islamic culture who were in service to imperialist governments) and from within, by those "gutless" clerics who side with the oppressors or those who busy themselves with the minutiae of religious practice but ignore attempts to weaken the influence of Islam.[45] He denounced Iran's constitution, written following the Constitutional Revolution of 1906, as anti-Islamic because it allowed for a monarchy and hereditary succession, which was "wrong and invalid."[46]

Khomeini argued that because Islam is a complete social, political, and religious system of laws governing every aspect of life, it is a religious obligation to have an Islamic government and qualified executor to enforce these laws. Only an Islamic government, led by a just and educated religious scholar, could stand up to oppressors and preserve Islamic order.

Khomeini's arguments against imperialism and the machinations of foreign governments certainly resonated with us and many other secular Iranians. After all, it had been only twenty-five years since the CIA coup that overthrew Mossadegh, and for over a hundred years, both the British and the Russians had been interfering in Iran's affairs to gain access to the country's resources and secure a route to the Persian Gulf. But Khomeini's them-against-us attitude toward non-Muslims and foreigners was disturbingly isolationist, and his anti-Semitism was, while not unheard of in Iran, ugly all the same.

---

45. Imam Khomeini, *Governance of the Jurist* (Velayat-e Faqi) , Institute for Compilation and Publication of Imam Khomeini's Works, Tehran, trans. Hamid Algar, no date, pp. 7 and 86. [Iran Chamber web site.]
46. Khomeini, p. 10.

He railed against the opulence and greed of the monarchical system. The *faqih* (the Islamic jurist chosen to lead the country) should not accumulate worldly wealth. Khomeini evoked Imam Ali (the Commander of the Faithful), the Shi'ites first caliph, who said that worldly possessions and rank were no more important to him than "the moisture that comes from the sneeze of a goat."[47] He said that it was the duty of Muslims to "save the oppressed and deprived" and "to take from the rich and give to the poor."[48]

Khomeini said that an Islamic government would not be like a police state "where the people are deprived of all security and everyone sits at home trembling for fear of a sudden raid or attack by agents of the state." Under an Islamic government, "all will live with complete security under the protection of the law."[49] But of course, that law would be *shari'ah* law.

Khomeini saw *shari'ah* law as an antidote to the stultifying, paralyzing bureaucracy of Iranian government that inevitably led to bribery and corruption. Under *shari'ah* law, he said, a case that might drag on for twenty years in a secular court could be settled in two days. But however expedient, the *shari'ah* law he was calling for specified stoning of married adulterers and cutting off the hands of thieves. It was speedy because it brooked no interference. Of course, he said, under this law, punishment would be the same for everyone, even the families of the Islamic government's leaders. It would be Draconian but equal.

As for equality between the sexes, the treatise did not actually address the rights of women or their place in an Islamic society. Women were rarely mentioned, except to say that "men and women

---

47. Khomeini, p. 25.
48. Khomeini, pp. 25 and 43.
49. Khomeini, pp. 46-47.

are friends and protectors of one another,"[50] or that married men and women who are adulterers should be stoned.[51]

Ali and I were just beginning to get acquainted with Khomeini's ideas, but the *Guardianship of the Jurist* had been circulating in Europe and the United States, as well as in Pakistan, Afghanistan, and, clandestinely, in Iran, for some time, gaining adherents among revolutionary Muslims.[52]

In October 1978, in an attempt to suppress the growing support for Khomeini's return to Iran, the shah prevailed upon Saddam Hussein to expel Khomeini from neighboring Iraq. It was a tactical error on the shah's part. Instead of disappearing into obscurity, Khomeini moved his operation to Neauphle-le-Château, a suburb of Paris where, because of his visibility in the Western media, he was in a far better position to manipulate the course of events.

Shortly after Khomeini's arrival in France, his aides took advantage of the advanced telephone systems to reach out directly to supporters in Iran and used the international press corps, eager for the ayatollah's every pronouncement, to broadcast his opposition to the monarchy. At the same time, Khomeini sought to allay the growing fears among Westerners and secular Iranians that the establishment of an Islamic Republic would simply trade one form of repression for another.

The televised interviews went something like this: the 76-year-old cleric, accompanied by his translator, would receive a journalist while sitting on the floor of a room furnished with little more than a carpet and the occasional bolster propped against the wall. His simple robe and turban and his Spartan surroundings served as a

---

50. Khomeini, pp. 66 and 71.

51. Khomeini p. 12.

52. Khomeini, p. 3, foreword by Hamid Algar.

tacit rebuke of the opulent lifestyle of his archenemy, the shah. The foreign journalist (who had to submit his questions in advance) was probably unaccustomed to conducting interviews while sitting on the floor and would seem to be at a slight psychological disadvantage. But even if he sat on a chair, he was likely to be uncomfortable. Khomeini had none of the ingratiating people skills of secular politicians and statesmen—Western or Eastern—or even those of his own earnestly personable translator, Dr. Ebrahim Yazdi. Khomeini didn't converse so much as pronounce, softly meting out even the harshest of his words in even tones, his mouth barely moving within the wispy frame of his long, white beard. He often did not deign to look directly at his interviewer, preferring instead to fix his gaze on the middle of the carpet. With each question, the journalist would lean forward a little, tilting his head at an angle in a vain attempt to make eye contact, putting himself ever so slightly off balance while his subject remained immovable.

On the evening news one night, before the fall of the shah, Ali and I watched as one such interviewer tried to find out what kind of leader the ayatollah would be if he were to assume control of the government. "Would you be a strongman?" he asked. He meant, of course, *would you be a tyrant, a dictator*? Dr. Yazdi, apparently unfamiliar with that expression, translated it not as *diktaator* or *farmaanrava-ye mostabed*, but as *mard-e ghavi*, a strong man. The ayatollah had no qualms about stating that he would indeed be a strong man.

It seemed the whole world was eager to find out if Khomeini would be a strong man or a strongman, and he was busy putting fears to rest. On October 26, he told Reuters, "In Islamic Iran, the clergy themselves will not govern but only observe and support the government's leaders." Unlike the shah's relentlessly opaque regime, which stifled all dissent, "[t]he government of the country at all levels will be observed, evaluated, and publicly criticized."

In November, he assured reporters that, when the shah left, he had no intention of running the country. "Neither my desire nor my age nor my position allows me to govern," he told a United Press reporter. "I am not interested in personal power," he told the *Guardian*. He assured the Paris newspaper, *Le Journal*, that, "It is the Iranian people who have to select their own capable and trustworthy individuals and give them the responsibilities. However, personally, I can't accept any special role or responsibility."[53]

Regarding women's rights, he assured German reporters that "these words that you have heard regarding women in the future Islamic government are all hostile propaganda. In the Islamic Republic women will have complete freedom, in their education, in everything they do, just as men are free in everything." He assured the *Guardian* that "women are free in the Islamic Republic in the selection of their activities and their future and their clothing."[54]

"He sounded so reasonable," we said. "Nothing could be worse than the shah," people said. After all, Khomeini is a man of the cloth. Religious people have ethics. We remained hopeful. Still, there were nagging doubts. Khomeini's pronouncements in the Western press were at odds with the ideas he had set out in 1970 in *The Guardianship of the Jurist*. Now, eight years later, what did Khomeini mean when he said that in an Islamic Iran, the clergy

---

[53]. "Democracy? I meant theocracy," a selection of quotes by Khomeini in various interviews and speeches before and after the 1979 Iranian Revolution, compiled by Dr. Jalal Matini in "The Most Truthful Individual in Recent History," *Iranshenasi*, Vol. XIV, No. 4, Winter 2003; translated and with an introduction by Farhad Mafie, *The Iranian*, August 5, 2003. www.iranian.com/Opinion/2003/August/Khomeini, accessed October 11, 2010.

[54]. Matini.

would not govern? What would an Islamic Iran look like? When he said that women would be free, what kind of freedom was he envisioning? Had he mellowed in the intervening eight years since he wrote his treatise, or was he not telling us everything?

Although we were worried about our future in Iran, we settled into the soothing domestic routine of our invented American life. However, we soon found that outside the bubble of our sabbatical existence, upheaval had become the norm, and not just in Iran.

First there was Jonestown.

On November 18, 1978, the four of us were spending a quiet Saturday evening at Essie and Julie's sabbatical rental in Berkeley when the evening news came on with reports of the shooting death of Northern California congressman Leo Ryan and four others on an airstrip near Georgetown, Guyana. *Where's Guyana? What was Ryan doing there?* The last time I had thought about Guyana—or its neighbors, Venezuela, or Suriname, for that matter—I was a teenager watching the Miss Universe Pageant.

Congressman Ryan had traveled to that South American country to investigate reports of the mistreatment of US citizens at the Peoples Temple settlement, in Jonestown, named after the group's charismatic leader Jim Jones. Family members of the cult's followers had complained of beatings, public humiliation, and imprisonment at the hands of Jones and his aides.

The day after the shootings, photographs of bodies began to surface, a sea of bodies, over 900 of them, all followers of Jones. At his behest, they had apparently participated in repeated dress rehearsals for mass suicide, should the Temple ever come under attack. This time, the punch he told them to drink was laced with cyanide. Jones's followers accepted this order; they gave the punch to their children, then lay face down on the ground with their arms around their loved ones, like some school air-raid drill, and died. All this was incomprehensible. That they followed such an obviously egomaniacal nut case as Jim Jones, to begin with, was equally unfathomable.

Nine days after Jonestown, on November 27, former San Francisco supervisor Dan White shot and killed Mayor George Moscone and Supervisor Harvey Milk. Dan White, an all-American, squeaky clean former police officer and firefighter who favored gun control, seemed an unlikely candidate for a murderer. As one of his acquaintances said, "If he were a cereal he would have had to be Wheaties."[55] That very ordinariness was chilling, nonetheless, because it masked such hatred. Knowing White's reasons—that the mayor wouldn't reappoint him after he resigned as supervisor and that he was resentful of Milk, an openly gay colleague who supported his replacement—didn't make his actions any easier to understand.

The events of that November cast a pall over our safe Davis existence, reminding us that the rest of the world was off-kilter, unpredictable, and tenuous. Anything could happen.

Back in Iran, it did. What had been unthinkable just a few years before was now reality. On January 17, we watched the network news footage of masses of exhilarated demonstrators in Tehran, brandishing copies of newspapers with the headline "*Shah raft*" (the shah left) in five-inch type. Barely two weeks later, on February 1, Khomeini arrived in Tehran. On February 11, the army declared its neutrality, thus yielding to the revolutionaries. (This day is now an Iranian national holiday.) On March 30, the Iranian people were presented with a referendum: Should the government of Iran be an Islamic Republic?

---

55. "Another Day of Death," *Time*, December 11, 1978.

Did the voters really know what they were voting for? What is the definition of an Islamic Republic? Why was there no other option? Had all those political factions taken to the streets only to have a single option? Had all those people died in the revolution defending their right to speak only to have yet another dictatorship define the issues and limit debate? According to the government, 98 percent of voters answered yes. But even if all those votes were cast in favor of an Islamic Republic, we will never know how many of those voters truly understood what an Islamic Republic would be.

30

....

THE DINNER PARTY

San Francisco: Spring 1979

The room was dark, illuminated only by track lights trained on the large table, an open triangle in the center of the room. Forty or fifty of us walked solemnly in single-file around the table, which was laid with thirty-nine brightly colored, boldly decorated ceramic plates and intricate table runners. The table was set for a dinner party, but unlike most dinner parties, the mood was not festive. Instead, it was hushed and reverential. We stopped briefly at each place, just long enough to take in the gleaming, gaudy, vulvar designs of the plates and the obsessively beaded and embroidered iconography of the table runners before moving on to the next setting.

We spoke in whispers, with little thrums of recognition or acknowledgement as we saw the embroidered names of the women, some well-known, some only vaguely familiar, some we had never heard of at all. Each of the thirty-nine plates, many adorned with unabashedly vaginal imagery, represented a woman from mythology or history, such as the Primordial Goddess and Kali; Eleanor of Aquitaine and Hildegard of Bingen; Sacajawea and Sojourner Truth; Margaret Sanger and Susan B. Anthony; Artemisia Gentileschi and Georgia O'Keefe. The floor in the center of the table's open triangle was covered with white ceramic tiles bearing the names of nine hundred ninety-nine other "women of achievement," many of whom had been long forgotten or marginalized by history.

This was *The Dinner Party*, a five-year labor of love created and executed by artist Judy Chicago with the help of a studio full of researchers and crafts people—ceramists, beaders, embroiderers, china painters, carpenters, and weavers.

Chicago wanted to pay tribute to women who "throughout history had prepared the meals and set the table," but never had a place at that table. In *The Dinner Party*, these thirty-nine women would be the "honored guests."

In honoring these women, Chicago also celebrated the "womanly arts." I had been an art major at UC Davis, so I was no stranger to the use of non-traditional materials. Many of the West Coast Funk artists on our faculty were enthusiastic proponents of the dumb and the ugly, urging us to put aside oils and canvas in favor of linoleum, sand, fiberglass and rusty found objects.

When, in my freshman year, William T. Wiley, challenged me to stop making "pretty" art and make something "dumb-looking," I complied by finding a surfboard-shaped piece of cardboard, covering it with a broken piece of yellowing foam rubber fished out of a dumpster, and encasing the whole creation in several yards of Saran Wrap.

"Yep, that's dumb, all right," he said.

My response was silence. Dumb silence.

Over the years, the alternative materials I had seen artists employ were primarily industrial—metals and plastics most often used by men to build and repair and eventually discard—but these alternative materials were different. Outside of the Bayeux Tapestry, Judy Chicago's *Dinner Party* was the first time I had seen traditional women's crafts elevated to high art.

In contrast to the frenzy of the decorated surfaces, silence was a major element of the show—the silence of the absent honorees, the silence of history about their achievements, the silence of the visitors as we contemplated all those centuries of that silence.

The Dinner Party was nearing the end of its three-month run at the San Francisco Museum of Art, what was supposed to be the first stop on a planned national tour. I had convinced Ali that we needed a break from monitoring and dissecting the news reports out of Iran so that the four of us could make the ninety-minute trip from Davis to see the exhibition before it closed. I wanted five-and-a-half-year-old Samira and four-year-old Sarah to experience the show, even if they couldn't yet comprehend the magnitude of it.

Although one unkind critic dismissed *The Dinner Party* as "vaginas on plates," the show was monumental, both visually and conceptually, in the wealth of historical information, the richness of the materials, the elegant execution of all the elements in so many different media, and the collective weight of these women's lives.

In the book that accompanied the exhibition, Chicago wrote of visiting a china painter whose home was throbbing with creative energy. Every surface was covered with her oil paintings, quilts, embroidery, and painted china, the flowers of which echoed those she had planted in her garden.

> "This woman had done all that work, trying as best she could to fit her creative drive—which could probably have expanded into mural-sized paintings or monumental sculptures—into the confined spaces of her house, which could hardly have held another piece of work.

The china-painting world…seemed to be
the perfect metaphor for women's domesti-
cated and trivialized circumstances."[56]

Reading these words, I thought of my friend Badri, Farzin's wife, and her apartment in Tehran, which, like the china painter's, was chockablock with her own handicrafts. A doctor's wife and the mother of two young sons, she worked long, intense hours as a surgical nursing supervisor, yet she had a frenetic energy that found its outlet in needlepoint, tapestry, crocheting, knitting and embroidery.

I thought of all my talented women friends in Iran who had so much energy and such a need to give back to their communities. What would happen to women with talent and energy in the Islamic Republic? What kind of future would they have? What kind of future could Samira and Sarah expect in Iran?

I knew what I wanted for them. I wanted them to know their foremothers. I wanted their voices to be heard. I wanted them to have a place at the table.

56. Judy Chicago, *The Dinner Party: A Symbol of Our Heritage*, Anchor Books/Anchor Press/Doubleday, Garden City, NY, 1979, p. 11.

31

PACKING UP THE DOLLHOUSE

Davis: Summer 1979

As the end of our sabbatical year approached, our land-lords wanted to know if we would be staying on. The prospect of staying in Davis was tantalizing. After all, this was where Ali and I met, fell in love, and married, where we were creative and care-free. This was where Ali had stayed up all night developing photos of safflower chromosomes, where I had ridden my bike to art class, one hand on the handlebars, the other clutching a five-by-six-foot canvas. Why couldn't we just be those people again?

I found many reasons to stay—the schools, the informality, the ease with which I did everything—driving, shopping, raising children, and communicating. Ali and I stepped up our discussions, drew up lists of pros and cons, and got nowhere. We asked friends and family if we should go back: my father ("Well, honey, I can't tell you what to do. I'm sure you and Ali will make the right decision."); Ali's IBB colleague, who had already left Iran and was living in New England ("Why do you want to go back? Everybody else is leaving. But, OK, if you decide to go back, you'll need the name of my vodka supplier."); my dental hygienist ("What? Are you crazy?"); Ali's brother Ahmad ("Of course, we would miss you if you stayed in California, but I have to tell you, it's not going to be easy for you in Tehran.")

Tehran had never been easy, not even for Ali, but especially not for me. My list of grievances against Tehran was long: the hellacious traffic that made every cross-town trip feel as if it could be our last, the insidious pollution that seeped into our pores, the Sisyphean bureaucracy that turned a simple request into an Everest expedition. But now, judging from the reports in the American media, there would be the added stresses of post-Revolutionary turmoil—the demonstrations and counter-demonstrations, and the horrors of the denunciations and executions.

What we knew of the new Tehran was unsettling. Even more unsettling was what we didn't know, namely how we would fit in. And why did we even think we needed to fit in? Why, when so many of our friends were fleeing Iran, would we want to go back?

Ali and I wrestled with three scenarios: (1) we all stay in Davis, and our make-believe lives become a reality; (2) The girls and I stay in Davis while Ali returns to Iran to scope things out, and we spend a fortune on long-distance phone calls as he tries to explain to me life in the Islamic Republic of Iran; (3) the four of us return to Iran and take our chances with the new regime. Each option had its drawbacks. For weeks, we circled back and forth in our deliberations in a kind of infinity loop, sometimes switching positions, never getting anywhere.

"Davis is so easy...so safe," one of us would say. "We'd be stupid to leave."

"Yes, but we have no jobs here," the other would say.

"OK, we have jobs in Tehran, but what if we're killed getting to or from them?"

"Come on, it's never as bad as it looks on TV."

"How can we be sure?"

"I'll go back, and if it looks like things are calming down, you and the kids can join me in a few months."

"I don't want to stay here without you."

"I don't want to be without you either."

"What if it is as bad as it looks on TV?"

"How can we be sure?"

Most sensible people, if they can't be sure about a volatile unknown, will opt for the safety of the known. We were not those people. We wanted to know if we could live in this new Iran, and the only way we could really know was to go back to Iran and make the decision together.

We packed up as much of our make-believe lives as would fit into four wooden crates—the respectable furniture, the La-Z-Boy recliner, the D'Nealian handwriting workbooks for grades 1 through 6, the doll house—as if we could transport some of that normalcy to Iran. Our friend Sharon sat on our living room floor performing astonishing feats of legerdemain, rolling up Ali's suits into tight bundles and stuffing them in boxes.

In the end, we went back because Iran was home. Our lives were there, our real, grown-up lives. Waiting for us in Iran were family and friends, an apartment that we owned, and a job for me in the English Department at Tehran University. More than that, there was unfinished business. Ali was not yet ready to let go of IBB, where he had invested all that creative energy, nor was he ready to give up his country. I was not yet ready to let go of my adopted country, one in which I had learned so much and had so much more to learn.

When I told my father of our decision to return to Iran, he was not concerned. "I know Ali won't let anything happen to you," he said. And, really, what could happen? After all, we were not supporters of the monarchy. We had done nothing wrong. There was no reason to believe that anyone would have it in for us.

32

SANANDAJ IN ATHENS

Athens: August 20 – September 1, 1979

After a few days in London, I left for the International Modern Language Association meeting in Innsbruck, Austria, and Ali and the children headed for Athens, where they would wait until I could rejoin them a few days later. Ali's J-1, or non-immigrant exchange visa, that he had used for his sabbatical year in Davis was due to expire soon, so he decided to make good use of his time in Athens and apply for a multiple-entry tourist visa from the consulate there. To do that, he had to rouse Samira and Sarah from their sleep at 5 a.m. so he could secure a good spot near the front of the long line of applicants, many of them Iranian, circling the consulate.

The girls were understandably grouchy and whiny from lack of both sleep and their mother. In addition to the children's protests, Ali had to endure the censure of a gaggle of Iranian matrons who couldn't understand why he had dragged two sleepy little girls out of bed only to make them stand in line for hours without a proper breakfast or anything to amuse them. The women gave Ali the fish eye as they comforted the girls with biscuits (which the ladies had in abundance, because no sensible Iranian woman would embark on such an errand without proper provisions).

After two hours of waiting, Ali was directed to the office of a kind and congenial consular official who readily agreed that Ali should have a visa.

"How about your wife and daughters?" he asked, as they were wrapping up the interview. "Do they need visas?"

"Oh, I don't have to worry about them," Ali explained. "They all have American passports."

"Oh, well…that changes everything," the man said, putting aside Ali's visa application. "In your situation, all this office can request is a green card. You're welcome to apply for that, but the process will take about two months."

"I don't really want a green card," Ali replied. "I'm not planning to live in the States."

"Well then, you can get your multiple-entry visa in Tehran. Our embassy is under construction, but when the visa section re-opens, it should be a very simple process."

Ali thanked the man and left empty-handed. He was disappointed that he had put the girls through this ordeal for nothing. It would have been safer to have a US visa in hand when we arrived in Tehran, just in case things didn't work out. Nevertheless, he had no sense of urgency about getting an American green card. Not having one was still a point of honor for him. In spite of the uncertainty about the political situation in Iran, when we made the decision to return, we did it with uncertainty but with the hope that the Islamic regime would move toward democracy. Ali was certain he could get another visa as soon as we were settled in Tehran. There was no reason to think otherwise.

In the three days they were without me in Athens, Samira and Sarah had gone native. They met me at the airport dressed in crinkly blue and white cotton dresses and embroidered sandals Ali had bought them at a handicraft shop. With their dark hair and eyes, they easily passed for Greek. On one of our outings, the girls ran ahead of us and scampered into a gift shop catering to tourists. The owner, thinking they were local ragamuffins, stopped them at the entrance, yelled at them in Greek and shooed them away. When the owner saw Ali and me following close behind, she realized her mistake and made a great show of welcoming all of us. By then, it was too late. We were not about to buy anything from a merchant who would discriminate against her own countrymen— however little they might be.

We took a day-long cruise from Piraeus to a nearby island on one of those awful boats packed with tourists, offering a tasteless lunch of rock-hard kebabs, stale pita bread, and wilted salad that adhered itself to aluminum dishes of questionable cleanliness. A young Iranian woman spotted us and started speaking Persian. She had a lonely joylessness about her, a heavy resignation that was immediately apparent. She stood on the deck with her back to the sea, the wind whipping her shoulder-length hair across her face, as Ali took her picture with her own camera.

"I'm not going back to Iran," she said. "This hair has to be free."

One afternoon, while the children were playing on the swings at a park near our hotel, we struck up a conversation with an Egyptian man who was vacationing in Athens. When he learned that we were on our way to Iran after a year in America, he asked what we thought of the shah.

"We're not supporters of the shah," Ali said. "Anything will be better than the monarchy."

"I'm curious," the man said. "You've been away for a year, but you're going back now. So…you support the Islamic Republic?"

"Iran is our home," Ali answered. "We're hoping the regime will become more democratic."

"Sure, we're concerned about freedom of speech," I said, "and women's rights, and of course, there are all these executions…."

The man shook his head and asked, "What did you think an Islamic Republic would be like?"

Two days before we were to leave Athens, we walked to an outdoor café. It was only 10:30 in the morning, but the old men sitting at tables under the trees playing checkers and backgammon were already on their second round of ouzo.

We settled into our chairs, hoping to enjoy these last few hours of irresponsibility. We were becoming very bad at irresponsibility. At a *taverna* the previous evening, we had dutifully smashed plates provided by the management for the amusement of tourists who thought that's what Greeks do, but our hearts weren't in it. We were becoming more and more fearful about returning to Iran. But at the same time, we wanted the uncertainty to be over. What *did* we think an Islamic Republic would be like? Why *were* we going home?

"I guess it's still too early for ouzo," Ali said as he studied the café menu.

As we waited for our coffee, my eyes traveled to a newsstand next to the café, where newspapers and periodicals were suspended from a wire between two trees. I realized I hadn't seen a paper for a couple of days. Actually, I had been enjoying a respite from news of Iran. Every news story brought more doubt and confusion, more second-guessing of our decision to return home.

In spite of myself, I lazily skimmed the front pages from a safe distance, until one image caught my eye. I had never seen this

photo before, but it was chillingly familiar: Men were lined up...
somewhere in a desert. I walked over to the newsstand for a closer
look. The image had been reproduced over and over on the front
pages of several newspapers—Greek, Italian, Arabic, English. As I
leaned closer, the grainy image came into focus—armed soldiers in
camouflage uniforms crouched on the ground, aiming their rifles
at blindfolded men—some of them already fallen, others doubled
over from the force of the bullets, but one still standing tall and
proud with his bandaged hand on his chest, waiting. I scanned the
English text: "Iranian government spokesman announced....mili-
tary trial....Sanandaj airfield....nine Kurdish rebels....two of the
shah's policemen...."

Eight years before, in Fatemeh and Asghar's courtyard, I stepped
over the dying sacrificial lamb at the doorstep and shut off a part
of my heart to ignore that animal's suffering. That sunny morning
in the Athens café, I pushed that photo of the summary executions
of eleven men on a desolate airfield out of my conscious mind and
stepped over the threshold leading back to Iran.

PART V: Dislocation

33

....

WELCOME HOME

Tehran: September 2, 1979

We arrived at Mehrabad Airport late at night, exhausted and disoriented. The lingering summer heat at midnight gave the dark Tehran streets an unreal quality, like a photographic negative. Driving home, with Ali's nephew Hassan at the wheel, we saw men in khakis with guns slung over their shoulders stationed at main intersections and traffic circles.

"Who are these guys?" I asked Hasan.

"They're *pasdaran*," he answered. The *Pasdaran e Enqelab e Eslami*, the Army of the Guardians of the Islamic Revolution (or Revolutionary Guards), was created in May 1979, just a few months after Khomeini took over. Their presence did not inspire confidence. Before the revolution, the only visible security forces on the streets were the blue-uniformed cops on the beat, and they carried billy clubs, not guns. I had never been afraid to walk in Tehran late at night, because no one carried guns. Now guns were everywhere.

As our car rounded the corner of our street, a shot rang out, startling the children.

"Get down," I shouted.

"Why are they shooting?" Sarah asked.

My heart pounding, I told the first lie that came into my mind.

"They're just shooting at birds."

"They shouldn't do that," shouted Sarah, who, outraged, began to cry. Was our four-year-old child crying because she feared for the birds, or did she somehow understand that it was not just the birds that were in danger? And how many more lies would I have to tell them? Clearly, I would have to get better at lying.

The night settled back into silence. When we arrived at our apartment, we were too tired for anything more than tea and a cursory look around. Devoid of our personal items, our cozy clutter, the place had a blank, brittle sparseness. It was unfamiliar, ours but not ours, with an unwelcoming emptiness that we would need to fill.

A front window had been left ajar, but in the dim light, everything else appeared in order, so we lugged the mattresses and bedding out of the storage room and spread them on the living room floor, where the four of us camped together.

When I opened my eyes the next morning, I revised my assessment. Very little was in order. In the bright morning light, I could see that a thick film of dust covered carpets, bookcases, and furniture. Last night's footprints were visible in the dust on the floors. All the houseplants were shriveled, and the soil inside their pots was shrunken and cracked. When I went into the kitchen to put the tea on, I noticed that on each of the painted metal cabinets, our "bachelor" tenants had, with some kind of stylus, etched indelible reminders to themselves: "tea"…"flour"…"pots and pans." Stuck to the outside of the kitchen window screen were the enmeshed remnants of a raw egg.

And the phone was dead.

When Ali went upstairs to Arash and Ladan's apartment to get the tenants' set of keys, he learned that the Indian engineers had left five months before, skipping out on the rent and the phone bill. Ali called the phone company from Arash and Ladan's apartment and learned that the outstanding bill was over $1,500 in calls to England and India. We would have to pay it if we wanted our phone reconnected.

While inspecting an empty bedroom closet, I came upon a cardboard package that had once held a 16 mm porn film.

"We'll hardly ever be here," our tenants had assured us.

We had heard what we wanted to hear: *"We won't be home long enough to do any damage."* What we should have heard was, *"We won't be here long enough to clean the house or remember where we keep the tea without defacing your kitchen cabinets. We will feel so guilty after watching porn films that we will need to make repeated calls to our wives in England. Oh…and as soon as things get dicey, we're out of here."*

I could hardly blame them for leaving. Why would they want to stay? I could only imagine the uncertainty that repeated demonstrations, shortages, closures, and sidelong glances from neighbors must have engendered. I was feeling fairly uncertain myself. *Why stay if you don't have to? That was the question, wasn't it?*

Hasan came back later that morning to see if we needed anything.

He took one look at us—jet lagged and forlorn—and at the condition of the apartment and sprang into action.

"Where's the vacuum cleaner?" he asked. "And I'll need a mop…."

"Wait, Hasan jaan," Ali said. "We can take care of this…or we'll hire someone…."

"You and Aunt Ellen are in no shape to do this, and it might take days before we find anyone to clean. I can handle this. You take the girls and go to Batoul's house, and don't come back until you hear from me."

We muttered a few perfunctory *taarofs* but quickly took Hasan up on his offer. He could handle this. He was no stranger to a mop. One of Fatemeh's six children, he grew up in a household where everyone pitched in, and he was part of an extended family where the children were always ready and eager to sacrifice their own comfort for an older relative.

We spent the day at the home of Ali's niece Batoul and, rested and well-fed, returned several hours later to find Hasan covered with dust and streaked with sweat, but smiling and triumphant.

With a now spotless house, we could begin the process of settling in, but we still had some nagging questions. Who had left the eggy calling card on the kitchen screen? Was it meant for the Indian tenants or for the owner's American wife? If Arash and Ladan knew about the departure of our tenants five months ago, why didn't they let us know? And if Arash and Ladan had received our keys from the tenants, why didn't they let themselves in and close the open window…or water the plants?

In the unforgiving light of that first morning back home, I saw that more than just the plants had withered. Something in me had died—my optimism, my sense of safety, definitely my trust in the neighbors upstairs.

Usually, when I returned home from a trip, I would feel energized by the prospect of new beginnings, new projects, a chance to apply what I'd learned, to reorganize and reinvent. But this time, I had no clear sense of forward movement. I didn't know where we were going.

34

SCHOOL DAYS

Tehran: Winter 1980

The school photo Samira brought home broke my heart.

It was a school snapshot taken February 3, 1980, a year after Khomeini's return to Iran and just five months after our return from Ali's sabbatical. Samira is standing in front of the blackboard with her first-grade teacher and four of her classmates. The one in the sweat suit is the only boy in the school, the son of the live-in caretakers. It must be chilly in the classroom because the teacher's plush jacket is slung over her shoulders. In another four months, the government will announce that all women who work for government agencies must wear a chador or a headscarf, manteau, and slacks. But for now, the teacher is not wearing hijab. She is sporting fashionable leather boots below her pleated skirt. Samira is the only child wearing red pants; the other girls are a study in blues and muted browns. Samira's gray sweater is at odds with itself, buttoned crookedly that morning in a rush to get ready for school. Her classmates are wearing their gray-blue school smocks, but both of Samira's smocks are at home, waiting to be washed. Her gaze is fixed somewhere in the middle distance. She has the beginning of a shy smile on her face. Her shoulders are hunched up to her ears, but then all the children look vaguely uncomfortable. They stand at attention, unsmiling, stiff, and uncertain, posing with their schoolbooks open in front of them as if they are waiting for the signal to begin a joyless recitation. The walls are bare. The only adornment in the photo is the arithmetic lesson chalked on the board behind them, two neat columns of unsolved problems.

When we returned from sabbatical, one of our first tasks was to find schools for the girls. We had always thought they would go to one of the private English language schools in Tehran, but after the revolution, we heard that these schools were not accepting new students. We didn't try to talk our way in. It doesn't matter, we said. We're both products of public schools. We're not elitists. A public school is perfectly fine.

We found a private preschool for Sarah not far from our house and an all-girls public elementary school for Samira on a side street next to the university. All government schools, even during the shah's time, were segregated by gender. On our first visit to the elementary school, we explained to the vice principal that we had just returned from the States, and Samira hadn't spoken much Persian for the last eleven months.

"It might take her a while to…," I began.

"Don't worry, *Khanum*," the vice principal said, with a wave of her hand. "We even have a Turkish girl, and we made *her* understand. We'll make your daughter understand."

A Turkish girl, even? Ali and I stared at her in disbelief. Did a school administrator really just say that?

She meant a Turkish-speaking Azarbayjani-Iranian girl, a member of a large ethnic minority, originally from the province of Azerbaijan but now living in communities throughout the country. While Azarbayjanis were integrated into every level of Iranian society and contributed greatly to the arts, literature, sciences, and politics, they were often the target of the Iranian equivalent of

Polish jokes. Perhaps the vice principal meant only that the little girl came into the school speaking nothing but Turkish and quickly learned Farsi there. However, her dismissive comment perpetuated a common stereotype. *If we can make a Turkish girl understand, we can certainly make* your *daughter understand.*

If she had said, "Don't worry. We'll teach your daughter," or "Your daughter will soon catch up," I would have been reassured that Samira would be entering a nurturing environment. But she had said, "We'll make her understand." *Is "to be made to understand" the same as "to learn"?*

The private pre-school classroom Samira and Sarah attended in Tehran prior to our sabbatical had been colorful, light, and airy. The teachers encouraged exploration, movement, and fluidity. Like their counterparts in American classrooms, their students used all their senses and experienced a variety of learning modes. They had learned not just through language and logical problems but also through movement, the arts, and social interaction.

The principal of the preschool made a special effort to engage parents as full partners in the education process, and he wasn't shy about offering parenting advice. One afternoon, as Ali and I waited for Samira to carefully and slowly descend the long staircase from her second-floor classroom, he suddenly appeared beside us.

"Let her fall," he said.

"What?"

"That's right. You're standing here at the bottom of the stairs waiting to catch her. Let her fall. She's perfectly capable of coming down the stairs, but she sees your fear. She's very shy and hesitant most of the time. You have to work on building her confidence."

"How can we do that?"

"It's easy," he explained. "You have to give her little jobs to do. For example, tonight, after dinner, let her serve the tea."

"You mean…carry the tea tray? What if she…."

"Drops it? So what? She drops it. It's not a big deal."

That night, after dinner, Samira served tea, grinning with pride in her new accomplishment.

The next afternoon, when we came to pick up the children, the principal was there to greet us.

"Whatever you did last night really worked," he said. "I can already see the change in your daughter."

The following week, at a parent meeting, the nursery school principal gave us a book on child development, a prize for being the Most Improved Parents.

Now, two years later, after our meeting with the elementary school vice principal, something told me Ali and I wouldn't be getting any awards at this new school.

What little I knew of Iranian public schools did nothing to assuage my anxiety. My overall impression was that they relied heavily on rote memorization, offering very little opportunity for individual exploration or creativity. However, I knew many Iranian immigrants, products of these same schools, who came to the United States and beat the pants off American students in math and science and carried volumes of classical poetry in their heads.

I pushed my concerns and prejudices out of my mind, ready to make this work, to make the experience a positive one for Samira. Indeed, in just a few weeks, her Persian language skills came back to her with such force that she was earning nineteen and twenty out of twenty on her homework and tests.

When the school announced the formation of a parent support

group, Ali and I eagerly attended the first meeting, hoping to learn more about the school and help in any way we could. The small meeting room was crowded with about seventy other enthusiastic mothers and fathers, most of the women without hijab, most everyone standing for lack of chairs. The principal talked about the need for donations and asked for volunteers to serve on a board. Just as we were about to approve the slate of officers, a commotion arose somewhere deep in the crowd.

"Wait, wait," someone yelled from the back of the room.

Soon a small, wiry woman in a gray chador emerged, elbowing her way to the center of the group. "Who are these people?" she asked.

The room went quiet. The principal stared at her. "What do you mean?" she asked. "They're parents just like you."

"We don't know them," the woman said, clutching her chador tightly under her chin, her face half covered. "How can we trust them with the money?"

"Khanum," the principal began, "I think we can trust them to...."

"Why? Why? What do we know about them?" the woman countered, peering out from her chador, her chin thrust forward, her eyes narrowing into slits. "We need to investigate them."

The prospective officers kept their composure.

"Fine. Investigate us," they said. "We have nothing to hide."

It was clear from her combative tone that the woman wanted the nominees to be investigated for not only any history of financial malfeasance but also for any involvement in the shah's regime. She very likely wanted to know if they were Islamic enough. All politics is local, and there is nothing more local than the neighborhood PTA. What had begun as a genuine expression of parental solidarity and support had ended in acrimony and suspicion. How many more selfless gestures would be quashed by strident accusations? How many tired, overworked parents would forgo volunteering at their children's schools rather than subject themselves to scrutiny by followers of Khomeini? Better to keep to one's self than to risk being suspected. *Vellesh kon, baba!* Let someone else do it.

Still, I wanted to be involved. I wanted to know how the Iranian public education system worked. The school was still unknown territory to me. It lacked transparency, as did so many government institutions in Iran. There were no invitations to volunteer in the classroom, no baking of cupcakes for birthday parties, no parent-teacher conferences, no sitting in tiny plastic seats at back-to-school night as there had been in Davis. You deposited your child in the morning, collected her in the afternoon, and hoped for the best.

I needed to have a mental image of Samira's classroom. It was unsettling to drop her off at school every day and not be able to imagine her environment, her classmates, or the rhythm of her day. At the very least, I needed to know why her school uniform was always filthy.

Ali and I decided to pay a visit to Samira's first grade teacher. We stopped by the office after school one afternoon to ask if we could see our daughter's classroom.

We were met with a blank stare. "Why?" the teacher asked.

"I'd just like to see where she goes every day," I explained. Had no other parent ever made this request?

"Very well. Follow me, please," she said as she led us up to the second floor.

One look at the stairwell and one of the mysteries was solved. The walls were black with layers of grime from years of heating oil and grubby little hands. I imagined Samira, shyly clinging to the banister, brushing against these walls four times a day. Apparently, the live-in caretakers had better things to do than wash walls.

"After you," the teacher said, with the air of someone patiently accompanying a fool on her errand. She watched as we looked around the room, her arms folded in front of her as if to say, "I could have told you there's nothing to see here."

The room was bare except for the teacher's desk; a blackboard and rows of wooden desks and benches bolted to the floor, each accommodating two students; and a framed photograph of Ayatollah Khomeini where the shah's had been. No bulletin board. No books. No examples of student work. No teaching aids.

Teaching aids! Perhaps we had something at home we could donate.

"Do you need anything for the classroom?" I asked.

"What do you mean?"

"Oh, I don't know…a globe, a map…maybe an electric tea kettle to demonstrate that science lesson on steam…."

"No, Khanum. We have everything we need."

And perhaps they did, but I doubted it.

Back in the States, American teachers found creative ways to enhance the textbook lessons and tap into every learning style as they tried to reach every child. However, as far as Iranian government schools were concerned, these other ways of learning were a superfluous distraction. First grade was a time to put aside childish things. It was a time for the intellectual rigor of bare classroom walls, of recitation and memorization, of linear thinking. Sure, there was plenty of oil money, but why waste it on classroom frills?

In spite of myself, I had to admit the Iranian system worked…

at least for Samira. She sailed through first grade, still shy and lonely, but victorious. She was a natural student, one who could have flourished in any system.

On the last day of school, the three of us went into the office to say goodbye to Samira's teacher. I wanted to thank her, but I was also hoping to hear some kind of assessment of Samira's first year.

"How did she do?" I asked.

"She didn't make first student," was the abrupt response.

That's not what we wanted to know. We wanted to know how she had progressed. We wanted someone to acknowledge that a child who had forgotten most of her Persian in September had easily made up for lost ground and was earning top grades within a matter of months. The emphasis on becoming first student was ludicrous. What about the individual achievements of all the other students? And how about a little sensitivity? Our daughter is standing right here listening to you.

I had always been proud of Ali, who was consistently first student from first grade through his senior year of college. Now I wondered about the other students and their parents, the students who had almost become first student, the students who struggled, the students who were disheartened by the endless competition, the students who were made to feel not good enough. Was this the system I wanted Samira and Sarah to grow up in?

Why was that school photo so heartbreaking? It wasn't just the fact that I had sent Samira to school without her uniform, although I cringe every time I see that crookedly buttoned sweater, a permanent reminder of my carelessness that morning. The photo was also a reminder of the barrenness of that classroom, the rigidity of that school system, and the choices we were making by returning to Iran.

Samira (second from right) with her first-grade teacher and some of her classmates, 1979.

35

THE YEAR OF TEACHING DANGEROUSLY

Tehran University: 1979-1980

On his first day back at work in September, Ali found Tehran University transformed into a clamorous bazaar of competing political movements. The hallways of the colleges of science, literature and engineering were filled with information tables manned by students of every political stripe—National Front, Islamic Society, Fedayeen, Mujahidin, Communist Tudeh Party—all selling books and tapes, passing out leaflets and hand-written newspapers, and arguing at the top of their lungs.

Following the ouster of the shah in January and Khomeini's return the following month, the country had been enjoying a period of relatively free speech. However, after the March referendum the previous spring that established the Islamic Republic, the hardliners were gaining ground. In August, the month before we returned from sabbatical, liberals and leftists were under siege by followers of the Hezbollah (Party of God) who were intent on helping Ayatollah Khomeini cleanse the country of Western ideologies and threats to the new regime. Even after the referendum, there was still no consensus about what such a republic should look like, and there were still those who questioned why there should be an Islamic Republic at all.

In spite of the referendum, Ali held out hope for a secular, progressive government. The dissent at the university was disquieting, but at least people were expressing themselves. Perhaps, he thought, some lasting good could come out of all the tumult.

Soon after our return, Ali was taking part in a funeral procession for a prominent progressive activist when he suddenly saw cars without license plates surrounding the mourners. The cars disgorged thugs who set about beating people and shutting down the procession. He ran to escape them and walked the ten blocks back to the university. When he got back to his office, he realized that he didn't have his university ID card. It must have fallen out of his pocket while he was fleeing. He was frantic. Not only would it be a hassle to replace, but the card also contained critical personal information, such as his birth certificate number and our home address. If it got into the wrong hands, it could be dangerous.

Later that day, Ali got a phone call in his office from a woman who said she had found his ID card and would bring it to him. The next morning, a young student without hijab arrived and handed him his card.

"Where did you find this?" he asked.

"Where did you lose it?" she replied.

"At the funeral procession," Ali answered.

"Then that's where I found it," she replied. "You're lucky it was I who found it."

The vigilant, suspicious parent we encountered at the PTA meeting had her counterparts among the IBB graduate students. While most students were respectful of their professors and intent on focusing on their research, a small but vociferous minority was busy making life difficult for those they deemed un-Islamic or progressive. They were intent on purging the last remnants of Fereydoun and Lisa Djavadi's influence, and that meant going after the other co-founders of the institute.

That fall, Ali was elected to the IBB's *shora-ye hamahangi*, a coordinating council consisting of three faculty members, three staff and three students. The council, formed in the heady days after the revolution, took over many of the institute's decision-making functions that were previously the province of the IBB director and the chair of the Cell and Molecular Biology Department. But many of their deliberations were unprecedented. For example, before the revolution, IBB administrators never had to decide how to deal with anonymous denunciations of professors posted on the IBB corridor walls because nobody denounced professors, anonymously or otherwise. But after the revolution, a handful of newly empowered Islamic students filled the hallways with hastily scrawled manifestos, crude caricatures, and slanderous accusations—all unsigned.

It was impossible to tell how many IBB students were involved in this enterprise or whether they were, in fact, IBB students. For all anyone knew, the authors could have been two or three students who changed their handwriting with every post, or they could have dictated their screeds to willing janitors or undergraduates. Who was to say? Ali's guess was that there were five or six of these writers out of the fifty or so IBB graduate students, but their anonymity permitted them to make outrageous, unfounded accusations that had more prominence than they deserved.

After much discussion, the coordinating council members decided that they would allow only signed postings to remain on the walls. However, the anonymous hardliners weren't going away without a fight. In defiance of the committee, they continued to post their unsigned manifestos and slurs. They branded a candidate for director of the institute as a puppet of the Djavadis and those who wanted to bring back the monarchy. They asked why, when this candidate was performing his military service, the shah signed an exit permit allowing him to leave the country to attend a scientific conference. They questioned no-interest home loans given by Fereydoun Djavadi to several professors and staff: was it from Djavadi's "own pocket or from the people's reserves?" Some of their questions were legitimate. What about that no-interest loan? Was it favoritism, or was it an attempt to provide young professors with a way to concentrate on their duties at IBB without having to get a second job?

Ali had actually raised this issue with Fereydoun Djavadi in the early days of IBB. He noted that scientists in other faculties on campus were so strapped that they took second and third jobs, teaching in other colleges, trading carpets, and importing automobiles to make ends meet. Ali advocated for some financial support that would allow IBB to hire the best scientists and allow them to focus on their students and their research. The question should not have been why a young professor should get a small no-interest loan but why the government couldn't make such a loan available to more professors in other departments so they, too, could concentrate on their teaching and research.

It's the job of university students to question authority. But the aim of these anonymous scribes wasn't to get answers. What they wanted was to clean house.

In the hopes of a return to civility and collegiality, Ali began taking down anonymous postings, like the drawing, scrawled in felt pen on the back of a calendar page, showing a giant hand dropping the shah (in full court regalia with a bloody ceremonial sword) into the "trash can of history," where the Djavadis and another founding faculty member awaited him.

One wag concocted membership criteria for a fake union, the "Syndicate of the Porters of the Institute," illustrated with a crude sketch of a Ph.D. making his way to the airport carrying two suitcases, one labeled "America" and the other "CIA." The text, satirizing the Western-educated faculty, referred to the three international conferences that IBB organized in the late 70s:

> "The purpose of the organization: to carry the suitcases and belongings of the international scientific community who come to Iran for symposia. The condition of membership: having a Ph.D. in any field but obtained from America. European graduates can also become members with permission from the head of the syndicate. Acceptance depends on good service and good dancing."

Some brave souls were supportive of the administration, or at least protesting the atmosphere created by the anonymous postings. One student wrote,

> "I hope that the brothers and sisters will prevent this behavior by any possible means. A fanatic is a person who in a general meeting doesn't have the courage to express opinions and then writes posts with no signature and lies and accuses others with no evidence. A fanatic is one who, instead of constructive criticism, without any reason swears at others."

When Ali began removing the anonymous posts, both for and against the faculty, he himself became the target of the anonymous scribes. One morning, he arrived at work to find, prominently displayed on a wall, a photograph of himself shaking hands with the empress. This encounter might have been incriminating if it had been on a yacht in the Caspian or a *soiree* at Niavaran Palace, but it was at a ceremony at which, along with other university colleagues in various disciplines, the empress presented Ali with a Tehran University research award. No matter. Optics triumphed over logic.

Ali removed the photo, and a few days later, he found a warning:

> "Mr. Estilai, I am respectfully informing
> you that from now on, the next time you
> want to remove posters, invite the American
> ambassador. In the meeting, it was agreed
> to remove insulting posts, not those stating
> facts."

Actually all the posts directed at professors were insulting. In the culture of Iranian universities, students routinely addressed professors as *agha ye doctor* or *khanum e doctor*. It had always been Mr. Doctor Estilai, never Mr. Estilai. But these hardliners were intent on taking their targets down a peg or two, likening them to bazaar porters who were at the beck and call of foreign scientists and dignitaries.

One such posting read (in Persian):

> "Mr. Estilai, in the older days, the posters
> were taken down by the SAVAK. Nowadays,
> they're taken down by people who claim
> they're democratic....Mr. Estilai takes down

the posters because he is afraid his monarchist tendencies will be revealed....Why take down the posters? Do you assume you understand more than others?....Perhaps you want to say it's your duty. Yes, it's correct. You, during Djavadi, had such a duty, but as Deputy Director and in cooperation with all the work that Djavadi has done. You are half responsible for one half of the crimes that the escapee Djavadi has committed.... Mr. Estilai, we advise you not to remove the postings because experience has shown that in spite of the agreement on the removal of the posters, people still want to read them. We will post so many that you will not be able to remove them, and we will reveal the facts. Remember, this is not *taarof.* Experience has proven that we are more stubborn than you are."

The author signed the screed with a large, blue thumbprint. *Go ahead, catch me if you can.*

Never mind that Ali did not have "monarchist tendencies." In fact, he himself had a history of wall postings that railed at the establishment. While in high school in Kerman, he and two of his friends produced a weekly *rooznameh-ye divari* or wall newspaper. Produced by hand with one of the boys' impeccable calligraphy and placed behind glass in an ornate frame, the newspaper contained poetry and essays that were read enthusiastically by their classmates. However, Ali and his cohorts sometimes ran afoul of the school administrators who didn't appreciate their anti-shah sentiments. The newspaper was removed several times, until the principal finally shut it down for good.

Having been a victim of censorship himself, Ali was not intent on shutting down debate, but he wasn't going to allow that debate to be taken over by anonymous thugs.

Ali never brought any of this turmoil home with him. After a day of dissent and false accusations, he would use his short commute to our apartment to put that ugliness out of his mind. By the time he parked the car and came upstairs, he was smiling and relaxed. He became clever at hiding his stress—and the reasons for it—but the stress was taking its toll, physically and mentally in the form of backaches, stomach ulcers, and lack of sleep.

Ali certainly didn't show me any of those IBB manifestos. He put them in a folder in the back of our filing cabinet. He especially did not show me the one that ended with, "By your conscience, don't remove this. Otherwise, you'll be shot by [Ayatollah] Khalkhali's bullet."

During a street demonstration, Ali saw a young woman in hijab directing a group of *basijis*, members of a volunteer militia in support of the Revolutionary Guards, on motorcycles. She was telling them which demonstrators to go after with their batons and chains. He watched as she ran alongside their motorcycles, pointing at people in the crowd. Suddenly, with a sickening clarity, Ali realized that he knew her. She was a graduate student at IBB, one of the Islamic hardliners who were critical of the institute's founders. Shocked and outraged, he ducked out of her line of vision and made his way out of the crowd. He was terrified, yet relieved that she hadn't seen him. He was sure that if she knew he had seen her in action, she would work harder to get rid of him.

We tried to keep all of our anxieties about the political situation from the children, but because of the turmoil at the university, we were constantly on alert. Sarah's pre-school and Samira's elementary school were near the campus. One day, I was having lunch with Ali in the IBB cafeteria when we heard gunshots outside. Soon after, Essie came rushing in and told us we should leave immediately and pick up our children because there was gunfire near Samira's school on 16th of Azar Street. Suddenly, the lack of amenities in Samira's first grade classroom was the least of our worries.

One night I dreamed that Ali and I were sitting in a quintessential *New Yorker* cartoon living room: matching stodgy armchairs, a floor lamp casting a pale golden light, French doors leading to a terrace—a comfy, middle-class tableau. We sat facing each other, engrossed in our newspapers. Just outside the French doors, I could hear Samira and Sarah screaming. People were beating them. Ali and I paid no attention. We continued to read as their screams grew louder.

"Should we do something?" I asked.

"There is nothing we can do," he said.

It wasn't just IBB students who were turning our world upside down. On November 4, 1979, a group calling themselves Students Following the Line of the Imam [Khomeini] seized the US Embassy in protest against the Carter Administration's allowing the shah to seek medical treatment in the United States. The students demanded that the United States hand over the shah so that he could stand trial in Iran.

When we first learned of the embassy seizure, Ali and I were not terribly concerned. After all, just nine months earlier, guerrillas widely believed to be leftists stormed the US Embassy, trapping 100 employees. That insurgency lasted only two hours. Ebrahim

Yazdi, then deputy prime minister of the provisional government, intervened and ordered Revolutionary Guards loyal to Khomeini to free the prisoners and provide continued protection for the Embassy.[57]

But this time there would be no intervention. The Revolutionary Guards posted at the Embassy entrance stood and watched as the students breeched the gates and stormed the "nest of spies," taking ninety Americans hostage. Ebrahim Yazdi, now the foreign minister, tried to mediate, but Khomeini decided to let the students have their way. The next day, Yazdi, Prime Minister Mehdi Barzargan, and the rest of the interim government's cabinet resigned in protest. Bazargan, who came to prominence as a deputy minister in Mossadegh's cabinet and helped force the British oil interests out of Iran, was himself a devout Muslim and follower of Khomeini. However, Barzargan saw the takeover of the Embassy as not only a bad political move but also a sign that his power to lead had been usurped.

The embassy takeover signaled not just Iran's split with the United States but also the deep division between Khomeini's hardliners and Bazargan's team, a more moderate faction. With these resignations, our hopes for a moderate government began to fade.

Given the United States' involvement in the 1953 overthrow of Mossadegh's government, many Iranians were suspicious of American Embassy personnel, believing most of them to be CIA agents. It didn't help that during the shah's time, one of the US ambassadors to Iran was former CIA director Richard Helms, a logical choice to help solidify the anti-Soviet base in Iran during the Cold War.

---

57. Ebrahim Yazdi, who received his Ph.D. from Baylor University and became a naturalized US citizen in 1971, was one of several foreign-educated Iranians in Ayatollah Khomeini's inner circle in Neauphle-le-Château.

However, we were certain that the hostage taking would not benefit Iran domestically or internationally. If the Iranian government had legitimate grievances, they should have clearly stated them to the US government. Instead, Khomeini seized on the United States' welcoming of the shah to create a critical emergency allowing the hardliners to stabilize their power.

Beyond the now iconic photos of blindfolded embassy personnel paraded in front of the press by their young captors, Ali and I knew very little about the hostages or what was going on in the "nest of spies." We did know that a number of hostages, women and African Americans, had been voluntarily released on humanitarian grounds at the behest of then Minister of Foreign Affairs Abolhassan Banisadr, and that the dedicated students were piecing together thousands of documents shredded by the other agents of the "Great Satan" in the moments before their capture. Those quiet images of patient students bent over mounds of shredded paper provided a sharp contrast to the chaotic scene outside the embassy, now covered with graffiti and hand-written banners. Demonstrations and marches sprang up all over town. Our daily lives were played out against an incessant, undifferentiated drone of protest.

One joke making the rounds at the time reflected many Tehranis' jaundiced view of the daily demonstrations:

Hundreds of protesters are marching in the middle of the street and shouting, "Death to America!....DEATH TO THE SHAH!....GOD IS GREAT! KHOMEINI IS OUR LEADER!"

When their numbers begin to spill over onto the sidewalk, one of the organizers yells into his bullhorn, "Don't spread out."

"Don't spread out!" roars the crowd.

Their frustrated organizer yells back, "'Don't spread out' is not a slogan!"

The crowd shouts, "Don't spread out is not a slogan!"

The Iranian New Year of March 1980 brought Khomeini's formal call for a purging of Western influences from the nation's universities. The previous winter had been bloody; rioting at universities in Tehran, Mashhad, Isfahan, and Shiraz had left at least twenty-six students dead. Kurdistan was also the scene of violent battles between the military and the Sunni Kurds who wanted autonomy for the Kurds and opposed the Shia-controlled central government. Led by the Sunni sheikh Ezuddin Hosseini, the Kurdish rebels were joined by several traditionally disaffected leftist groups. Those pesky leftist groups that were forced underground during the shah's era were not welcome in the Islamic Republic either: the Fedayeen-e Khalq (People's Sacrificers), the Mujahedeen-e Khalq (People's Crusaders) and the Tudeh, Iran's pro-Moscow Communist Party. All of them, like the moderate nationalists or pro-democracy secularists, had helped topple the shah and were angry at being marginalized. Ultimately, the clergy benefited from the monarchy they opposed: centuries of brutal political repression had stifled civilized debate. With the exception of those brief periods when Mossadegh was in power or perhaps when Cyrus the Great was busy dictating his declaration of human rights, the Iranian people had not experienced civic dialogue that did not end in incarcerations, bloodshed or executions.

The current dialogue was as much about class warfare as it was about ideology. But while both the leftists and the clergy professed to support the *pa barahneha*, the barefoot ones, it was Islam that easily captured their hearts and minds—and their meager pocketbooks. After decades of clandestine operations, the leftist groups were no match for the ubiquitous clergy, with its 1400 years of open and unfettered access to a mostly illiterate audience, its network as intricate and complex as the tile work on a mosque and as serpentine as the corridors of the bazaars.

Intent on eradicating the troublemakers, Khomeini ordered the shutdown of opposition activities on university campuses, as well as preparations for closure of the universities. These measures were intended to not just stifle debate but also to prepare for a cultural revolution, a general "Islamification." "It is not the Western power we must fear," Khomeini told his followers. "It is American ideas."[58]

That spring, one American idea in particular only served to consolidate anti-Western sentiment. On the afternoon of April 24, I was in the garden when Ali came running downstairs. "You won't believe this," he said. "US helicopters in Iran!"

"Where?"

"In the desert...near Tabas," he said, shaking his head in amazement.

As improbable as it was, Operation Eagle Claw was chillingly real. From news reports later that evening we learned that the mission to rescue the American hostages in Tehran had been foiled by a deadly dust storm that left the charred bodies of eight American soldiers in the desolate desert. The evening news featured a video of Iranian soldiers jeering at the blackened corpses lying in the sands of Tabas.

The failed rescue only served to fuel Iranian paranoia about the United States and its cohorts in Iran; several Tehranis noted that, while the helicopters were making their way to Tabas, someone had left the lights on in Amjadieh Stadium, a few blocks away from the U. S. Embassy, the "Nest of Spies."

58. John Kifner, "Iran Declares a 'Holy War' Against Ideas From the Left," N. Y. Times, April 27, 1980.

As the academic year wore on, Ali felt increasingly lonely at IBB. By the spring of 1980, ten of his closest colleagues, among them Liza and Fereydoun, had left the country. Gone were the informal communal lunches in the cafeteria and the easy banter in the hallways.

One afternoon, feeling especially adrift, Ali went to his friend Manoucher's office to say hello. As soon as he sat down, his old friend began complaining about the Djavadis. "Why them?" he asked. "Why should they have had all that power?"

"Manoucher, these are your friends," Ali said. "You know what they've accomplished, how they served the university—and they took nothing for themselves."

Manoucher responded with a verse from the Qur'an.

Ali looked at him in disbelief. "Manoucher, this is me you're talking to. You don't need to recite the Qur'an to me. I grew up with it."

Manoucher didn't answer; he didn't feel he needed to convince Ali. The divisions were becoming clear. Animosities were growing. Neckties were coming off. Headscarves were going on. Colleagues were taking sides, and Manoucher felt he was on the winning one.

If Manoucher had been religious prior to the revolution, he kept it to himself. Whenever he came to our house, Ali would ask him what he wanted to drink—whiskey, vodka, wine? "Whatever you're having," he would say with a grin.

Ali was stunned by how easily his old friend seemed to have changed his views. He made a great show of being very Islamic. Which one had been the real Manoucher all those years, the live-and-let-live, vodka-drinking secularist, or the bitter Qur'an-quoting Islamist? It was one thing to watch the university and IBB taken over by Islamic fundamentalists but quite another thing to see that takeover abetted by people we assumed shared our values.

We heard on the news that Ayatollah Sadeq Khalkhali, the "hanging judge," was planning to visit Kerman. During his tenure as the sole judge of the Revolutionary Courts and later as head of the anti-narcotics campaign, Khalkhali was ultimately responsible for the speedy trials, some lasting as long as a minute, and the summary executions of hundreds of prisoners. Pouran, who was visiting us in Tehran, shuddered and said, "What misery is this ayatollah going to bring down upon the heads of us poor Kermanis?"

I took refuge from the turmoil in books, and in Voice of America on our short-wave radio, turned low so the neighbors wouldn't hear. The only place I felt safe was at home. When I made my way home from the university, up the stairs to our apartment, I felt that my last refuge was inside my own skull.

My friend Katie Black in California used to send me subscriptions to the *Atlantic Monthly*. Of course, the magazines arrived not monthly but erratically, subject to the whims of the postal service, which made them all the more special when I discovered them beneath a pile of letters under the mail slot in the downstairs entry. Each issue was a cultural care package. I stopped whatever I was doing and devoured them on the spot. I especially loved the short stories by John Sayles. The desolate places that Sayles wrote about, the lonely stretches of highway through the American heartland, were exotic to me. He portrayed a world of CB radios and big rigs, of abandoned houses and junked cars, cornfields and barns and beaten-down people. It was not a world I knew, but I found myself nostalgic for these places I had never seen.

Sayles wrote a series of stories about a character named Brian McNeil, a young adventurer who hitchhikes across the country from New Jersey to California with a wanderer's receptivity to new experiences, a youthful American openness, wary but non-judgmental. Along the way, in South Dakota, Brian wakes up to find himself in the middle of a Buffalo pen, a mangy roadside attraction long ago bypassed by the Interstate. He falls into a job with a crew of hard drinking horse castrators with names like Bad Heart, Blackroot and Jim Crow. The Midwest was a foreign country, and Brian was the quintessential American innocent.

Another story, "I-80 Nebraska, m.490 – m.205," is populated by truckers with CB handles like Alabama Rebel, Scorpio Ascending and Axle Sally. I could hear their flat, whiny drawls and arcane lingo on their CB radios as they navigate the Interstate through North Platte, "Lincoln town," and Omaha, "the big O town." At the time, I was listening to a lot of Waylon Jennings, Willie Nelson, Kris Kristofferson, and Merle Haggard, and their songs could have been the soundtrack to these stories. It was the quirky characters and their haphazard journeys that enticed me. Their world was at once exotic and familiar, grungy, and wholesome, circumscribed by circumstances yet open to possibilities, and about as far away from Tehran as you could get.

Even as late as the spring of 1980, I thought I could continue on in my *bi hijab* fashion, venturing outside modestly dressed but without a scarf or manteau. But when Ali and I attended a demonstration, chador clad women began shouting at me for not wearing any hijab. After the government declared hijab mandatory for women working in government institutions, Ali and I decided that we would not be those people in my *New Yorker* cartoon dream. There was something we could do.

We made the decision to leave, at least temporarily. With Essie and Julie, we went to the Swiss Embassy to apply for Swiss visas and arrange for our tickets from Bern to the United States to be given to us on the plane. That same day, we went to Julie and Essie's house in Karaj for dinner. After dessert, while the children played indoors, we sat outside on the terrace drinking tea and enjoying the soft, balmy night, bright with shooting stars. The shortwave radio was playing in the background, tuned to the BBC World Service—its tinny, bottom-of-the-well-sound offering a familiar counterpoint to our conversation. As we frequently did that summer, we talked about leaving: *Do we really have to leave? For how long? What will happen to our lives here? What if we were to stay?* We were only half-listening to the radio when we heard, "Today in Kerman...." We all leaned closer.

"....four people were stoned to death."

We stared at the radio in disbelief. Hangings and firing squads were becoming everyday occurrences, but stoning?

"Sexual offences....adultery....two men and two women."

These people were not members of the shah's secret police, or his generals or cabinet members or other enemies of the current regime. These were not political dissidents. They were two women in their fifties accused of prostitution, a father of six charged with homosexual acts as well as adultery with one of the women, and a 22-year-old man accused of raping a 10-year-old girl.

After a summary trial, the prisoners were placed in holes dug expressly for their execution and buried up to their chests. Sacks were placed over their heads, and five especially chosen people—one of them the presiding judge of a revolutionary court—hurled stones at them until they died.

That night on the terrace, and for many nights thereafter, I could feel the sickening thud of the rocks against the victims' heads, see the bodies slump over one by one, hear the crowd jeering.

We heard later from a nephew in Kerman that one of these five executioners was the son of one of the women. This was what Pouran had feared when she heard that Ayatollah Khalkhali was visiting Kerman. If we were not convinced before that we needed to leave Iran, we were certain now.

36

....

BAREFOOT IN ZURICH

Zurich: July 30, 1980

On our second day in Zurich, still reeling from the scene at Tehran's Mehrabad Airport, Julie and I take the four girls and make our way to the American Consulate. We crowd into the small office of the same consular official who met my plane. He is less harried today, slouching comfortably behind his desk, affable, polite, but resigned. Julie and I sit stiffly, straining forward to hear him say, very gently, that there is nothing the American government can do about getting our husbands out of Iran.

Of course not. Ali and Essie aren't citizens. They don't even have green cards. What difference would it make? The American hostages are citizens, and they're still stuck in the Embassy.

We ask what we need to do to apply for our husbands' green cards. The official hands us the forms, which we quickly fill out and give back to him to keep until Ali and Essie can get out of Iran and complete the process—if they ever can.

That evening, I call Ali from the hotel, hoping to hear that he'll be on the next plane to Zurich.

"What happened? Did you get it straightened out?" I ask.

"Not yet," he answers.

"Who'd you see?" I ask.

"Essie and I went to the Prime Ministry," he says, guardedly.

"What did they say?"

"Look, it's going to take a little longer," he says.

"How much longer?" I ask, not able to disguise my anxiety.

"I don't know. Please just try to enjoy Zurich until I get there."

Enjoy Zurich?

"Why won't they let you leave?"

"I'll call you tomorrow," he says.

Then he talks to Samira and Sarah. I watch their faces carefully as they answer their father's questions, see their tentative smiles as they each answer, "Yes, the hotel is nice....Yes. I will....I will....I love you, too." Their eyes fill with tears, but they do not break down.

It will take a little longer, he had said. Everything in Iran takes a little longer, I think bitterly. The Iranian term for bureaucracy is *kaghaz bazi*, paper game. It is the national pastime, with soccer a close second. Under both the shah's regime and the Islamic Republic, bureaucratic posturing, foot-dragging, or just plain busy work complicated the simplest act. You might say the paper game stifled the economy and crippled productivity. On the other hand, it provided billions of hours of gainful employment to those engaged in creating, shuffling, signing, copying, stamping, filing and, often, losing those papers. Whether it was ordering a telephone line, retrieving one's own possessions from customs, obtaining a translation of a foreign diploma, or just buying pots and pans, day-to-day business was rarely easy for the customer.

Nothing was transparent. Before the revolution, one of our Iranian scientist friends once said that he couldn't work in Iran any longer because "Iran has no database." Of course, there were databases; they just weren't shared freely. Officials were in their jobs to protect information, not disseminate it.

In 1976, as a graduate student, I decided to investigate Tehran University's main library. The library is the heart of any university, or should be. I had easy access to the English Department's small library and the one in the basement of the Faculty of Literature, but I wanted to see what treasures the main library held. I wanted to wander among the stacks, to hear my footsteps echo as I walked along the aisles, to choose a book at random and savor it, put it back and find another.

As soon as I entered the building, I came face to face with a receptionist behind a large wooden counter.

I nodded to her as I walked toward an entrance gate to the main reading room.

"Yes, Khanum, what do you want?" she asked as she stopped me.

"I just want to look around," I said.

"What are you looking for?" she demanded.

"I don't know. I suppose I could start with the English Literature section."

"Which book?"

"Well, I won't know until I find it," I answered.

"I'm afraid you can't go in without permission," she said.

As a married couple, Ali and I had one of our first confrontations with Iranian bureaucracy in 1971 after the household goods we had shipped from the States four months earlier finally arrived at the customs office in south Tehran. Ali looked around the cavernous building with its rows of clerks' windows and long lines and realized he had no idea where to begin. There were no signs or personnel to direct him. Suddenly a man came up to him and offered to help. He wasn't a customs employee but a self-employed gofer, much like the free-lance guides who station themselves outside of historical monuments scanning tourists for an easy mark.

"Hello, sir. Are you here to pick up a shipment?" he asked.

"Yes, I have four small crates."

"You're going to need thirteen signatures to release your belongings. I can get them for you in ten minutes."

"How much?" Ali asked.

"One hundred tomans ($14)," he replied.

Ali scanned the long lines again and figured it would take him at least three hours to get those thirteen signatures. One hundred tomans was a bargain.

Sure enough, ten minutes later the gofer handed him the signatures. But Ali wasn't finished yet. He had to find his shipment and have it inspected. He went to yet another warehouse filled with towers of crates stacked on pallets. Fortunately, one of the customs agents on duty was another long-lost classmate, this time from Ali's high school days in Kerman. The agent opened the crates and rummaged through our meager assortment of dishtowels and photo albums, until he came to the books. Ali tensed; he knew that, if anything, our books might be of interest to the government. While we were careful not to ship leftist or anti-government literature, we could never be sure what the shah's secret police might find subversive.

"Usually, we take four or five books at random for the authorities to review," the agent explained, "but I'll let you choose the books."

Ali thought for a moment and then picked out five of my textbooks, fairly certain that the shah's secret police would not feel the need to defend the country against early Italian Renaissance art or anthropological monographs on the Trobriand Islanders.

A few weeks later, the customs office sent Ali a letter saying he could retrieve the books. However, Ali never went back for them. That trip to the warehouse was as close as he ever wanted to get to the censors' scrutiny.

But our most prolonged encounter with Iranian bureaucracy was our battle to get our telephone. It was worse than the nine months it took for Ali to get his first paycheck from the university. It was worse than trying to get my UC Davis diploma translated and evaluated by the Ministry of Education.

When we bought our apartment, we knew that our building did not yet have a telephone line. We had heard that it was sometimes difficult to get one, yet we were hopeful that we would have a phone within a few months.

We were very naïve.

As soon as we moved in, we paid 3000 tomans (about $430) to the government telephone office for a phone line. We were told that we would have to wait until the telephone office decided to offer service to our area.

Ours was an established neighborhood, at least ten years old. However, no one on our side of the street had a telephone. The neighbors had been waiting for years, to no avail. We persevered; yet two and a half years later, we still did not have a phone. It meant that the girls and I couldn't be in contact with Ali when he went out of town on business for weeks at a time. It meant walking four or five blocks to a pay phone on a noisy street to call the doctor when the girls had chicken pox or whooping cough.

Finally, we had had enough. Our neighbors in the building had

had enough. We decided to resort to *party bazi*.

Party bazi means exploiting one's personal connections. It is more than just networking, another social skill at which Iranians excel. Very little gets done unless you know someone who can grease the skids, who can provide just the right introduction to a vacant apartment, a competent hairdresser, a popular physician. Rather *party bazi* implies favoritism via personal connections for one's own gain.

Ali asked Lisa and Fereydoun, his influential colleagues at IBB, to intervene. They sent Ali, our upstairs neighbor Ashkan, and another professor, the owner of the third apartment in the building, to talk to the chancellor of the university. The chancellor sent the three of them to an army general who agreed to meet them in his office. The general condescended to make the arrangements for the phone line, letting the three university professors know he was doing them an enormous favor. It still took another six months for the lines to be installed, but when they were, all the neighbors on our side of the *koocheh* benefited.

On the morning the installers came from the Ministry of Post, Telegraph and Telephone, I happened to be down in the *koocheh* on my way to the greengrocer's. I had to weave through a gaggle of neighbors who had poured into the street, talking animatedly as they watched the workers digging up the sidewalk.

"Are you getting a telephone, too?" I heard one portly man in his undershirt ask another.

"Yes, finally! I can't believe it," his neighbor answered, beaming. "What do you think happened?"

"I don't know, but somebody on this street has a donkey that moves."

When a person has the influence and connections to get a difficult job done, Iranians say *kharesh mire* – his donkey finds the way, meaning his donkey gets the job done. I quickly navigated past the gaggle of neighbors, hoping that none of them would ever suspect it was our donkey that had found the way.

Now Ali and Essie clearly need a donkey that could find the way, and fast. That's how things work. That was how Ladan was able to visit her husband when he was in prison—she used Ali's influence with the university chancellor who used his influence with who knows who to….

Prison. No, don't even think about prison. They are not going to prison.

Over the next few days in Zurich, Julie and I try to distract the nervous children, taking rides around town on the streetcars, nervously devouring the best French fries we had ever had, visiting a topless beach. We hadn't specifically planned to visit a topless beach, but somehow here I am, sitting glumly on the shore of Lake Zurich, feeling awkward and overdressed in my conservative one-piece bathing suit, a prudish refugee from the Islamic Republic of Iran. Samira and Sarah play half-heartedly at the shore. They are a bit puzzled by the topless ladies, but they ignore them. What they really don't understand is why we are having a day at the beach when their father is stuck in Iran. I have no answer for this.

Too exhausted to contemplate another long plane ride, and still hoping that Essie and Ali will join us soon, Julie and I decide to stay a few more days in Zurich. Julie contacts some Swiss friends, Gerhard and Frieda, a scientist, and his wife in their fifties, who live in a village just outside of town. Julie tells them our story, and they invite us to stay with them in a small town outside the city. For two days, the six of us are soothed by the ordered solidity of their household. They feed us and commiserate. Frieda takes us to the zoo, where we sit entranced watching the chimpanzees, and to the *Kunsthaus* where we see a retrospective of the work of Ernst Kirchner, a victim of another oppressive regime. Kirchner was a German artist whom the Nazis branded one of the "degenerates," an enemy of the state, a German version of *taghooti*. Unable to exhibit his work, he killed himself in 1938.

Reluctantly, we leave the sanctuary of Gehhard and Frieda's home and return to Zurich to make plans for a return to the States. Zurich stands in gleaming contrast to our messy lives. We are a disheveled, rag-tag bunch, the six of us, frazzled, rumpled, and often snappish. The normally outgoing Sarah is now as shy and quiet as her sister. Both are stoic, but when the hotel manager accidentally spills hot coffee on Samira's lap, she permits herself an angry, righteous crying jag. Crossing the street with my children, I almost walk in front of a tram.

Zurich, however, is orderly and spotless. Even its sidewalks are immaculate. On our last outing in the city, I watch from a streetcar window as a young woman walks barefoot for several blocks along the sidewalk. She boards our streetcar and sits down opposite us. When she crosses her legs, I see that her bare feet are still clean.

37

....

PAPER GAME

Tehran: July 29, 1980

While Ali and I were saying goodbye at Mehrabad Airport, Essie called his friend Hussain and asked for a ride to the Prime Minister's office. The letters given to them at the airport had directed them to the Prime Ministry's Office of Prohibited Exit. All the way there, they told each other that, surely, there must be some mistake, and the obvious error would soon be corrected.

After sitting in the car for an hour waiting for the building to open, they made their way to that office. They showed their letters to a receptionist who told them to wait in an adjoining room for Brother Tavakoli.[59] Ali and Essie had expected that, arriving so early, they would be the only people with such a problem, but when they entered the small, drab waiting room they were surprised to find it crowded with about twenty other petitioners sitting shoulder to shoulder on the government-issue metal chairs that lined the room. As they entered, a few of the men nodded at them in acknowledgement before returning to their conversations. Ali and Essie didn't know the others but gathered from their well-tailored suits and courtly demeanor that they were educated and wealthy.

---

59. In the egalitarian spirit of the revolution, officials of the Islamic Republic were often addressed as Brother or Sister, especially when they did not have an advanced degree or a title.

They found some seats and waited for a couple more hours until Brother Tavakoli finally arrived. He was a young man, tall and slim, with a short beard, who adhered to the standard Islamic Republic dress code: dark suit with a white, banded shirt collar, buttoned to the top. He didn't invite anyone into his private office. Instead, he made his way around the room, conducting each interview standing in front of the petitioner, well within earshot of everyone else. As he questioned each person, the others watched and listened attentively, anxious for some clue to their own predicaments. From their replies, Ali and Essie learned that among this sullen group were former members of the Majles (the Iranian parliament), former military officers, former factory owners, and other former big shots from the shah's regime. At the end of these encounters, each man left silently, eyes downcast, still not knowing why he wasn't allowed to leave the country.

Even as the crowded waiting room began to thin out, the atmosphere remained close and muggy. It was yet another hour before Brother Tavakoli made his way over to Ali and Essie. He stood in front of them, impassively reading the letters they handed to him. He was not impolite, but he was not respectful, either. He had the attitude of one who suspects that everyone else is a potential thief—that if you weren't guilty, you wouldn't be sitting there.

He took Ali and Essie's letters and asked for their identity card numbers and their parents' names. He disappeared into another room and returned a few minutes later, this time asking for their telephone numbers. Ali gave him our home number, since Essie's house did not yet have a telephone line.

"Go home. We'll call you."

When Ali and Essie protested that their families had left the country and they needed the issue resolved immediately, Brother

Tavakoli abruptly answered, "No, we can't do anything now. Just wait for our call."

In the early afternoon, Essie and Hussain dropped Ali off at our apartment. When Ali opened the door, he found his brother Reza and his wife Pouran. They had made the trip to Tehran a week ago to say goodbye to us and help us close up the house. Confident that we were all safely on our way to Zurich, they were in the midst of packing up to return to Kerman. They couldn't stand staying in the empty apartment without us, and were anxious to leave. One look at Ali's ashen face told them no one was going anywhere soon.

"What happened?" asked Reza.

Ali didn't answer. He just headed for the bathroom, doubled over in pain. In a fight or flight response to the day's stress, his stomach was conducting its own purging.

When he came back, he told them the story.

"What are you going to do?" asked Pouran, handing him a glass of very strong tea.

"First, I'm going to lie down," said Ali, emptying his pockets of coins and scraps of paper and dumping them in a pile beside the telephone. He rummaged in the storeroom for a pair of pajamas, changed his clothes and stretched out on the living room floor, weak and enervated. Unable to sleep more than a few minutes, he got up and went looking for the scraps of paper he had put next to the phone.

"I had a telephone number right here," he yelled. "Where is it?"

"I'll find it, I'll find it," Pouran said, racing into the storeroom and retrieving it from Ali's desk. Pouran had just been doing what she always did in response to stress—straightening up.

"Please, never touch my things," shouted Ali.

Pouran disappeared into the kitchen to make more tea.

The Prime Minister's office called at 6 p.m.

The man at the other end said, "We have received a letter from the *Komite ye Paksazi* [Purging Committee] that prevents you from leaving the country."

"Well, what does it say?"

"We can't tell you what the letter says."

"At least tell me who wrote the letter," demanded Ali.

"We can't tell you that either. But if you bring us a letter from the committee authorizing your release, you can leave the country."

Why would the university's Purging Committee want to make trouble for them? They hadn't done anything. They were respected members of the faculty.

Ali remembered that he knew one of the members of this committee, Dr. S., a university administrator he had known from his undergraduate days at the College of Agriculture in Karaj. If anyone could solve this mystery, he could.

38

LINES IN THE SAND

Tehran, July 30, - August 27, 1980

The next morning, Ali met Essie at the University, and they headed for Dr. S's office in the administration building. Essie and Ali's personalities had always complemented one another. When faced with conflict and bureaucratic machinations, Ali was often rebellious and easily upset; Essie's public vibe was non-combative, affable, and ingratiatingly respectful. That morning, they were behaving true to form.

Essie ambled into the office ahead of Ali, smiling, his hand outstretched.

"Salaam, Agha-ye Dr. S," Essie began. "We have met before. I am…."

"Of course I remember you, Dr. Meisami, Dr. Estilai," Dr. S. said, smiling as he got up from his desk to greet Ali and Essie.

Ali was in no mood for pleasantries. "Do you think you've found thieves or counter-revolutionaries?" he asked.

"What do you mean?" the man asked, clearly taken aback.

"The letter your committee wrote…the letter that's preventing us from leaving the country. Thanks to you, we're *mamnou'ol khoroudj*. Our families left the country yesterday, but we're stuck here."

"What's this nonsense?" the official replied. "We haven't written such a letter. Of course, after the revolution, we went through all the professors' files, and if we found a SAVAK agent or senators or ministers from the shah's era, we expelled them. But we certainly didn't write any letters about the two of you. If the university has two decent, distinguished professors, they're you two gentlemen. I advise you to find out who wrote that letter."

Leaving Dr. S's office, Ali and Essie stepped out into the bright summer sunlight, as much in the dark as when they had arrived.

"I think he's probably telling the truth," Ali said. "But the Prime Minister's office said they had a letter from the Purging Committee. If it's not the university's purging committee, then whose purging committee is it?"

"Let's go see Dr. K.," said Essie. "Maybe he knows something."

They walked across the campus to the Institute of Biochemistry and Biophysics, and made their way to the third-floor office of the director.

Dr. K. was an associate professor that Ali and others had hired three years before. At first, Dr. K. had sought to ingratiate himself with the IBB founders, inviting Lisa, Fereydoun, Ali, and other colleagues and their families to his ancestral home, a 45-minute plane ride from Tehran. Ali and I weren't able to accept his invitation, so we will never know how hospitable he might have been. However, after the revolution, his demeanor changed. His relationships with the founding faculty became decidedly chilly. With many of IBB's senior professors leaving the country, he soon became the director.

When Ali and Essie arrived at Dr. K.'s office, they found him polite but wary. They asked him if he knew anything about a letter from the Purging Committee.

"No, gentlemen" was the reply. "I know nothing about this."

"Then, may I use your phone?" asked Ali.

"Of course," Dr. K. replied, handing him the phone.

Ali dialed the number of the Prime Ministry. After several minutes, he found someone who would talk to him and explained the situation: he, Essie and Majid had been prevented from leaving the country; their families were allowed to leave; and the Prime Minister's office had a letter from a purging committee, but no one could or would tell them who wrote it or what it said.

Not really believing that he could get the information he needed over the phone, Ali braced himself for the usual bureaucratic dissembling. Instead, the man at the other end of the line was very forthcoming. "Yes, sir," he said, "I have your folder right here. However, this letter is not from the university's purging committee; it's from the Institute's purging committee."

"But the Institute doesn't have a purging committee," Ali answered, dumbfounded.

"Well, it appears it does. This letter was signed by several members of the Institute." While the man at the other end of the line read the list of names, Ali studied Dr. K.'s face. Two of the signers were Dr. K.'s graduate student and his staff research associate, and the chair of this purging committee was a research associate in the Faculty of Engineering who also happened to be the husband of Khanum S., herself a research associate in the Institute. The fourth signer was a professor in the College of Fine Arts.

Hanging up the phone, Ali looked at Dr. K. and said, "How can you plead ignorance about this? There's a purging committee in your own institute and you didn't know about it? Your own graduate student and research associate signed this letter, and you weren't aware of it?"

"I'm telling you, I never knew anything about such a letter," replied Dr. K.

"Well, when was this committee created?" asked Ali.

"I know nothing about any committee."

There was no point in sparring with Dr. K. The institute Ali had helped create was conspiring against him. He suddenly understood the gravity of those libelous, childishly scrawled messages posted on the Institute's walls.

Tehran: August 1, 1980

"*Parti nadari?*" Ali's sister Fatemeh asks. "Don't you know anyone?"

With the memorable exception of securing the neighborhood telephone lines, we had not played the *party bazi* game. But if ever there was a time for *party bazi,* family and friends reckoned it was now.

"You know some ministers, don't you?" asked his brother Reza.

He was thinking of the Minister of Agriculture and the Minister of Post, Telegraph and Telephone. Both were graduate students at UC Davis when Ali was there, and one had been Ali's roommate for a year. He and the agriculture minister had always been on good terms, although their worldviews and politics were vastly different. Ali explained that, right now, his problem was relatively small, but it could easily become a bigger problem if he were to involve these two government officials. He might face more scrutiny, and he would definitely be beholden to them.

Hoping that reason might win out, Ali, Majid and Essie strategized about meeting with members of the Institute's Purging

Committee. They knew who wrote the letter, but they still didn't know what they were being accused of. They decided to start with the chair of the committee, who agreed to meet them by the steps in front of the entrance to the Faculty of Science.

"Mohandes S.?" asked Essie, when they saw a lone figure approaching them.[60]

"Yes," he replied icily, clearly wishing to be elsewhere. "You wished to speak with me?"

"Yes," Essie replied, smiling in his usual genial manner, hoping to keep the discussion friendly. "We just learned that your committee has succeeded in getting us declared *mamnou'ol khourudj*. Would you please tell us why you have done this?"

Dispensing with the usual pleasantries, Mohandes S. picked up a stick lying on the ground and began to scratch a crude diagram in the dirt.

"Look, it's very simple," he said, gesturing to the dusty column of circles he had created. "Here's the shah," he said, pointing to the topmost circle. "And here is the empress. And below them are Lisa and Fereydoun Djavadi, then the Institute, and then all of you. All of you are *vaabasteh* (connected, dependent)."

Ali smiled and said, "May I have that stick? I'd like to draw a diagram for you."

He drew three circles. "This is the shah. This is Mohandes Riazi, your boss when he was the Dean of the College of Engineering. As you well know, he was also the speaker of the Majles, for fifteen years a trusted servant of the shah. And this is you," he said, pointing to the third circle. "Using your logic, I can say that you

---

60. *Mohandes* is an academic title bestowed on graduates of engineering, architecture, and agriculture programs.

are connected to the shah. However, this type of comparison is irrelevant," Ali continued. "We are university professors, academics. We don't have loyalties to the shah's regime."

For the last nine years, Ali had scrupulously steered clear of political involvement. True to his liberal sympathies, he had avoided showing support for the shah's regime, even when this avoidance might have aroused suspicion. After the shah dissolved the *Mellion* (Nationalists) and *Mardom* (People) parties in 1975 and created the *Rastakhiz e Melli* (National Resurgence) Party, the university administration encouraged professors to sign the party's membership roll book as a show of support. When the dean of the Faculty of Science, Dr. Sheybani, strolled through the corridors during his daily perambulations, he would buttonhole every passing professor and invite him to sign the book. Refusing to sign would have alerted the SAVAK. Instead, Ali avoided that side of the building for several months, until the membership roll was packed up and sent to the Prime Minister's office.

"Yes, you're all academics," countered Mohandes S., dismissing Ali's argument with a wave of his hand, "but you all benefited from that regime."

"What do you mean, *benefited*?" all three of them asked at once.

"For example, Dr. Estilai, when you went on sabbatical last year, you continued to receive your administrative bonus as deputy director of the Institute."

"What?" cried Ali. "Did you even research this? Two or three months before I went on sabbatical, I wrote a letter to the university saying that I would be on leave and asking them to discontinue my administrative bonus. When I returned from sabbatical, I found out the university was late in processing the letter and kept on depositing the bonus in my Tehran bank account for three months. When they realized their mistake, they withdrew the funds. I never saw a penny of that money."

"OK, but you and Dr. Meisami got interest-free loans from the Institute," said Mohandes S., angrily.

"And this definitely should be a point in our favor," said Ali, smiling. "Charging interest is forbidden in Islam." Mohandes S. was not amused.

Four years previously, Ali and I had bought our tiny *me'mar saz* apartment for 800,000 tomans, or about $115,000. The *Bank e Omran* was giving professors first-time-buyer loans of 600,000 tomans at seven per cent interest. But we, like a lot of young academics' families, needed another loan to bridge the gap. Fereydoun Djavadi organized an interest-free loan of up to 200,000 tomans for Ali, Essie, and Ashkan, our friend who had just been released from prison. We could have borrowed the full amount but instead took a loan of 150,000 tomans (about $22,000) and put in our own 50,000 tomans—all of our savings.

"That's right," Ali said. "During the last four years, the university regularly deducted the loan payments from our paychecks. I, personally, have repaid all but 44,000 tomans of that loan."

Undaunted, Mohandes S. played another card. Turning to Essie, he said, "Dr. Meisami, you imported mice from Israel for your research."

"You've got to be kidding," Essie said.

He wasn't. Those pesky Zionist mice just would not go away.

Ali, Essie, and Majid said they were deeply disappointed that they were never informed of these charges. The university had permitted them to leave, they argued, so this committee should not be trying to stop them.

Mohandes S. looked at them. For a moment, it seemed he had no more cards to play. Then he asked, "Are you ready to resign?"

They were taken aback at the abruptness of the question, but it took only seconds for all of them to make up their minds.

Yes, we'll resign.

"Good. If you give me your letters of resignation," S. said, "I'll be sure to get permission for you to leave the country."

So this is what the committee wanted. There were no real wrongs to redress, just a need to clean house, to purge the recalcitrant, to eradicate the logical, to dispense with the secular, to get rid of anyone who was not sufficiently Islamic.

Standing there outside the Faculty of Science, under the gaze of Mohandes S., Ali, Essie, and Majid silently took pieces of paper from their briefcases and wrote their letters of resignation.

Balancing his tablet on his knee, Ali wrote, "Since the university is no longer a place of research and teaching, and since my family is out of the country, I hereby submit my resignation from Tehran University."

They handed their letters to Mohandes S. and walked away.

39

FIRSTBORN

Zurich: August 6, 1980

I had spoken to Ali in the morning, only to hear yet again that he doesn't know when he'll get out of Iran. There is nothing more we can do in Zurich, so Julie and I decide to leave for the States. She and her girls are off to Berkeley; Samira, Sarah and I are heading for Maryland to stay with my sister Katie and her family in Silver Spring. I look forward to collapsing on Katie's couch, lazing on her back porch, luxuriating in the humid, lush green of her backyard. I want to hear the cicadas sing and the screen door slam shut as the children parade in and out in body paint and hats made of newsprint.

She will say, "Tell me again about your lentil soup. I love to hear about it."

She will tell me everything will be all right. She will distract me with sewing projects and trips to the Smithsonian. We will compare notes on a past we didn't share. You see, I didn't always have a sister—not until mid-March 1973, when I was four and a half months pregnant with Samira.

One afternoon, Ali picked me up from National University in the village of Evin, north of Tehran, to take me home for a late lunch. As he steered the car down the steep hillside, I busied myself opening the stack of mail he had brought along. One large manila envelope was from my father, who was constitutionally unable to put creases in letters he thinks are important. I tore it open and pulled out seven nearly margin-free lined pages filled with my father's angular handwriting. The letter was addressed to both of us. Skimming the first page eagerly, I caught random phrases: "this may shock you"...."an older sister"...."he was already married."

"My God, you're not going to believe this," I said to Ali.

"Read it to me," he said, negotiating the winding road.

Balancing Dad's letter on my pregnant stomach, I began to read out loud. I was unprepared for the words I heard coming out of my mouth. My father was telling me something that he himself had learned only ten days before he wrote the letter. He was telling me that in 1945, while he was serving in the U. S. Army in France, my mother fell in love with a Marine who was also a reporter for *The Washington Post.* Less than three months before my parents were married, my mother had given birth to a daughter whom she had given up for adoption. When the relationship began, she hadn't known that the child's father was already married. My father explained that, given the temper of both the times and my Italian grandparents, there was no way she could have kept a child born out of wedlock.

This other daughter, Katie Berg, had been searching for Mother for several months and finally found her address. She immediately contacted her, and they corresponded and talked on the phone for about two weeks before my mother broke the news to my father. Katie was now planning to visit my parents in California that summer.

"She is a lovely person," my father wrote, with characteristic openness and kindness. "She would like to write to you. She was raised as an only child and would now like to know her brother and sister."

My parents grew up in Ellwood City, Pennsylvania, a small steel mill town north of Pittsburgh. They went to the same high school, and my mother's best friend was my father's younger sister Shirley. Dad was voted the Best Boy Dancer and Best Dressed Boy of the Class of 1938. Mother, the county spelling champion, was voted Prettiest Girl and Dramatic Girl of the Class of 1939.

My parents became engaged in 1941. In October of that year, my father was drafted into the army and shipped to Camp Croft in South Carolina for basic training. Thinking that he would be in the service for only a year, they planned to get married after he was discharged. But less than six weeks later, the Japanese bombed Pearl Harbor, and Dad's battalion was shipped out to Iceland. From there, he was sent to England, then to France—part of the forces that invaded Normandy in June 1944. He spent the rest of 1944 slogging through the French hedgerows and establishing bridgeheads until he was wounded in January 1945 and transported back to England. When he had recovered, he rejoined his battalion in France as part of the Army of Occupation.

When he was finally discharged in July 1945, Dad went to see Mother in Washington, D.C., where she was still working at *The Washington Post*. Wearing loose fitting clothes to disguise her pregnancy, she told him that she didn't want to get married right away because she had been offered a job at a newspaper in California. She would work there for a while, and they would get married when she returned after Christmas.

Actually, she didn't go to California. Instead, she entered the Florence Crittenden Home for unwed mothers in Washington, D.C. The home arranged for Dad's letters to be sent to an address in Alameda, California, and then forwarded to her. Her letters to him were, in turn, first sent to Alameda where they were postmarked and forwarded to Ellwood City.

Because her job at *The Washington Post* paid only a subsistence wage, she needed to find a way to pay for her confinement at the Crittenden Home. She was too ashamed to go to her parents or friends. The only resources she had were the war bonds my father had bought and the $600 my father had managed to save working at the steel mill the summer before he was drafted. This money was safely tucked away in a joint account they had opened at the U. S. Postal Service before he shipped out. That $600 was exactly what she needed to pay the Crittenden Home; she took out the $600 and handed it over to the social worker.

On November 18, 1945, Mother gave birth to Katie, and six weeks later, on December 30, she gave her up for adoption. That same day, she took the train home to Ellwood City. The Best Dressed Boy and the Prettiest Girl celebrated New Year's Eve at the Elks Club and were married exactly one month later on February 1st.

The elaborate ruse was successful. For all those 28 years, my father never suspected anything—even when Mother said, "Oh, let's just leave that $600 in the postal account," even when she said, "I used that $600 when you were away at school in Kentucky." My father, the cock-eyed-optimist accountant, never audited his own operation. But when the deception was revealed, here he was, clearly elated to be sharing this news of a new family member with me.

As Ali and I made our way home, I felt lightheaded, giddy, displaced. The road leveled off, but my stomach hadn't. My first thought was that I was no longer the firstborn, no longer the only daughter, a status that somehow had made me feel secure all these years. Until I read my father's letter, I had no idea how tightly my self-image was bound up with my sense of an immutable position within my family. So often as a child, when I felt slighted by a parental decision or attitude favoring my younger brother, I was comforted by the knowledge that I was the only girl, the firstborn, my brother's opposite, and that, loved or unloved, I held a unique position. Now I had to re-evaluate and redefine that position.

"Well, that explains a lot," Ali said as he pulled into our garage.

I knew what he meant—my mother's moodiness, her fiery outbursts, her glacial silences. Mother's behavior had always seemed strange to Ali. What had become commonplace for me was, for my husband, far beyond the range of normal behavior. Perhaps some of her rage was the result of carrying the secret of Katie's birth for twenty-eight years.

I couldn't be by myself that afternoon. After Ali dropped me off at home and returned to work, I called up my friend Christa and went to her house, glad to be distracted by her clamoring children. Uncharacteristically, I didn't share my news. I hadn't really processed it yet.

Somewhere I had picked up that "firstborn-is-special" mythology. I'm sure my mother had told me that a woman always has a special feeling for her firstborn child. Well then, whom did she mean? How many firstborns can a woman have?

I tried to imagine how my mother must have felt all these years. My mind replayed so many conversations we had about sex, marriage, and children. I thought back to a summer at home from college when I smugly dismissed a neighbor's daughter, unmarried and pregnant, as stupid for not having the "good sense" to use birth control. What had my mother thought hearing this judgment?

I was now twenty-six and expecting my first child. What had my mother felt at twenty-four, having to give up her own first child? What had she felt when I was born? Had I been a replacement? This Katie was born November 18, 1945, and Mother had relinquished her six weeks later on December 30. Did that explain the gray cloud of anger and depression that hovered over my mother every year just before Thanksgiving and stayed beyond the holidays? Is that why Christmas at our house was always so joyless, why she never liked the gifts we gave her? This other first daughter's birthday was the same day as my childhood best friend's. Had my mother remembered that other birthday every year as I shopped for my friend's present, or had she successfully blocked it out?

Everything shifted off-center. Our entire past as a family had to be re-evaluated in the light of this new discovery. Not only did the introduction of Katie into our circle upset the delicate symmetry, it also caused me to question basic assumptions I had about my mother as a person, to see her as someone who existed apart from her role as my mother, someone with her own history, her own set of battles. Occasionally, as a small child, I experienced heavy flashes of recognition during which I clearly saw my mother as an individual entirely separate from me. But those moments were fleeting, and I quickly reattached my mother's existence to my own. Once again, she was detached from me by this revelation, a separate and distinct person with a private history.

Dad, however, seemed rejuvenated. "I love your mother more than ever," he wrote. "It's like living in a new world." He was proud that, after years of alcoholic binges, he had been sober "when she really needed me." After Mother told him about Katie, they talked day and night for three days. "It was probably the calmest conversation we ever had together," he said. It was also very likely the longest.

Theirs had been a dismal marriage. My father's affectionate advances were routinely rebuffed. To me, it had always seemed that their relationship was unbalanced, tilted in her favor. He pursued her; she retreated.

The overwhelming silences of our home life were broken most often by Mother's angry tirades, frequently directed at my father, whom she considered her intellectual inferior. The bleakness of their relationship suffused everything. Ours was a family of largely unconnected individuals. My parents, my younger brother and I pursued our own lives, each seeking a way out of our environment—my father through alcohol, my mother through mystery novels and solitaire, and my brother and I through fantasies of a bohemian life beyond suburbia. Although dependent on and answerable to one another, we lacked a positive sense of involvement in each other's lives.

While my father felt that this revelation had brought him and my mother closer, I felt left out—perhaps because it was my father and not my mother who told me the story. I wondered why my mother had not written that letter herself. After all, this Katie Berg was her child, her secret to reveal. Why did she abdicate this responsibility?

I remembered that August morning eighteen years before when I awoke to find my father home from work and my mother gone. Dad had explained that during the night, while I was asleep, he had left me in the care of a neighbor and taken Mother to the hospital, and I now had a baby brother. Suddenly I was eight years old again with the same anxious feelings: How could she have gone to the hospital without my knowing it? Why had they left me out of this important experience? I felt distanced from a momentous event that I had wanted to be part of. Now it seemed that my father had once again assumed the role he had eighteen years ago, that of announcing the birth of a sibling.

However, to Mother's enduring credit, once Katie contacted her, she no longer felt the need to keep this 28-year secret. Newly liberated, she immediately set about making plans to have Katie meet the entire family.

During the next few weeks, I wondered what my new sister was like. She didn't really have a face yet. I had a hazy image of a thin, dark, relentless young woman. I was curious but wary—until her letter arrived.

When Katie's pictures tumbled out of the envelope, I recognized her immediately. There were Mother's eyes, dark curly hair, and shy smile. There were also my long limbs and tendency to slouch. Family resemblance is irresistible. I no longer felt wary or displaced but connected, part of a new symmetry.

In the summer of 1974, Ali, Samira, and I traveled to Washington, D. C., where Katie lived with her husband John, and their two young children, Amy and Adam. We talked non-stop for two days.

Had we grown up together, Katie and I might have asserted our individuality by concentrating on our differences. Instead, we marveled at what we have in common. And there is so much we have in common: a love of learning languages, painting, literature, travel, a laissez-faire approach to housekeeping, exotic food, the dark candies in a bag of Kraft caramels.

In fact, talk of food seems to weave in and out of the most serious conversations. "Tell me again about your lentil soup," Katie will say. "I love to hear about it." My remark that her kitchen smells like Grandmother's will lead to questions about the grandparents she had never met and my anise-flavored, garlic-infused childhood summers with them. During our visits, we try out new recipes and discover new restaurants. Each special meal remembered adds to our common history. These shared meals are a way of finding who we are and forging a common past.

We are different though. As an adolescent, I used to spend hours dreaming of my favorite rock star or movie idol. I was fascinated to find out that Katie never wasted her time on these fantasies. Instead, she saw The *Wizard of Oz* forty-three times. I poured over

Teen Magazine; she collected all the Oz books.

Very soon after I met Katie, I began to delight in referring to my sister in conversation. These references became so natural that I never stopped to consider whether or not my listener already knew about my sister. "When I was at my sister's house…." "My sister's children…." "My sister and I…." It was a joy to be able to say these words.

Inevitably, the friend or in-law who heard this off-handed reference would say, "Sister? Wait a minute….I didn't know you have a sister." At this point, I had a choice of two responses: "Oh, really?" or "Neither did I." The decision between these two replies was crucial. My answer depended on a variety of factors: how well that person knew my family history, how sensitive I thought that person was, how much I felt he or she cared to know about me, and how much I felt I needed to explain.

If a friend asked, "Well, what's she like?" I knew I'd made the right decision.

It's very difficult to anticipate the reactions of friends to the story of my sister. Often people that I have assumed would be sophisticated enough to accept the news and be happy for me appear shocked, while those that I expected to be scandalized are pleasantly surprised. One such unexpected encounter occurred in the mid-seventies when Ali and I were in California visiting old college friends, a couple very much like ourselves—an Iranian Ph.D. married to an American teacher. The after-dinner conversation turned to our travel plans, and I mentioned that on the way back to Tehran, we would stop in Washington to visit my sister. Our Iranian friend looked puzzled and said, "I don't remember you ever saying anything about a sister. She wasn't at your wedding was she?"

Something made me want to take the "Oh, really" approach,

but Ali intervened. "It's a very interesting story," he said, looking at me expectantly. Dutifully taking his cue, I delivered my story, telling our friends that before my mother was married she had a child whom she had given up for adoption. As I explained how my sister had searched for and found us, I saw our friends' expression change from perfectly understandable surprise to discomfort. They were plainly sorry that they had asked.

Later, I tried to analyze what went wrong with that encounter. What reaction did I expect from these educated, worldly friends? Obviously, I had hoped for, if not unconditional acceptance, certainly an open mind regarding this new person in my life and the exciting possibilities inherent in this unique relationship. At the very least, I expected healthy curiosity. Instead, I got polite rejection.

By revealing my mother's story, I had violated a taboo. I had revealed an aspect of my mother's sexual history that normally would have remained private. In spite of or because of the fact that I was telling them how happy I was, my friends were embarrassed for me.

In the case of my in-laws, I had to risk stepping on all sorts of conventions and religious beliefs. I was concerned about how I would explain Katie to Ali's traditional Muslim family. At the same time, I knew I would never want to keep secret someone who had become so much a part of my life. I began referring to my new sister casually and frequently in conversation.

One day, when we were alone, my sister-in-law Naazi quietly and carefully remarked that she thought she heard me say that I didn't have any sisters. What was this about a sister? When I told her the story, she accepted it with that even calmness characteristic of Ali's family. I believe that she was genuinely happy for me. Naazi probably felt that every woman should have a sister. Or perhaps that very Iranian preoccupation with parentage and family made my sister's search and my acceptance of her so understandable. I think Ali's family had always felt I was bereft having only one brother. Naazi, who had grown up with four brothers and two sisters, who had seven children of her own, could certainly understand and share my joy in this new connection.

By telling Naazi, I didn't really have to tell the story again because she took care of telling the rest of the family. As it turned out, no one in the family seemed shocked. The Estilais proved to be far worldlier than some of my university-educated friends in the States.

Ellen (left) and her sister Kate Berg in Chevy Chase, Maryland, circa 1976.

40

BAREFOOT IN SILVER SPRING

Silver Spring, Maryland: August 1980

"Are you trying to find out if Daddy is dead?" asked Samira. Her toast and orange juice sat untouched as she studied me across the breakfast table, taking the measure of my mood as I quickly searched *The Washington Post* for stories about Iran. I had never before heard that irony in her voice.

"Daddy is not going to die," I said firmly as I put down the paper and looked at her, hunched in her chair, her pale, pinched face revealing all the stomach-churning anxiety I had been trying to hide.

She seemed, just then, much older than her seven years. It was about six years too soon for that sardonic half-smile and mordant humor. She shouldn't have had those dark circles under her eyes, either.

We all had dark circles under our eyes when we arrived at John and Katie's three nights before. Katie had been appalled at how thin I had become—thin and brittle and strung out. It was a relief to collapse and be taken care of, but there was no respite from our worries.

Samira, Sarah, and I had talked briefly with Ali two days before, but he still had no idea when he would be able to get out of Iran. He had spoken with Katie and asked her to take Samira shopping for a birthday gift from him.

At the toy store, Samira surveyed the Barbie dolls but was unmoved. She opted instead for a cuddly, round, red-haired baby doll with bodily functions. When it drank, little orange dots appeared on its diaper. We got Sarah a doll, as well. Her favorite one, inadvertently packed away in a storeroom, was, like her father, stuck in our apartment in Tehran.

The previous day, we cobbled together a birthday party for Samira, a week late. It was much more subdued than the raucous double birthday celebration for Julie and Samira that we had planned to have on our arrival in Zurich, but it was a welcome respite from the constant rehashing of the events of that awful morning at Mehrabad airport. Katie made sure there were paper hats for all the children and a homemade chocolate cake. We forgot to take photos, perhaps because no one really wanted to record our grim attempts at celebrating.

The news from Iran was also disheartening. In addition to the 24/7 coverage of the hostage crisis, the American newspapers were reporting executions of Iranians accused of conspiring to overthrow the revolutionary government.

In Washington, American on-lookers pelted pro-Khomeini Iranian demonstrators with eggs and soda bottles in front of the White House. With all this anti-Iranian feeling, I began to feel unsafe and conspicuous. One day, when Katie and I took the children on an outing in the city, I asked her, "Do you think people can tell we're Iranian?"

"No," she said, laughing, "but listen to yourself."

"What?"

"The children are Iranian, not you. Remember?"

Then why did I feel Iranian?

By late August, the novelty of being back in the States had begun to wear off. I had started to smoke again just before we left Tehran, and now I was bumming cigarettes from the pack John left on the mantle. Like people who don't count the calories consumed while they eat standing over the sink, I had convinced myself I wasn't really a smoker if I didn't actually buy the cigarettes. One day, I oafishly took the last one. My disappointed but gracious brother-in-law said nothing when he came home from work and discovered the empty pack on the mantle.

I craved American comfort food, and I ate it nervously. When John and Katie went out to celebrate their 10th anniversary, I made a large macaroni and cheese casserole for the four children and me, and I ate half of it.

I knew we couldn't stay at John and Katie's forever, no matter how generous and patient they were. Ali was still in the dark about his situation, so it might be months before he could join us. Katie and I talked about my next step. Should I enroll the children in school? Should I be looking for a job? If so, what kind of job? Should I take the civil service exam? Where should I look for an apartment and how would I pay for it? What if I have to sign a lease? What should I do about winter clothes for the children? And where would Ali want to live? That is, if he ever got out of Iran.

When Ali was able to call us again, we decided it would be easier for him to find a job in California, where he had more contacts. He was hoping to find work at UC Davis. Perhaps his major professor could help. He was also concerned about putting too much financial pressure on John and Katie. "Go to California and wait for me there," he said. The next day, I let my parents know that the girls and I would be coming to stay with them.

On August 27, the day I left Silver Spring for Claremont, Ali wrote:

I do not think a thing like this was necessary for me to realize how much I love my beautiful wife and two children. My dear Ellen, my love, my wife, my friend, I know that we may have hard days ahead of us, but I am ready to do everything just to be with you and the children. I also know that we are going to make it in spite of all the difficulties that one may foresee. Do not worry and start the new life with hope and enthusiasm. Get yourself and the children started and I promise to be with all of you soon. I know you have had a rotten deal these days and I do not know what to write to make you happy. The only thing I can say is that with the power of love there should not be any problem you and I cannot solve. We owe it to our children, and for their sake too we are going to be as strong as ever.

41

A DEPARTURE NOT
FORBIDDEN, ALMOST

Tehran: August 1980

The day after they handed Mohandes S. their hastily scrawled resignation letters, Ali, Essie, and Majid went to see Dr. Arefi, the chancellor of the university, to get his official acceptance. Actually, they mostly saw the back of his head. For the greater part of their meeting, he stood staring out the window with his back to them. Arefi, who was also Ayatollah Khomeini's cardiologist, had little sympathy for their plight. His main concern was to purge the university of liberal professors.

"After you settle your affairs with the institute, I will accept your resignations."

Ali opened a bank account for the loan repayment, which was to be funded by the rental of our apartment. His brother Reza, who had power of attorney, would give Ali's research assistant the money to make the monthly payments to the university.

A few days after Ali, Essie and Majid received formal acceptance of their resignations, the IBB Purging Committee wrote to the National Purging and Healing Committee informing them that, "in view of the complete settlement of the accounts" of the three professors, "it is declared that their departure is not forbidden."

Ali and Essie took that letter to the National Purging and

Healing Committee. They needed that office to write a letter to the Prime Minister's Office. They found a willing official who immediately wrote a letter to Brother Tavakoli saying that their departure was no longer a problem, that "the exit of [the three professors] has been deemed to be without hindrance. Therefore, it is requested that you will order the necessary action with respect to the lifting of [their] exit prohibitions." He signed it, sealed it in an envelope, and handed it to Ali and Essie.

With the ink barely dry and buoyed by a newfound confidence, Ali and Essie immediately set off to deliver the letter to Brother Tavakoli. "This is going well," said Essie, beaming with relief. "We'll drop off the letter, then get some chelo kebab. Tonight, we'll call our wives and tell them we'll be seeing them soon.

They found Brother Tavakoli in his office and handed him the envelope, sure that this nightmare was almost over. Tavokoli read the letter and, without saying a word, tore it into small pieces. Ali and Essie watched as their only copy of the letter cascaded into the wastebasket.

"What are you doing?" cried Ali.

"This letter is no good," said Tavakoli. "The gentleman who signed this just called to say that his office no longer has the authority to issue such a letter. The authorizing legislation expired three days ago, so you'll have to wait until the Majles reauthorizes them."

"How long will that take?" asked Essie.

Brother Tavakoli shrugged. "Weeks, months…the Majles is in recess. Who knows when they'll get around to it?"

Even Essie couldn't hide his disappointment behind a sunny smile. There was no point in arguing with Brother Tavakoli. Exhausted, they left his office and went to Essie's house in Karaj to recuperate, regroup, and plan their next strategy. But they didn't know what to do next. They had explored all possible avenues of redress. For now there was nothing that could be done.

42

······················

A DIFFICULT DAY, A STRANGE AFFAIR, A CHAOTIC WORLD

Haraz Road: Late August, 1980

"You're going on a trip?…Now?"

Ali could hear that familiar, impatient edge in my voice. He had called me at my parents' house in Claremont to tell me that he was taking a respite from his paper games to go to the north of Iran with Farrokh, an old friend from UC Davis.

"Why now? What's happening with your exit permit?"

"For now, I've done everything I can," he answered. He didn't tell me it might be "weeks, months, who knows?" before he could get permission to leave.

He knew that a road trip with a college pal might sound to me like a frivolous waste of valuable time, but he had to get out of Tehran. After more than a month of shuttling from office to office, from one unsympathetic functionary to another, with no results, Farrokh insisted he take a break.

"You look awful," Farrokh told him. With a candor former roommates allow each other, he surveyed Ali's gaunt face, ashen skin, and bloodshot eyes and announced, "You're coming with me to Gorgan."

Farrokh's mother and most of his seven siblings lived in Gorgan, a town about 250 miles northeast of Tehran, near the Caspian Sea. With its mild climate and lush forests, Gorgan promised a welcome respite from both the steamy oppressiveness of Tehran and the cold intimidation of its bureaucracy. Not having the energy to *taarof*, Ali went home to pack his suitcase.

Of course, I knew that Ali needed this trip. We had visited Farrokh's family a few years before, and I was enchanted by their gracious, seemingly effortless hospitality, the after-lunch naps on cool, pristine sheets followed by languid afternoons with tea and fruit on sun-filled terraces, the easy banter of siblings at elaborate lunches and dinners, all masterfully orchestrated by Farrokh's mother.

The two friends took off in Farrokh's car and headed for Gorgan via the Haraz Road, a major route from Tehran to the Caspian Sea region. With Mount Damavand looming in the distance, they navigated the narrow, winding road along the Haraz River, through the barren landscape of spectacular craggy rock formations and dizzying views of deep gorges.

However, Ali was too preoccupied to notice the scenery. He was remembering all the times he had traveled to the north as a high school student, undergraduate, university researcher, husband, and father. His thoughts turned to his first trip, when, as a fifteen-year-old, he was chosen to go to the Caspian resort of Raamsar, to attend a summer camp for the top students in each province. He remembered his youthful optimism, his pride in representing Kerman, and his unshaking faith that if he just worked hard enough he could do anything, be anything...even a professor at the University of Tehran.

He was never one to wax dramatic, but now Ali allowed himself some maudlin flights of fancy as he played each scene of the last month's travails over and over in his head. He imagined never being able to leave, never again being able to see the children or me. He pictured us moving on in America without him.

Fortunately, Farrokh was the perfect traveling companion to distract him. Tall and lanky with a casual elegance, he exuded an easy confidence. Farrokh had always been unflappable. Years ago, in Davis, Ali tried to teach me to drive. He started with the basics: you can't go faster than the car in front of you. My first lesson ended when I made a too-sharp turn into our alley and went faster than the neighbor's fence in front of me, taking out a few redwood planks. I was certain I was unteachable. As Ali and Farrokh helped me repair the fence, I despaired of ever learning to drive.

"Of course you can learn to drive," Farrokh said. "I'll teach you."

On the day of my lesson, he lounged in the passenger seat, nursing an extra-large Coke while I issued a stream of caveats about my ineptitude.

"Just turn on the ignition," he said.

"You're sure you're not afraid to be driving with me?"

"Just GO!"

Now, as Farrokh navigated this dangerous road, he provided Ali with that same sense of confidence and equilibrium. Each time his anxious guest veered near the precipice of despair and self-pity, each time he looked down into the gaping maw of What-If, Farrokh's quick, incisive wit and infectious laughter drew him back from the brink.

For the seven-hour journey, Farrokh had stocked the car with tapes of classical Persian poetry sung by popular Iranian singers. Ali played one of these tapes over and over, a *ghazal* by the fourteenth century Persian poet Hafiz that speaks of change and loss. In it, the poet laments his falling out of favor and the pain of separation from his beloved. He asks the wine bearer to bring him wine to soothe his pain. When he asks a "clever person" if he sees what's going on, the response is, "a difficult day, a strange affair, a chaotic world." In other words, live with it. "In this earthly world, there is no human being" Hafiz said, no genuine person, no helper. "Another world must be constructed, and anew, a human being." The poet concludes by saying that Hafiz's tears are worth nothing in terms of the richness of love, "because in this sea of love, all seven seas are but a dewdrop."

Change was all around. People that Ali had expected to behave humanely had disappointed him: students conspired against professors; professors turned a blind eye to the slandering of colleagues; old friends supplanted solidarity with suspicion. Pure science was displaced by dogma.

Ali was not just separated from the children and me. He was also cut adrift from his life's work, from the institute he had helped create, from a future he had envisioned for himself, a future in service to his country. It was not his country anymore.

43

....

PURIFICATION AND HEALING

Tehran: September 15, 1980

Fresh from his restorative sojourn in Gorgon, Ali returned to Tehran determined to make something happen. He and Essie knew that it was ridiculous to sit around waiting for the government to enact new authorizing legislation for the country's Purging and Healing Committee. Nothing in Iran ever got done waiting for the government to do it. (Installing our telephone line was a prime example.) So while Ali was gone, Essie had been using his affable charm to arrange a meeting with one of the members of the IBB Purging Committee, Professor Ayatollahi in the Faculty of Fine Arts. If the national committee couldn't act, perhaps this man had the influence to make it happen. By all accounts, he seemed not only well connected but someone they could talk to. At least it was worth a try.

Ali and Essie met Dr. Ayatollahi at his office. After the usual pleasantries, Essie recounted their story: their lack of guilt; their willingness to resign; their separation from their families. Dr. Ayatollahi, sitting behind his desk, listened intently, nodding sympathetically from time to time. Clearly, he wanted to have this issue resolved. When Essie had finished, Ayatollahi took his pen and scrawled a note on a university memo pad to the National Office of Purging and Healing. It read:

In the name of God

Brother Mirzaee,

Since the purging group of IBB has studied the files of the gentlemen Ali Estilai, Esmaeel Meisami and Majid Tehrani and has cast its verdict, therefore, please cause a letter to be written to Mehrabad [airport] and nullify their prohibited departure. I thank you.

Habibollah Ayatollahi

Ali and Essie immediately took this letter to the National Purging & Healing committee, but the person they talked to refused to write a letter to the Prime Minister's office because he didn't have the authorization from the Majles. "It cannot be done," he said. "You'll have to wait."

They raced back to Ayatollahi's office and told him his letter didn't work. They needed more than just *party-bazi*, they needed a justification, a loophole, a clever, elegant detour. Ayatollahi thought for a few minutes and then, without saying anything, he began writing.

"In the Name of God

Respectfully, the decision of the purging group of the Research Institute of Biochemistry and Biophysics (IBB) regarding the lifting of the prohibited departure of gentlemen Dr. Meisami, Dr. Estilai, and Dr. Tehrani, was made before the expiration of the authority of the purging group. It is therefore fitting that by any means their prohibited departure from Iran be lifted.

Also, since their wives and children are waiting for them outside the country, it is not deemed advisable to keep them waiting any longer.

That's it.

God be with you."

That was it. But was that it?

September 2, 1980

The next day, Ali and Essie took professor Ayatollahi's letter to yet another Ayatollahi, (perhaps a relative of the one at the university) at the National Group for the Purging and Healing of Departments. He gave them a letter to take to Brother Tavakoli at the Prime Minister's Office saying that the letters of Ayatollahis #1 and #2 regarding the "nullification of the prohibited exit status... are sent to you for any appropriate action."

That's it.

Tehran: September 10, 1980

Ten days after their meeting with Dr. Arefi, the university chancellor, Ali, Essie, and Majid drove to the Institute to pick up the letters accepting their resignations. They also received copies of the original letter written by the IBB Purification and Healing Committee asking that the three professors be prevented from leaving the country until they could be properly investigated. This was the first time that they saw a formal statement of the accusations against them: connections to the previous regime and financial corruption, specifically unpaid no-interest loans.

That letter was dated June 4, 1980—almost two months before that awful day in the airport. For two months, the three professors had worked side by side with three members of the Institute's purging committee, all of whom knew that they were under investigation but did not see fit to tell them. They knew that Ali and Essie were planning to leave the country and would be stopped at the airport, in front of their families, and be turned back, and they let that happen.

And how much investigating of the three professors went on during that time? Precious little, very likely. Their only connection to the previous regime was that they worked with Liza and Fereydoun Djavadi; their "financial corruption" was the loans that were common knowledge in the Institute. The committee didn't come up with any other wrongdoing because there was nothing to uncover, and they knew that. They simply wanted to discredit them, and force them to resign.

"Your resignation from the university position of full-time associate professor is accepted," Chancellor Arefi wrote to each of them. "Your employment with Tehran University is terminated and you will have no further position with the university."

This was the university where Ali had dreamed of teaching, where he had worked sixteen-hour days to help build the Institute into a first-class research facility, the likes of which the university had never seen.

No further position. With one antiseptic letter, it was all over. There was no "thank you for your nine years of exemplary teaching and research," no "thank you for helping create the Institute of Biochemistry and Biophysics," no "thank you for mentoring your graduate students," no "thank you for your groundbreaking high school textbook," and no "thank you for your part in revolutionizing the way the biological sciences are taught in Iran."

Ali wasn't the kind of revolutionary they were looking for. He pocketed his letter and headed for home, happy that at least now he could rejoin his family

September 11, 1980

Ali and Essie's travel documents had been sent to the Passport Department, where they had been held captive since that day in July when they were prevented from leaving with us. It took them more than half a day of cajoling to get the passports released. Ali and Essie then went to the Swiss Embassy to renew their expired visas. They remembered that July day, more than two months before, when the four of us waited in the embassy's courtyard, thinking that the hot sun and the jostling crowd of visa seekers would be our greatest inconvenience.

The congenially world-weary embassy official with whom we had first met was nowhere to be found. The woman who took his place that day had never met Ali and Essie and had no knowledge of their cases. She looked at their passports and quickly handed them back.

"Your visas are expired," she said.

"We know. That's why we're here," said Essie. "We'd like to get new ones."

"No, I'm sorry," she replied. "I can't give you new visas."

Ali and Essie were frantic. "It's not our fault. We couldn't use the old ones," Essie explained. "Our government put a hold on our passports."

"Sorry, we're not issuing visas at this time."

"Can't you just extend the old ones?"

"Sorry. You can try again in a few weeks."

"Come on," Ali shouted. "You mean to tell us we've spent over two months cutting through Iranian red tape only to be stopped by the Swiss?"

One of the official's colleagues heard Ali and Essie's loud protests and came out of her office to investigate. "Oh, I remember these gentlemen," she said. "They were here with their American wives." She took their passports and a few minutes later returned with their visas.

September 15

With visas in hand, Ali and Essie set off to buy new tickets to Bern. They gave their passports to the travel agent, who would in turn send them to the airport police. The airport police would call them if any problem arose. However, since Ali was leaving the next day, he didn't have time or strength or patience for any more problems to arise, so he and Essie drove to Mehrabad Airport to speak with the police officer in charge. He checked their papers carefully and politely assured them that everything was in order.

September 16, 1980

On the afternoon before Ali's departure, about twenty friends and family members crowded into our apartment to say goodbye. Around five or six p.m. the same airport police officer called.

"Agha-ye Doctor Estilai, it seems you are *mamnou'ol khoruj*."

Ali froze. "What do you mean? We were just there a few hours ago and you told us everything is OK"

"I'm sorry sir. I can't say anything. If you want to know more, you'll have to come to the airport."

"But we have official letters…."

"I'm sorry, that's all I can say."

Ali's sister Fatemeh was watching him carefully during this conversation, seeing his face turn from ashen to red to yellow. When he hung up the phone, she lit a cigarette and brought it to him, but he waved it away. "I've gone almost two years without a cigarette, and I'm not going to let these bastards ruin that, too."

When he could breathe normally, he called Essie, who was still in his office at the university collecting his things for his own departure two days later. He immediately rushed to our apartment and the two of them drove to the airport and stormed into the police station, all the while thinking how they were going to tell their wives that they were once again *mamnou'ol khorouj*. The officer on duty directed them to another office where a bearded man in a gray suit was sitting behind a desk. He looked at the two red-faced men and nodded.

"Hello, sir, I'm Ali Es...."

"Estilai, yes I know," the man said. "Actually, there is no problem. You can leave. You both can leave."

"But what happened?" asked Ali.

The man just shrugged and smiled, as if to say, *what does it matter? You can go. Don't push it.*

When Ali and Essie went back to the police station, the officer didn't have any explanation either.

"Agha, my flight is leaving in six hours," said Ali. "Please give me my passport. I'd feel better if I had it with me."

"I'm really sorry, sir," replied the officer. "I understand, but I can't do that. But look here," he said, opening a drawer beneath the counter, "your passport will be right here. You can tell the night shift officer where it is."

Could it really be that easy? You just open a drawer, take out the passport, and I'm on my way?

Is that it?

44

....

WHAT ARE *YOU* DOING HERE?

JFK Airport: October 7, 1980

By the time Ali finally reached JFK Airport, it had been seventy days since he last saw the girls and me—seventy days of uncertainty, hope, rejection, anticipation, despair, and humiliation. Especially humiliation. His dream of being a professor at the university he loved was extinguished forever. Everything he had worked for those last nine years was gone, along with his good name. If he hadn't persevered; if he had been just a little less tenacious, a little more despondent; if the Swiss embassy official hadn't remembered them and issued the visas; if Essie hadn't been so relentlessly optimistic and enlisted the aid of Ayatollahi #1; if Ayatollahi #1 hadn't found that loophole, and if the Iraqis had bombed Mehrabad Airport sooner, he and Essie might never have made it out of Iran. Ali left Tehran in mid-September, less than a week before the Iraqi attack on the airport that triggered an eight-year war. Essie got out a few days later, just ahead of the Iraqi fighter jets.

Ali arrived in Zurich and waited for Essie. When they reunited, they went to the U. S. Embassy in Bern to apply for permanent residency; the paperwork that Julie and I had begun was waiting for them. However, because it would take two weeks for their visas to be processed, and they were almost out of money, they took a train to Bremerhaven, Germany, to stay with Essie's niece and her husband.

When at last he arrived at JFK with his visa, Ali still faced uncertainty. He knew the immigration officers at JFK could still deny him entrance. He had become used to last-minute setbacks, and it wasn't until they stamped his passport that he began to relax just a little. Now, after being fingerprinted and interviewed at immigration, he had just one more hurdle, the baggage check at customs. As he lifted his luggage onto the counter, the customs officer, a middle-aged woman, took one look at his Iranian passport and said, "What are *you* doing here?"

"I have come to reside," he answered.

It was a stilted, formal response to a mean, churlish question. I know what Ali's voice sounds like when he is confronted with overbearing bureaucratic authority—or even just the security guard at the entrance to a gated community. I can hear the words emerging faint and dry from his throat, slowly and deliberately, each syllable receiving equal weight.

The customs officer was unimpressed with his elegant word choice. After all, the American hostages had been "residing" in Tehran for 339 days. Ali watched as she slowly and methodically inspected every item in his bags. She was so meticulous in her search that Ali was sure he would miss his connecting flight to Los Angeles. He hadn't fought so hard to get back to his family just to be foiled at the last minute by one woman's prejudice.

"Open this one," she barked. "OK, now that one." Rummaging through his collection of Persian classical music tapes, she said, "You *know* you can't bring these into the country, *don't you*?"

"No, I didn't know that," he answered, "but if you have to take them, go ahead."

The inspection was dragging on for so long that the woman's supervisor, who had been quietly observing from a distance, came over and stood behind her. "What's the problem?" he asked her.

Eager to be done with his inquisitor, Ali didn't wait for her explanation. "Look, I understand how you feel," he said to the woman, "but it's not my fault they took the hostages. I'm running away from that system, myself. I just want to rejoin my family."

With that, the customs officer softened. She put the music tapes back in Ali's bag and waved him on. Because he had borne the brunt of her ill humor, the Iranian woman and young girl who were next in line had a much easier time of it.

After translating for them at customs, Ali shared a taxi with the woman and her daughter to catch his connecting flight at a distant terminal. When the little girl asked her mother a question, the taxi driver turned to Ali and asked, "What language is that?"

"It's a language you probably don't want to hear these days," he responded. "It's Persian."

"Persian?"

"Yes, we're from Iran."

"Eye-ran? Hey, I don't give a shit," the driver said, with a philosophical pragmatism shared by taxi drivers the world over. "You wanted a taxi. I was available. Your money's as good as anyone else's."

I don't give a shit was hardly the welcome he had envisioned, but for the time being, it would have to do.

PART VI: When Was the Last Time You Were in Iran?

45

MEHRABAD, AGAIN

Tehran: March 16, 2006

It's one a.m., and we are due to land at Mehrabad Airport in about thirty minutes. The four of us, Ali, Samira, Sarah, and I, left Los Angeles nearly twenty-four hours ago, eight of those spent in the surreal neon and steel limbo of Frankfurt International Airport, alternately nodding off on each other's shoulders and jerking awake in the noisy departure lounge.

We sleep fitfully on the six-hour Lufthansa flight from Frankfurt and awaken to the rustle of our fellow passengers preparing for landing as the pilot announces that, in the Islamic Republic of Iran, women must observe the Islamic dress code. We, like most of the passengers on this flight, have timed our journey to coincide with Nowruz, the Iranian New Year, which is four days away. Too bad we couldn't time the hour of our arrival. With so few international flights to Tehran, we have no choice but to arrive in the dead of night.

The four of us have celebrated the last twenty-five Iranian New Years in California, first in Bakersfield, then in Riverside, sprouting our wheat, dying our eggs, taking photos around the traditional *haft sin* table laid with coins, dried jujubes, garlic, vinegar, wheat germ pudding, apples, dried sumac berries, sprouted wheat, and fresh herbs—things that begin with *sin*, which corresponds to the letter S in English. We would gather on the first day of spring at whatever time the vernal equinox occurred that year—at ten at night or five in the afternoon or 3:47 in the morning. We would turn on the Los Angeles Iranian television station and wait for the countdown. We would help jam the phone lines to Iran, calling our relatives in Kerman and Tehran with Nowruz wishes, saying *yes, ensha'allah, perhaps next year we will be there.…yes, we will try.… yes, we miss you, too.*

We did miss them. Our own Nowruz celebrations were bittersweet. Sure, we stocked up on Iranian pastries from the bakeries in Tehrangeles or Orange County. I made *sabzi polow ba mahi*, the traditional herbed pilaf served with fish. But there was no massive *khooneh takooni*—literally the shaking of the house—that month-long cleaning marathon in which the entire country turns itself inside out and back again, banishing winter's sooty, grimy bleakness. No *chahar shanbe soori*, jumping over burning sagebrush on the last Tuesday night of the year, exchanging one's winter sallowness for the fire's red glow. No two-week holiday with *deed o baz deed*, visiting and being visited in return. No daily round of lunches and dinners, no picnics in the country beside a running stream on *sizdah be dar*, the thirteenth day of the new year, when it's bad luck to stay indoors.

It's too late to worry about bad luck.

The last time the girls and I were in Mehrabad Airport was almost twenty-six years ago, on Samira's birthday, when we left Ali behind. For far too many years after that fiasco, Samira's birthday would include an annual reminiscence of the worst day of our lives in the worst year of our lives—of how scared we were, of how long it took to be reunited. For a long time, the pain of that story was immediate and real. It became our family legend, to be recited annually, until these recitations faded into a kind of shorthand and finally into no words at all. Gradually, it dawned on us that it was unfair to Samira to have these memories play any role in her celebration, so we put those thoughts aside and let her have her day, unencumbered by the weight of that sadness, disappointment, and fear. But we did not forget any of it. And now, the weight has become immediate and real again.

As our plane begins its descent, I watch the Iranian women as they prepare for landing, fishing headscarves out of their purses, stealing glances at their tired, sallow faces in tiny mirrors. They survey their sleep-smudged mascara and faded lipstick but make no move to reapply it. I've heard that the authorities no longer make women wipe off their make-up, but perhaps these women don't want to tempt fate. It seems they are making a choice between looking their best for their awaiting loved ones and preventing the ire of the passport and customs agents. The women adjust their scarves and wait.

I pay particular attention to the headscarves—whether they are sheer or heavy, if they are draped casually or knotted firmly under the chin so that no wisp of hair is visible. I'm trying to gauge how repressive the Islamic Republic might be by how tightly the scarves are tied. I've been following this tightening and loosening and tightening again from a safe distance for twenty-six years now. It's a complicated dance, one step forward, two steps back, just enough room to spin before being knocked off balance again. I follow the reports in the Western press and the stories of friends and relatives just returned from Iran; grandmothers, my seventy-something sister-in-law Naazi among them, accosted by the Morality Police and chastened for allowing their scarves to slip too far back on their white hair; young women made to scrub off their make-up or arrested for wearing sunglasses.

My current image of proper hijab comes from a photo hanging above our piano that Ali took in 1993 when, after a thirteen-year absence, he went back to Iran by himself for a scientific conference. In that photo, twenty-four family members are standing in the mid-September heat of his sister Fatemeh's garden in Kerman. Some of the men are in shirtsleeves, their collars open. Others are wearing suits, their jackets unbuttoned. The men are, of course, tieless, because to wear a tie in the Islamic Republic is to invite accusations that one is not only un-Islamic but also *gharbzadeh*.[61] But it's the women that I marvel at. In that oppressive heat, they are wearing long, heavy, loose-fitting raincoats with big shoulder pads. Some have generous scarves; others, because they have just come from work, wear the *magna'eh*, that handy wimple that doesn't slip and slide like a scarf. One little girl stares out from the center of the picture; she's the only female not wearing hijab because she is not yet nine years old.

That little girl is Nina, the daughter of Minoo and Mansour, Ali's niece and nephew. Twelve years after that photo was taken, Nina and her family visited us in Riverside. They came from Canada, where they had been living for the last few years, to spend the Christmas holidays. This meant that every Estilai within driving distance spent that Christmas at our house. That holiday was an extended slumber party, with fourteen people in our small home occupying every available bed, pullout couch and air mattress spread out over our three bedrooms, study, dressing room, living room and family room.

And of course, there was much discussion about the family and

---

61. One professional group routinely ignores this convention; Iranians say that one way to recognize a physician is by his tie.

that photograph hanging above the piano.

"You know," Minoo said, "Nobody is wearing big, bulky coats like that anymore. You really shouldn't let hijab stop you from visiting Iran."

"OK, fine," I said, "but it's hard to find the time. There's so much going on at work. I'm not sure Samira and Sarah can get that much vacation. And our Iranian passports have expired. It's so difficult to renew them. And then of course, there are all the gifts we'd have to take. I have no idea what anyone wants."

Minoo has little patience with procrastination and wimpy excuses. Like her mother, Pouran, she is a single-minded go-getter who leaves little to chance. Years later, while visiting her brother's family in Northern California, she would make the toilet training of her twin niece and nephew her primary mission. Like the twins' aversion to their potty chairs, she felt our ambivalence about visiting Iran had gone on long enough. She'd had it with our vacillations. *Get off the pot. It's safe to go back. The Iran-Iraq war has been over for seventeen years. People need to see you. They need to see your daughters. Your daughters need to see them. You need to go back.*

She and Mansour downloaded the necessary forms from the web site of the Islamic Republic's Iranian Interest Section, housed in the Pakistani Embassy in Washington, D.C. So that his uncle wouldn't procrastinate further, Mansour started filling out the forms and made sure Ali completed them.

Minoo marched us down to Costco and supervised the taking of photos for our Iranian passport applications. We owned no headscarves, so the girls and I used the black wool shawl with red cabbage roses that Ali brought back from his trip to the Soviet Union in 1979. Since we couldn't be sure of the official position on makeup, we decided it was safer to skip the lipstick and mascara. Samira and Sarah had youth on their side, but the photo of my pinched, pale, tired, foreign-looking face was the worse for that decision.

It took eight hundred dollars and nine months to obtain all the necessary documents for the four of us. (My passport took six months longer than the rest of the family's, very likely because I was the only naturalized Iranian citizen.) This long wait provided more than enough time to find the appropriate hijab for our trip. Samira ordered three identical, voluminous ankle-length coats from Nordstrom, which were quickly vetoed by her cousin Manijeh.

"These are too bulky," she said. "You want to be stylish."

Samira exchanged them for three shorter, shiny black all-weather coats, and we each chose a different colored wool pashmina to complete the ensemble.

* * *

When our plane lands at Mehrabad Airport, Ali does the passport shuffle, gathering up our Iranian ones and making sure our American ones are discreetly out of sight. The girls and I put on our scarves and secure them tightly under our chins. With my headscarf in place, I begin to adopt a studied public demeanor—a kind of defensive narcissism, the feeling that my every gesture is being evaluated.

As we move toward the plane's exit, I almost run into the middle-aged Iranian woman ahead of me when she stops abruptly, the end of her scarf caught on the Velcro of one of the seatbacks. I free it for her and she turns to thank me. Pointing to her scarf, she says in Persian, "As if we needed this." Her hijab is already annoying her and she isn't even off the plane yet.

Considering how we left Iran in 1980, it is impossible not to feel a little paranoid as we approach passport control. Any passport control booth in any airport has that effect on me, but here I find myself conjuring up scenes of bureaucratic evil, of police appearing out of nowhere to escort us to a small, windowless room. *Come with us. Do not say anything. Do not make a scene.*

When we began seriously planning for this trip, Samira checked the US Department of State's travel warning, which advised US citizens to "carefully consider the risks of travel to Iran." Among the many risks were the threat of harassment and kidnapping of US citizens and large-scale demonstrations against the United States. The State Department warned that, although the Swiss Embassy protects US interests in Iran, the Iranian government "does not recognize dual citizenship and generally does not permit the Swiss to provide protective services for US citizens who are also Iranian nationals [that is, all four of us]. In addition, US citizens of Iranian origin [like three of us] who are considered to be Iranian citizens have been detained and harassed by Iranian authorities."

There is no reason why anyone should harass us or detain us, we said. People like us go back and forth to Iran all the time. Still, what do we know?

* * *

The passport control hall is old and shabby, with dirty stone-clad walls and dark brown paneling. While in line, we see a small office with two rows of chairs set perpendicular to a desk. In the middle is a coffee table with an Isfahani woodblock-print tablecloth and a sugar bowl. "Every business meeting begins with tea," I explain to the girls. "Some things never change." That familiar sight gives me an irrational sense of wellbeing. To my fearful, sleep-deprived mind, this small scene of imminent hospitality is a good omen.

There are only three people in line ahead of us when the passport official leaves his post. I am tempted to think he has gone for reinforcements. When he returns, wiping his brow, I think he might be nervous about what is going to happen next. *But what do I think is going to happen next?* When our turn comes, we open the gate and advance to the passport booth. Ali gives all our Iranian passports to the agent. The man quickly stamps Samira, Sarah, and Ali's passports and hands them back to each of them. He stamps mine and gives it to Ali. *Done! We're outta here.* But then he looks at me and says to Ali, "Wait, I need to see hers again."

Ali hands me my passport and tells me to give it to the agent. *What's my strategy here? Do I demurely avert my gaze to demonstrate that I am a modest woman? Or do I look him straight in the eye to show him I have nothing to hide? If so, how long do I hold my gaze? Smile or no smile?* I choose the direct-gaze/no-smile option. He checks my passport signature and waves me through.

It's now nearly two-thirty a.m. We retrieve our luggage from the baggage claim and wrestle everything—eight suitcases, four carry-ons, purses, and briefcases—onto four carts.

I had been shopping for months. It is impossible to travel light to Iran, especially after twenty-six years away. Every Sunday since November, I have clipped coupons for creams, cosmetics, vitamins, chocolates, and Tums. I was a weekly regular at Target and Rite Aid, with side trips to T. J. Maxx, K-Mart, and Sears. By early February, I still wasn't finished, so Manijeh, a champion shopper, offered to help. We descended on Ross Dress for Less in Orange County for shirts and ties, sweaters, purses, soaps, perfumes, and men's cologne. There were so many friends and family to shop for that we compiled an Excel spreadsheet with 184 names, which also served as a handy aid for remembering which nephew's spouse or niece's grandchild was which. Manijeh and her husband Majid volunteered to help us label all the gifts, and pack and weigh the suitcases, a job that took the four of us a day and a half.

Here at Mehrabad, we get into the nothing-to-declare line, hoping the customs agent will not think we are planning to open a small drug store or boutique. We approach the agent, a fortyish woman in a black chador, who surveys our mountain of baggage.

"What's all this," she asks.

"Gifts for a family of 300 people," replied Ali, exaggerating just a little. The girls and I can discern the tension in his voice, the stiff formality in his delivery.

"When was the last time you were in Iran?"

"It's been thirteen years for me and twenty-six for my wife and daughters."

She stares intently at the four of us for a few seconds, then at the four carts of luggage. "Twenty-six years. That's a long time." Then suddenly she smiles and waves us through. "Have a good visit... and Happy New Year."

Mehrabad, place of kindness...at least for now.

The Estilai siblings and their spouses, left to right, back row: Ghasem and Reza; middle row, Asghar Agha (husband of Fatemeh), Fatemeh, Ali, Nazee, Ahmad, and Sakineh; front row: Ellen, Mina (Ghasems's wife), and Pouran (Reza's wife), Persian New Year, March 2006.

Samira, Ellen and Sarah in front of the Tehran Museum of Contemporary Art, 2006.

EPILOGUE

January 2023: Riverside, California

I have been Googling "protests in Iran" nearly every day since the death of Mahsa Amini, the young Kurdish Iranian woman who died in police custody in Tehran on September 16, 2022, just six days shy of her twenty-third birthday. She had been arrested by the morality police for allegedly not wearing her hijab properly. Soon after, protests began in the Kurdish city of Saqqez, her hometown, and amid cries of *zan, zendegi, azadi*—woman, life, freedom—quickly spread across the country, ultimately involving 150 cities in all of Iran's 31 provinces.

It's hard to get information. The Iranian government frequently shuts down the Internet, so it's often impossible to contact our relatives. The news we do get from western sources is searing, every day more horrific than the day before. I have to take it in small doses. Rubber bullets and birdshot are fired into protesters' eyes at close range. Young women are pushed from rooftops. Children are shot in the back. The mother of one of these boys, left alone to mourn, says, "I read your books to an empty bed." The Human Rights Activists New Agency has estimated that over 500 protesters have been killed, 70 of them minors. In December, the Iran International website said 18,170 protesters had been arrested, including 565 students. As of January 7, four young men have been executed for their part in the protests, and three others have been sentenced to death. Injured demonstrators have been arrested in emergency rooms or sometimes taken by ambulances straight to jail. Some of the injured who were not arrested avoided emergency rooms altogether and simply called doctors abroad in a desperate form of telemedicine.

Yet amid all this horror, there is hope. We see grainy videos of long-haired girls, twirling and swooping and skipping to protesters' chants, tossing their headscarves on bonfires. For their entire lives they have been denied the right to dance in public, let alone without their heads and bodies covered.

Silhouetted by these bonfires, they have become two-dimensional symbols, just like their chador-wearing countrywomen are symbols for the regime. I want to know them as individuals, not silhouettes. I want to hear how they can be this brave. I want to know what they say to their mothers when they walk out the door to join the demonstrations. How can their mothers let them go? How can they not let them go?

Because this is what it will take for Iran to become a free, democratic society: women and girls, and the men and boys that support them, crossing those thresholds every day, not knowing if they will come back.

Protests against hijab are almost as old as the Islamic Republic itself, beginning even before hijab became mandatory. But this new generation is different. Although foreign media often portrays Iranian women as weak victims, meekly adjusting their chadors and head scarves, cowering before their fathers and brothers, acceding to all their demands, Iranian women are weak only on paper. We can see, by the way they have led the revolt so far that, despite the laws that circumscribe their lives, they are strong in spirit and determination, in raw social power.

Long before headscarves were flung on these bonfires, hijab was a flashpoint. It has always been used to define women's place in society. For centuries, hijab was the tangible manifestation of women's modesty, but when Reza Shah outlawed hijab in 1936, its absence symbolized progress and modernity. In 1941, after Reza Shah's abdication, his son allowed women to wear hijab if they chose to, but it also became a symbol of class differences, of Westernized elites versus their more traditional sisters. For the last four decades, hijab has symbolized the iron grip that the Islamic Republic has over the private lives of its people.

In 2012, the Iranian film *A Separation*, a film about leaving, won the Academy Award for best foreign film. The story begins after the main characters have decided to divorce because the wife, Simin, wants their eleven-year-old daughter to be educated abroad, but the husband, Nader, does not want to leave his father, who suffers from Alzheimer's. Nader agrees to let Simin go but will not give the necessary consent for her to take their daughter with her.

This film about two people who love and respect each other but reluctantly agree to separate could easily have descended into shrill melodrama, but screenwriter/director Asghar Farhadi and his actors created believable, multi-dimensional characters whose struggles are at once quintessentially Iranian and completely familiar to foreign audiences.

The film transcended not only political and cultural differences but also Iranian censorship rules. According to Islamic law, women are not required to wear hijab at home among members of their own family. In real life, a father-in-law is not forbidden to touch his daughter-in-law. But when her ailing father-in-law latches onto Simin's wrist and doesn't let go or when Nader shoves the cleaning lady out the door, the actors are violating the Ministry of Culture and Islamic Guidance's edict against physical contact between male and female actors. Asked how he was able to circumvent this stricture, the director explained that the censor is a human being, after all, and that he sought to make a film so compelling that the censor would forget about that rule. Indeed, he did make such a film. So strong were the performances that even "house hijab," that cinematic convention of women characters wearing scarves and coats inside their own homes, even when alone or with family members, failed to distract or annoy me.

One reason that Simin's house hijab makes sense in the story is that every time we see her in her apartment, she is on the verge of leaving it. She is temporary. Her coat and headscarf underscore her transience.

Hanging in our kitchen is a color photograph that Ali's dear friend Farzin gave us on our last visit to Iran, in 2008. It's a close-up of parched earth. A slurry of mud has dried and cracked in the relentless heat and formed a crazy-quilt layer of jagged shapes on top of the soil, like a jigsaw puzzle being pulled apart. In the center, a tiny, opportunistic clump of scrubby but vibrant green shrub has found an opening and pushed itself through the dry, hostile barrier.

I had admired the photo as we were leaving Farzin's house after a party. His son, a well-known photographer, had taken it. With typical Iranian generosity, Farzin took the photo off the wall and gave it to me. "I keep a copy of this in my office," he said. "I tell my patients, 'There's always hope.'" He was talking about surviving grave illness, but he might as well have been talking about Iran itself.

A little over a year after that last visit, Iran erupted in demonstrations following the June 2009 presidential elections. When the government announced the landslide victory of the hardliner incumbent Mahmoud Ahmadinejad, supporters of his opponent, Mir-Hossein Mousavi, protested the vote count and took to the streets, giving rise to the Green Movement—two years before the Arab Spring protests. Over and over we watched the viral video of young demonstrator Neda Agha-Soltan, the life draining out of her as she went from being a vibrant philosophy student to a symbol of the protest. Ali and I monitored the television and Internet for a few weeks until the struggle faded away. In the face of the regime's ruthless retaliation, progressive Iranians retreated. Who could blame them? Certainly not those of us watching the bloody clashes from abroad in the safety of our living rooms.

Ali and I are now bystanders to political and cultural events in Iran. We have settled into a diasporic routine. We used to have a satellite dish that picked up Persian-language TV stations; now we watch BBC Farsi and Voice of America. We scan the papers for any mention of Iran: sanctions, signs of rapprochement, bellicose public posturing, speculations about secret overtures, air pollution, gas prices, the rate of exchange for US currency, and boycotts of overpriced pistachios. We go to Iranian film festivals. We watch Iranian television sitcoms on YouTube. We travel 40 miles to an Iranian grocery store to stock up on essentials for Persian feasts.

Ali has created a garden—not the enclosed, orderly *chahar bagh* of formal Persian gardens, but a free-form, rambling entanglement of his childhood favorites: sweet lemon, roses and passionflower; and in the spring, *sabzi khordan*, an array of pungent fresh herbs that will take the top of your head off; a grove of mulberries (*toot*) he calls our *tootestan*; and pomegranate trees tucked in every available corner. In his hospitable fashion, he planted six of our twenty pomegranate trees near the sidewalk, and three more in the alleyway, so that neighbors and the occasional FedEx delivery person can help themselves.

We ask each other: what would it be like if we had never left

Iran? What would it have been like to raise our children there? We'll never know. Samira and Sarah will never know what it would have been like to take part in their elementary school's *jashne takleef,* the coming-of-age celebration for nine-year-old girls that marks their eligibility for marriage. They will also never know what it feels like to censor themselves lest they be jailed for their ideas. I'm glad they will never know these things. But then again, they will never know what it would have been like to grow up among a hundred first, second and third cousins, coming and going, giving and taking, fighting and making up.

Sometimes I feel guilty about leaving Iran. I know that we made the right decision for the four of us, but with every WhatsApp call from our Iranian relatives, I feel a pang of remorse. They never complain, they never reproach us for leaving, but I feel guilty just the same.

Perhaps that's why *The Separation* resonated with an American-Iranian like me and with so many other Iranian expatriates. We all are dealing with some level of separation—from family, country, culture. Iranians who remain in Iran can also feel separated, shut out of the political process, isolated from the world by economic sanctions, or alienated by their failure to realize their dreams, but those of us leading bi-cultural lives outside of Iran feel this sense of separation most acutely. We are at once Nader and Simin, longing for both restraint and freedom, needing to stay and needing to go.

Enforced hijab was the catalyst for our leaving, but our decision wasn't just about hijab. The veil was a scrim stretched across a stage where a multitude of injustices played out every day. I have followed its evolution and permutations over the years, looking for clues to the political landscape. On our visits to Iran in 2006 and 2008, I saw that hijab had evolved from a social leveler that accorded its wearers anonymity to a vibrant vehicle for self-expression. Many Iranian women have continued to push against the restrictive dress code, devising clever responses to it. In her 2005 memoir *Lipstick Jihad*, Azadeh Moaveni writes about the evolution of hijab since 1979, when the black chador was meant to be the great equalizer, when women couldn't draw attention to themselves. "Parliament never officially pardoned color, sanctioned the exposure of toes and waistlines," she observes. "Young women did it themselves, en masse, a slow, deliberate, widespread act of defiance. A jihad, in the classical sense of the word: a struggle."

Ali's grandniece was one of several young women who joined the struggle; she opened a shop in Tehran selling colorful, whimsical alternatives to the classic manteau and wimple. Photos of the 2013 collection showed her clad in leggings, dresses with comparatively low necklines and dusters in colorful prints, sometimes formfitting, sometimes voluminous, all with a hip bohemianism.

If women could wear these newer versions of hijab with impunity, it was most likely in the upper-class neighborhoods of Tehran. Even there, they were subject to the whims of the morality police. In south Tehran or the provinces, they would be more likely to be ridiculed, harassed, or jailed. Banned or mandated, shunned or embraced, hijab became emblematic of how a male-dominated society imposed its views on women. The reimagined manteau was a sign that Iranian women were beginning to take control of the discussion.

I think of my sister-in-law Sakineh on the steps of Ray's Pizza Pantry in pre-revolution Tehran, whipping off her chador, giving a silent rebuke to the officious manager who refused her entrance. Modesty is in a person's heart, she said.

The modern manteau is another kind of silent rebuke, but I always wondered what was in the hearts of young Iranian women. Would they be satisfied with a bit of nipped waist or exposed collarbone, a flash of leggings? Apparently not any longer. For many, these new fashions were part of a larger struggle, slow and deliberate, that has been playing out for decades. The creative spirit prevailed for a while. Just as Scheherazade beguiled the sultan with her stories and Farhadi won over the censor with his cinematic artistry, young Iranian women reimagined hijab while conforming to the letter of the law. The election of President Ebrahim Raisi brought a crackdown on violations of hijab laws. But with the death of Mahsa Amini, young women are not asking for reform. They are demanding the abolishment of not only mandatory hijab but also the oppressive government that it represents.

Forty-three years after we sat on Essie and Julie's patio in Karaj and listened to the BBC report of that stoning in Kerman, the Iranian judicial system remains repressive, mercurial, and arbitrary. Iran is second only to China in the total number of executions performed annually. In 2015, Iran executed 694 people between January 1 and September 15, the highest per capita rate of executions of any country.[62] In 2021, Iran executed at least 314 people[63] and more than 500 in 2022.[64] Among the many crimes that carry the death penalty are the usual murder, rape, child molestation and spying, but also pornography, and deployment of firearms during a

62. Colm Lynch, "Iran Wins World Record for Most Executions Per Capita." Foreign Policy, October 21, 2015, www.foreignpolicy.com, accessed January 21, 2023.

63. "Death Penalty 2021: State-sanctioned Killings Rise as Executions Spike in Iran and Saudi Arabia," Amnesty International, May 24, 2021, accessed December 10, 2022, https://www.amnesty.org/en/latest/news/2022/05/death-penalty-2021-state-sanctioned-killings-rise-as-executions-spike-in-iran-and-saudi-arabia/

64. "Iran Surpasses 500 Executions in 2022." Foundation for Defense of Democracies, December 8, 2022, www.fdd.org, accessed January 21, 2023.

crime, as well as the crimes of apostasy, enmity toward God (*mo-harebeh*), blaspheming the prophet or the imams, recidivist theft, recidivist consumption of alcohol and drugs, and even extra-marital relations and same-sex relations.

Critics of the regime, many of them peaceful student demonstrators, journalists, and bloggers, continue to be imprisoned, tortured, and executed. Religious minorities such as Baha'is and Sunni Muslims have been harassed, imprisoned, or executed, accused of "espionage for Israel" or "insulting religious sanctities" or "evangelizing Muslims."[65,66,67]

Iranians' lives will not change until they have the freedom to express themselves without fear of government reprisals, until they have a government that cares about all of its people, regardless of gender, religion, ethnicity, sexual orientation, and political persuasion. Iranians are on their way to making this change.

Regarding change, some Iranians like to cite *The Conference of the Birds*, by the Sufi poet Farid-al-Din Attar (d. 1230). I heard this story more than once on our last trip to Iran. It is an epic poem in which the birds of the world come together in search of Simorgh, the King of the Birds. After a grueling journey across seven valleys (which correspond to the Sufis' seven stages of enlightenment), what had been a band of thousands is reduced to thirty birds. After crossing the last valley, the Valley of Nothingness, and obliterating their sense of individual self, the thirty birds meet Simorgh. But instead of seeing Simorgh, they see a reflection of themselves.

---

65. Amnesty International Annual Report, 2014.

66. Human Rights Watch, "Religious Minorities," www.hrw.org, accessed January 23, 2023.

67. Mahmehr Golestaneh, Parvasha and yadegarha (Iranian Baha'is executed, 1978-1992), November 1992. During these fourteen years, 251 Baha'is were executed.

They saw how they themselves

were the Great Simorgh.

All along, Simorgh was in fact

si, thirty, *morgh*, birds.

Simorgh tells them,

Come and obliterate yourselves in Me,

become Me to find yourselves once more."[68]

That story was told to me not with joy but with sardonic resignation. For those storytellers, the tale was not only about Sufi enlightenment, submission, and oneness with God but also the latent power of a people exhausted by revolution and war. The *si morgh* were finally Simorgh. They were the ones they had been waiting for.

Now, in 2023, these young protesters are not waiting anymore.

---

68. Attar, *The Conference of the Birds*, translated by Sholeh Wolpé, New York, W. W. Norton, 2017, p. 331.

ACKNOWLEDGMENTS

Years ago, when I was a graduate student in English Language and Literature at the University of Tehran, one of my professors, the late Dr. Nahid Sarmad, was the first person to tell me that I was a writer. I cherished that thought but filed it away. Decades later, Mike Foley, my writing instructor at UC Riverside Extension, told me the same thing. This time I didn't delay.

I was fortunate that, just as I was beginning my writing career, the Inlandia Institute came into being, giving rise to a vibrant writing community in Inland Southern California. I can't imagine how I might have fared as a new writer without the many opportunities it has provided: author readings, dialogues with writers, community programs, writing workshops, and publication in workshop anthologies. I have greatly benefitted from workshops led by Ruth Nolan, Stephanie Barbé Hammer, Jo Scott-Coe, Alaina Bixon, Charlotte Davidson, James Ducat and Allyson Jeffredo, all of whom provided a safe, supportive, nurturing environment where writers could flourish. I am grateful for the staff of Inlandia: office assistant Kimi Palacios, programs and marketing manager Janine Pourroy Gamblin, publications manager and copy editor Maria Fernanda Vidaurrazaga, and especially executive director Cati Porter for her perceptive editorial hand and her steadfast belief in and support of this book. I am indeed fortunate that *Exit Prohibited* has found a home in Inlandia.

Many of my fellow workshop and writing group participants also provided feedback for portions of this book, among them Surekha Acharya, Joanne Andrew, Hong-My Basrai, Frances Borella, the late Deenaz Coachbuilder, Carlos Cortés, Charlotte Davidson, Jane Ellis, Nan Friedley, Jane O' Shields Hayner, Lynda Hogan, Joan Koerper, Karen Rae Kraut, Robin Longfield, Suzanne Maguire, Katrina Mason, Juanita Mantz, the late Marcia Muldoon, Christine Pence, Judith Turian, Nancy Van Deusen, and Frances Vasquez. Joanne, Judith, Karen Rae and Katrina generously gave feedback on multiple drafts of the entire manuscript. Katie Black, Dr. Helen Davaran, Dr. Hasan Javadi and Nahid Javadi, Dr. Mohsen Mehran, Kathryn Morton and the late Dr. Tom Morton, my sister Dr. Kate Berg, brother-in-law John Berg, and niece Amy Berg also provided critical feedback and encouragement. Dr. Mahtash Moussavi, Dr. Parviz Sabour, and the late Dr. Esmail Meisami shared memories of IBB. The late Dr. Julie Scott Meisami, a Hafiz scholar, provided a translation of lines from the poet.

I am grateful to my friend, Dr. Bahram Grami, who spent countless hours diligently fact-checking, proofreading, and making technical edits on two drafts of this book. He also provided invaluable assistance with the transliteration of Persian words. I am also indebted to Gayle Brandeis for her sensitive, expert guidance and developmental editing of an earlier draft.

Above all, I am thankful for the love and support of my first readers, my daughters Samira Estilai Mathieu and Sarah Estilai Wiebel, and especially my husband Ali Estilai, who urged me to embark on this third career and tell our story, and who read every page countless times. In so many ways, without him there would be no story.

Special thanks also go to the publishers of journals in which sections of this book previously appeared. Portions of Chapters 1, 5, 26 and 34 were woven into a collage essay that appeared in "Persian Lessons," *SHARK REEF*, Issue 32, Summer 2018, sharkreef.org/non-fiction/persian-lessons/. Chapter 12, "Going with the Grain," appeared as "Kerman, 1971" in *Slouching Toward Mt. Rubidoux Manor*, Issue 3, Summer 2010. Chapter 15, "Wild Rue," appeared in *Phantom Seed*, Issue 4, September 2010.

ABOUT THE AUTHOR

Ellen Estilai has spent much of her career collaborating with artists, writers, and agencies to strengthen communities through the arts. She has served as the executive director of the Riverside Arts Council and the Arts Council for San Bernardino County, and has taught English language, literature, and writing in universities in Iran and California. Her essays, short stories, and poetry have appeared in numerous journals and anthologies. Her chapbook, *The Museum of Missing Things*, is forthcoming from Jamii Publications in 2023. Because Ellen and her husband have been immigrants in each other's countries, her writing frequently explores the joys and tribulations of the immigrant experience. She lives in Riverside, California.

Photo credit: Ali Estilai

ABOUT INLANDIA INSTITUTE

Inlandia Institute is a regional literary non-profit and publishing house. We seek to bring focus to the richness of the literary enterprise that has existed in this region for ages. The mission of the Inlandia Institute is to recognize, support, and expand literary activity in all of its forms in Inland Southern California by publishing books and sponsoring programs that deepen people's awareness, understanding, and appreciation of this unique, complex and creatively vibrant region.

The Institute publishes books, presents free public literary and cultural programming, provides in-school and after school enrichment programs for children and youth, holds free creative writing workshops for teens and adults, and boot camp intensives. In addition, every two years, the Inlandia Institute appoints a distinguished jury panel from outside of the region to name an Inlandia Literary Laureate who serves as an ambassador for the Inlandia Institute, promoting literature, creative literacy, and community. Laureates to date include Susan Straight (2010-2012), Gayle Brandeis (2012-2014), Juan Delgado (2014-2016), Nikia Chaney (2016-2018), and Rachelle Cruz (2018-2020).

To learn more about the Inlandia Institute, please visit our website at www.InlandiaInstitute.org.

INLANDIA BOOKS

Writing from Inlandia annual anthology series

These Black Bodies Are... edited by Romaine Washington

Pretend Plumber by Stephanie Barbé Hammer

Ladybug by Nikia Chaney

Vital: The Future of Healthcare, edited by RM Ambrose

Güero-Güero: The White Mexican and Other Published and Unpublished Stories by Dr. Eliud Martínez

A Short Guide to Finding Your First Home in the United States: An Inlandia anthology on the immigrant experience

Care: Stories by Christopher Records

San Bernardino, Singing, edited by Nikia Chaney

Facing Fire: Art, Wildfire, and the End of Nature in the New West by Douglas McCulloh

In the Sunshine of Neglect: Defining Photographs and Radical Experiments in Inland Southern California,1950 to the Present by Douglas McCulloh

Henry L. A. Jekel: Architect of Eastern Skyscrapers and the California Style by Dr. Vincent Moses and Catherine Whitmore

Orangelandia: The Literature of Inland Citrus edited by Gayle Brandeis

While We're Here We Should Sing by The Why Nots

Go to the Living by Micah Chatterton

No Easy Way: Integrating Riverside Schools – A Victory for Community by Arthur L. Littleworth

Milton Keynes UK
Ingram Content Group UK Ltd.
UKHW010845010224
437095UK00014B/456